Digital Pedagogy
with ICT and Learning Technologies

Digital Pedagogy
with ICT and Learning Technologies

Atanu Das PhD (Engineering)
Head, Department of MCA
Former Head, Department of CSE
Netaji Subhash Engineering College (under MAKAUT, West Bengal)
Kolkata, India

Rajib Bag PhD (Engineering)
Professor and Head, Department of CSE
Dean, Student Affairs
Supreme Knowledge Foundation Group of Institutions (under MAKAUT, West Bengal)
Mankundu, Hooghly, West Bengal, India

CBS Publishers & Distributors Pvt Ltd
New Delhi • Bengaluru • Chennai • Kochi • Kolkata • Mumbai
Bhopal • Bhubaneswar • Hyderabad • Jharkhand • Nagpur • Patna • Pune • Uttarakhand • Dhaka (Bangladesh) • Kathmandu (Nepal)

Disclaimer

Science and technology are constantly changing fields. New research and experience broaden the scope of information and knowledge. The authors have tried their best in giving information available to them while preparing the material for this book. Although all efforts have been made to ensure optimum accuracy of the material, yet it is quite possible some errors might have been left uncorrected. The publisher, the printer and the authors will not be held responsible for any inadvertent errors or inaccuracies.

Digital Pedagogy
with ICT and Learning Technologies

ISBN: 978-93-89688-47-4

Copyright © Authors and Publisher

First Edition: 2020

All rights reserved. No part of this book may be reproduced or transmitted in any form or by any means, electronic or mechanical, including photocopying, recording, or any information storage and retrieval system without permission, in writing, from the authors and the publisher.

Published by Satish Kumar Jain and produced by Varun Jain for

CBS Publishers & Distributors Pvt Ltd

4819/XI Prahlad Street, 24 Ansari Road, Daryaganj, New Delhi 110 002, India
Ph: 011-23289259, 23266861, 23266867 Fax: 011-23243014   Website: www.cbspd.com
e-mail: delhi@cbspd.com; cbspubs@airtelmail.in

Corporate Office: 204 FIE, Industrial Area, Patparganj, Delhi 110 092
Ph: 011-49344934   Fax: 011-49344935   e-mail: publishing@cbspd.com; publicity@cbspd.com

Branches

- **Bengaluru:** Seema House 2975, 17th Cross, K.R. Road,
  Banasankari 2nd Stage, Bengaluru 560 070, Karnataka, India
  Ph: +91-80-26771678/79   Fax: +91-80-26771680   e-mail: bangalore@cbspd.com
- **Chennai:** 7, Subbaraya Street, Shenoy Nagar, Chennai 600 030, Tamil Nadu, India
  Ph: +91-44-26680620, 26681266   Fax: +91-44-42032115   e-mail: chennai@cbspd.com
- **Kochi:** 42/1325, 1326, Power House Road, Opp KSEB, Power House, Kochi 682 018, Kerala, India
  Ph: +91-484-4059061-67   Fax: +91-484-4059065   e-mail: kochi@cbspd.com
- **Kolkata:** 6/B, Ground Floor, Rameswar Shaw Road, Kolkata 700 014, West Bengal, India
  Ph: +91-33-22891126, 22891127, 22891128   e-mail: kolkata@cbspd.com
- **Mumbai:** 83-C, Dr E Moses Road, Worli, Mumbai 400018, Maharashtra, India
  Ph: +91-22-24902340/41   Fax: +91-22-24902342   e-mail: mumbai@cbspd.com

Representatives

• Bhopal	0-8319310552	• Bhubaneswar	0-9911037372	• Hyderabad	0-9885175004	• Jharkhand	0-9811541605
• Nagpur	0-9421945513	• Patna	0-9334159340	• Pune	0-9623451994	• Uttarakhand	0-9716462459
• Dhaka (Bangladesh)	01912-003485	• Kathmandu (Nepal)	977-9818742655				

Printed at Glorious Printer, Jhilmil Industrial Area, Delhi, India

to

Prof (Dr) Saikat Mitra
Honourable Vice-Chancellor
Maulana Abul Kalam Azad University of Technology
West Bengal, India

Preface

The globalization of the world economy and different educational regulatory bodies (MHRD, HEI, UGC, AICTE, NCERT, NAAC, NBA, BCI, NCI, NCTE, etc.) are driving remarkable changes in education system. There is a worldwide paradigm shift in teaching–learning process. Over the centuries before digital technology, education evolved into a system that used paper technology in a variety of highly sophisticated ways to satisfy its mission to develop and recognize knowledge and skills.

A very few books on digital pedagogy are available in the market though there is a good number of books on pedagogy. The digital pedagogy books are the edited volume book chapters and typically these are research focused. Standard text and reference books on digital pedagogy are not available in the market. The mode of teaching–learning process has been changed from input–output-based education to outcome-based education. In recent years, worldwide extensive reforms are being undertaken to bring about essential changes in education in terms of what to teach (content) and how to teach (knowledge delivery) and how to assess (student learning and the educational processes). In this transition period, the teachers are required to update and adapt themselves with modern teaching–learning processes and technology innovations. The teachers and instructors required a ready reference book on digital pedagogy which will be helpful to adopt them with effective digital practices. This book is written considering their needs. This book is written primarily for the teachers (orientation) who are in the teaching profession at school, college and university level. But all concerns (like guardians, students, academic administrators, technology-based system developers, educational entrepreneurs, educational researchers, etc.) associated with education must enrich themselves with the knowledge of paradigm shift concerning innovations in ICT and other learning technologies. After a market survey, it has been observed that this type of book is not available in the market. The book covers all the possible aspects that the teachers are facing in their practical professional life when they are trying to apply digital technologies in teaching–learning process. Teachers will get confidence and be adapted to digital learning practices. This book is written for the whole teaching fraternity like for school teachers, for all types of college teachers at undergraduate and postgraduate levels, for the teachers from teachers-training institutes and finally for the students at all levels.

This book is well organized with *twelve* chapters. The first chapter is the introductory chapter which indicates the flavour of this book. The second chapter covers the present learning theories and their explanation in educational philosophies and psychology. This chapter also presents different instructional strategies, an explanation of instructional theories, an illustration of the taxonomy of educational objectives. The third chapter is highly related with the previous chapter. After acquiring the knowledge of learning theory, pedagogical practice is required. This chapter presents the different teaching–learning styles and their effectiveness. It also discusses the role, duty and responsibilities of a teacher. The fourth chapter is the heart of this book, namely digital pedagogy which is based on the recent trends of pedagogy in the digital age. It provides all the knowledge about new pedagogy in the present time. Education is in an interesting transitional phase between its 'ICT-free' past and its 'ICT-aware' future. So, the fifth chapter is written on the critical understanding of ICT. It introduces the various types of issues concerned with the use of

ICT and explains the precise application of ICT in learning. Open educational resources (OERs) are the freely available resources that are mixed with the conventional education practices to assist training, knowledge gaining, evaluating and research functions. The sixth chapter has been focused on OER. It introduces the concept of open learning, OERs, MOOCs, flipped classroom, etc. and also explains the blending of technology with existing educational paradigms. With the availability of huge learning resources, we face many challenges to deal with them in the effective and efficient management of those educational resources. Chapter seven presents the technological supports in the name of the learning management systems for the above purpose.

With the use of computer and internet, the teaching–learning process has changed the dynamics of education. Teachers are using modern technology to replace old models of standardized, rote learning and creating more personalized, self-directed experiences for their students. Chapter nine is written on emerging learning technologies. After going through this chapter learners will be aware of almost all the emerging learning technologies. Modern age digital tools facilitate offering the learning content on demand and oriented towards learner's knowledge and expectations and content may be customized as per learner's requirements. These practices are covered in the eighth chapter on personalization and adaptive learning. It also covers the self-regulated personalized learning pedagogical model and its implementation methods, adaptivity and personalization in mobile learning towards student modeling. To design efficient and effective course content, a coherent framework for the variety of tools and production methodologies can be provided by courseware engineering. The title of chapter ten is courseware engineering which introduces the concept of courseware engineering, structure, and development process of courseware. It also describes the courseware life cycle model and courseware evaluation methods.

The technological innovations in education must be assessed from its effectiveness perspectives. The ultimate fruits are to be realized in the educational system and in the students' performances. The trends of education systems are rapidly changing and the outcome-based education (OBE) framework has already been accepted worldwide. This OBE framework will change the traditional practices of curriculum design, education delivery and assessment for the enhancement of higher order learning and professional skills. Chapter eleven is written on OBE and regulatory practices. It introduces the concept of OBE system and the parameters along with the attainment of OBE. It also explains how the OBE is useful to identify the curricular gap followed by the evaluation of continuous improvement in teaching–learning process. On the other hand, chapter twelve presents the latest trends of rubrics-based students' assessment planning for students' performance evaluation. Different students' assessment methods and corresponding performance indicators of the students' activities are analysed in detail in this chapter.

The authors are optimistic that this book will satisfy all the requirements of the learners to adapt themselves with digital pedagogy and teachers to find appropriate tools and practices for effective educational interactions today.

Atanu Das
Rajib Bag

Acknowledgements

We have pleasure to bring the book *Digital Pedagogy with ICT and Learning Technologies* for the readers who wish to be acquainted with latest educational practices in light of technology innovations in the field of information and communication technology (ICT).

We would like to thank our students who are our source of inspiration that drive us to develop this book keeping in mind their academic requirements in changing educational scenario. We would like to thank our respective college authorities for the opportunity to involve us in the related practices. We would also like to express our sincere gratitude to all my colleagues for their wonderful academic association and support. We also like to gratefully acknowledge our research scholars Koyel Chakraborty and Sonali Banerjee (both from SKFGI) for their support during development of this book. However, our family members deserve the most gratitude for their sacrifice to make this project successful in a very short period of time.

We are also thankful to CBS Publishers & Distributors Pvt Ltd and their entire team for bringing out this book in time. Suggestions for the improvements of this book will be gratefully acknowledged.

We hope this book will fulfil the requirements and expectations of our intended readers. Even then, if some anomalies appeared, we feel extremely sorry for those unintentional mistakes.

Atanu Das
Rajib Bag

Contents

Preface *vii*

1. Introduction — 1

1.1 Pedagogy and its Importance *1*
1.2 Changing Educational Scenarios *2*
1.3 Evolution of ICT Proficiency with Tools in the Digital Era *3*
1.4 How can Technology Help in Pedagogy? *4*
1.5 Digital Pedagogy Definition and Significance *6*
1.6 Learning to Teach and Teaching with Technology *7*
1.7 Affordances and Constraints in Teaching with Technology *8*
1.8 Indian National Policy on Education (NPE) *8*
1.9 National Mission on Education through ICT (NMEICT) *10*
1.10 Expected Outcomes of this Book *11*

2. Learning Theories — 13

2.1 Introduction to Learning Theories and Educational Philosophy *13*
2.2 Educational Psychology and Learning Theories *14*
2.3 Instructional Theory *24*
2.4 5E Pedagogical Model *26*

3. Pedagogical Practices — 28

3.1 Learning Styles *28*
3.2 Teachers' Role *36*
3.3 Duties and Responsibilities of a Teacher *37*
3.4 Teaching Styles *41*
3.5 Typical Teaching Rules to Remember *44*
3.6 Discussions *44*

4. Digital Pedagogy — 47

4.1 The Digital Age *47*
4.2 Components, Processes and Performances of Innovations in Pedagogy *48*
4.3 Activity System for Balance in Digital Pedagogy *51*
4.4 New Principles of Digital Pedagogy *51*
4.5 New Pedagogies *54*

4.6 Instructional Technologies 55
4.7 Taxonomy of Digital Tools and Learning Resources 57
4.8 Hybrid Pedagogy and Blended Learning 59
4.9 Remarkable Debates 60
4.10 What Digital Pedagogy is Not? 62

5. Critical Understanding of ICT 65

5.1 Digital Technology and Socioeconomic Context 65
5.2 Challenges of Integration of ICT in School 67
5.3 Aims and Objectives of Indian National Policy on ICT in School Education 67
5.4 IT @ School Project 68
5.5 Components and Objectives of National Mission on Education through ICT 68
5.6 Microsoft Windows and Office Software 70
5.7 Internet and Educational Resources 76
5.8 Technopedagogic Skills 81
5.9 Practical ICT Tools 82
5.10 Using ICT Tools (for Content Preparation) 85
5.11 Preparing Learning Designs (Template included) 88

6. Open Educational Resources 94

6.1 Open Learning 94
6.2 Technology and Open Learning 95
6.3 Open Educational Resources and their Usefulness 96
6.4 Widely used OERs 98
6.5 Advantages and Disadvantages of OERs 102
6.6 OERs in Action—A Practical Example from the K-12 Sector 103
6.7 Online Professional Development for Teachers 103
6.8 OER and Digital Pedagogy 103

7. Learning Management Systems 105

7.1 LMS Introduction 105
7.2 Computer- and Web-based Training (CBT/WBT) 105
7.3 Sharable Content Object Reference Model (SCORM) 107
7.4 Content Management Systems (CMS) 108
7.5 Learning Management System (LMS) and LCMS 110
7.6 Moodle 112
7.7 Google Classroom 117
7.8 Canvas 118
7.9 Facebook (Social Network) as LMS 121
7.10 Consortia (University) in Higher Education 122
7.11 Next Generation Digital Learning Environment 123

8. Personalization and Adaptive Learning — 126

    8.1 Personalization of Learning *126*
    8.2 Benefits of Personalized Learning *127*
    8.3 Personalized Learning Environment and ICT *127*
    8.4 Personalization of Learning and Prevailing Schools *128*
    8.5 The Self-regulated Personalized Learning Pedagogical Model *129*
    8.6 Adaptive Learning Models *132*
    8.7 Benefits, Limitations and Future Prospects of Adaptive Learning *132*
    8.8 Adaptivity and Personalization in Mobile Learning towards Student Modeling *134*

9. Emerging Learning Technologies — 137

    9.1 Emerging Technologies in Education *137*
    9.2 Intelligent Tutoring System (ITS) *138*
    9.3 ICT-based Distance Education (DE) *139*
    9.4 Virtual Learning Environments (VLEs) and Augmented Reality *140*
    9.5 Wearable Technology (WT) *141*
    9.6 Gamification *141*
    9.7 Mobile Learning *142*
    9.8 Cloud Computing *143*
    9.9 Internet-of-things (IoT) *145*
    9.10 Educational Data Mining (EDM) and Learning Analytics (LA) *146*
    9.11 Machine Learning (ML) and Student Modeling *147*
    9.12 Sentiment Analysis and Deep Learning *148*
    9.13 Cybernetics *149*
    9.14 Cyber Security *150*
    9.15 Big Data *151*
    9.16 Entrepreneurship Using Emerging Learning Technologies *152*

10. Courseware Engineering — 156

    10.1 Introduction to Courseware Engineering *156*
    10.2 Problem with Traditional Approaches to Courseware Development *157*
    10.3 Practical Goals and Development Dimensions *157*
    10.4 Pedagogical Model *158*
    10.5 Content Structure and Layout of Courseware Engineering *158*
    10.6 Courseware Development Process *161*
    10.7 Courseware Development Life Cycle *164*
    10.8 Courseware Quality Assurance *167*

11. Outcome-based Education and Regulatory Practices — 169

    11.1 Outcome-based Education and Its Requirements *169*
    11.2 Accreditation and its Usefulness *172*
    11.3 Parameters of OBE and Attainments *174*
    11.4 Continuous Improvement in Teaching–Learning Process *176*
    11.5 Curriculum and Teaching–Learning in OBE *177*
    11.6 Processes Followed to Improve Quality of Teaching–Learning *180*
    11.7 Pedagogy of Faculty Development Programmes (FDPs) *183*
    11.8 Role of ICT on OBE *183*

12. Rubrics-based Students' Assessment Planning — 186

    12.1 Students' Assessment *186*
    12.2 Examination Systems Reforms in Higher Education *188*
    12.3 Rubrics for Assessment *191*
    12.4 Continuous Comprehensive Evaluation (Peacock CCE Model) Rubrics *193*
    12.5 Assignments Rubrics *194*
    12.6 Laboratory/Practical Works Rubrics *194*
    12.7 Seminar/Presentation Rubrics *195*
    12.8 Mini Project/Project Phase-I Rubrics *196*
    12.9 Major Project/Project Phase-II Rubrics *197*
    12.10 Viva voce/Interview Rubrics *199*
    12.11 Use of ICT for Students' Assessments *200*

Bibliography — 205
Index — 209

Chapter 1

Introduction

Objectives of this chapter
- To introduce the concepts of pedagogy and digital pedagogy.
- To explain the importance of digital pedagogy with respect to changing educational paradigms.
- To introduce the concept of ICT as a groundbreaking learning technology tool to augment the need of the modern era.
- Explain the importance and usefulness of learning technologies with respect to pedagogical needs towards the evolution of information and knowledge of society.
- Review Indian Nation Education Policy and National Mission Education through ICT to justify the development of this book for teachers' education in the Indian context.

Expected outcomes of this chapter
After going through this chapter learners will be able to:
- Understand pedagogy, ICT, digital pedagogy and other related concepts necessary for going through the next chapters of this book.
- Explain why learning technologies are important in the changing social and education scenarios at the national and international level along with the educational policies and mission.
- Analyse the plan of designing instructional materials (maybe digital).
- Assess the performance of ICT tools in learning activities.

1.1 PEDAGOGY AND ITS IMPORTANCE

The term **'pedagogy'** is originated from the ancient Greek word **'*paidagogos*'** meaning the slave who led children to school. This is universally known as the **'art or science of teaching'** or **'approach to teaching'**. It is the study of how knowledge and skills are exchanged during learning with interactions among the participants (i.e. teachers, learners) of learning actions. Pedagogical theories and practices significantly influence the growth of learners acting as an agent or recipient of knowledge facilitated by teachers. Teachers take the center stage in the traditional learning environment whereas learner-centered education presumes to place the learners and their needs in focus.

Teachers design their strategies, actions, and judgments **using the pedagogical theories** of learning, interest and background of individual learners besides analyzing the students' needs. The design may be extended further to include liberal and skill-specific vocational education. Learners' background knowledge, experiences, situations, and environments are the key constituents for designing instructional strategies. Hence, the pedagogy varies with the learners.

The principles used in adult education are known as **'andragogy'**. The term is inherited from a Greek word which means 'leading man' in contrast to 'leading children' by which pedagogy was defined. According to American educator Malcolm Knowles, the theory and practice of lifelong education of adults are the objective of andragogy. Teachers act as a facilitator of learning based on humanistic and self-directed approach. This **'Socratic method'** is based on two-way argumentative dialogue (questions–answers) between individuals to draw out critical thinking and ideas. Hypothesis elimination is the way by which better hypothesis is identified by eliminating contradictions.

1.2 CHANGING EDUCATIONAL SCENARIOS

With the advent of information and communication technologies, two key concepts, namely **information society**, and **knowledge society**, are getting popularity from school level to cross-national level to project the education systems a global standard. Education must consider the information and knowledge processes by computer-supported cooperative learning in collaborative knowledge acquisition and problem-solving. The majority of the jobs worldwide are information-oriented and hence they are structured to produce information in the well-accepted global information economy rather than material products. Purposefully formatted and structured data is generally known as information whereas knowledge includes cognitive states required in interpreting processed information. Knowledge reproduction is much costlier than information reproduction because the first one requires training, apprenticeships, logical deduction and interpretations. Rules of thumb, intuitions, experience, insights, and judgments are the elements by which knowledge is reproduced and codified. Such knowledge is known as **'tacit knowledge'**. It is dependent on motivation, attitudes, values, and social contexts.

The learning process is 'technology push' if the knowledge acquisition process is driven by potentials of technologies without the forceful need from the perspective of the learners, teachers and learning contents. This approach is dominant almost all over the world with respect to the introduction of ICT in education. Educational institutions are investing in ICT infrastructure and materials blending them on traditional teaching methods and materials by extending and modernizing educational practices. Local and central governments along with government-funded institutions are often taking initiatives to host portals (i.e. infrastructure, examples: http://www.eun.org, http://www.kids.gov/k_states.htm, https://onlinecourses.nptel.ac.in) offering e-learning (learning through electronic devices) materials. The implementation of new pedagogical methods is highly demanding in light of easy access to huge quantities of educational content for new age teaching–learning.

Digital Contents Allow Learners

- Easy access to learning materials
- Faster turnaround for time-sensitive tasks
- Use of links (through hypertext or digital texts and hypermedia) to navigate more information in detail

- Inclusion of multimedia instead of plain text
- Collaborative discussion of tasks and solutions on a continuous basis.

These digital learning (or e-learning synonymously afterward) contents take driving force in this changing education scenario. Setting **instructional goal and clear targets** are the starting points in the design of instructional materials or contents. The key questions (Atkin et al., 2001) need to be addressed in this path are:

- What do you want to learn?
- Where are you now?
- How can you get there?
- How do we test what you have learned?

Education systems have been changing very rapidly all over the world during the last two decades especially. Traditional teacher-centric leaning is getting replaced by learner-centric educations. This paradigm shift is systematically encapsulated under the umbrella of outcome-based education in recent times where different outcomes parameters are defined by regulatory bodies and quantitative evaluation of the outcomes need to be enumerated.

1.3 EVOLUTION OF ICT PROFICIENCY WITH TOOLS IN THE DIGITAL ERA

Information proficiency is defined as the technical skill related to information functions whereas ICT proficiency is the technical skill related to information technology (IT). The intersection of the two along with the knowledge domain is actually the practical ICT proficiency. The following Fig. 1.1 illustrates this actual meaning of ICT proficiency. The word practical indicates the application of IT and information manipulation for knowledge acquisition and generation purpose.

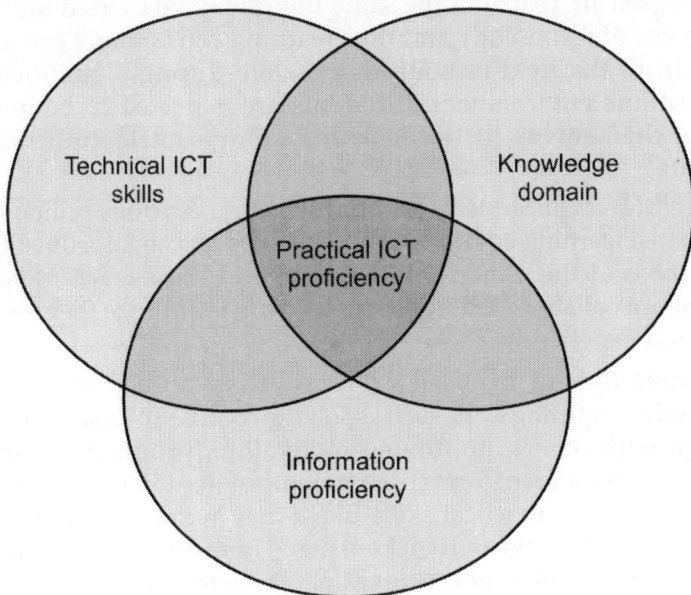

Fig. 1.1: Practical ICT proficiency

Evidence of associated knowledge potentials with respect to learners' outcomes takes place in the cell entries with the presumption that learners are using one or more ICT tools in the indicated column. The performance assessment of the ICT tools may be carried out with this framework if learner-specific software applications are available. This conceptual framework has the potential to measure skills, knowledge, and attitudes relevant to ICT utilization by learners.

Knowledge potential can greatly enhanced by ICT tools. There are various categories of tools which significantly contributing in this digital era. Table 1.1 presents the knowledge potential with respect to learning activities with present state of literal descriptions.

1.4 HOW CAN TECHNOLOGY HELP IN PEDAGOGY?

Technology can help in many ways in pedagogy. The following are the major benefits which we can expect from technological use in classrooms.

- *Improves knowledge retention*: Technology helps learners to participate actively (through interactivity) within and outside the classrooms with increased interest to use new methods through a blending of technologies. Retention of learners' knowledge will increase because of active participation in various learning experiments with different forms of technology.
- *Encourages individual learning*: All students in a class hardly learn in the same way since the abilities and learning style of all are rarely found the same. So the requirement of different students are often varied which can be fulfilled by using the great opportunities of technologies. Students can relook difficult concepts or skip ahead if they want and hence they can learn at their own speed. The technology has the potential to address individual learning through personalization addressed in a later chapter.
- *Improves engagement*: Teaching the same thing may be carried out in a new way through the use of technology and thus learning can be more fun and enjoyable. A virtual trip to the field of study is possible through 'gamification' in both online and offline environments. Students are expected to be more interested and engage themselves in the learning compared to traditional learning environments.
- *Encourages collaboration*: Students can participate in various online forums, blogs and other virtual learning environments (VLEs) by sharing documents and projects along with ideas at the same level (or class) and cross-level interactions. These facilities enhance collaboration skills and learners encourage themselves to acquire knowledge and experience.
- *Lifelong learning through technology*: Twenty-first century modern-day lifelong learning includes acquiring skills such as solving complex problems, critical thinking, collaborating with others, improving motivation, productivity and leadership besides developing different forms of communications. Lifelong survival of students is dependent on many practical skills like e-mail writing, creating presentations, internet, and multimedia networks usage, identifying authentic sources of information, keep up online etiquettes as per law, etc. Technology can facilitate the easy acquisition of those lifelong skill sets.

Table 1.1: Knowledge potential with respect to learning activities

Knowledge potentials →	Access, assemble, and reorganize knowledge	Critically interpret, analyze, and evaluate knowledge	Collaborate on projects and teamwork	Solve complex problem	Generate knowledge	Communicate, present, and disseminate	Select appropriate knowledge tools and evaluate their impact
Knowledge construction tool kits and database environment	Making inferences using, e.g. SIMCALC	—	—	—	—	—	—
Semantic organization tools	—	—	—	Using qualitative analysis software	Constructing reasoning chains using concept maps	—	—
Dynamic modeling tools	—	Scenario simulation	—	Using an optimization model for decisions	—	—	—
Interpretation tools, e.g. visualization and search tools	Web searching and organizing using browser	Using data mining tools to drill down to highly granular information	—	Interpreting data using visualization tools	—	—	Selecting ICT tools for a medical experiment and evaluate tool impacts
Communication, collaboration, and presentation tools	—	—	Using groupware	—	—	Using PowerPoint in net meetings	—

Note: The table structure was substantially adapted from Anderson and Plomp (2002). The table contains some changes to improve clarity.

- *Benefits for teachers*: Teaching fraternity is benefitted greatly by saving a lot of time because of ICT usage through the ways like virtual lesson plans, grading software, online assessments, online individualized students' progress tracking. The time may be utilized for helping those who are struggling, covering topics beyond curriculum, cocurricular and extracurricular activities. Access to massive open online resources regularly helps teachers to upgrade their knowledge and skills to fulfill all stakeholders' needs.

This list is not exhaustive and only indicative. New benefits are emerging with the progress of learning technologies towards the enrichment of pedagogy. The interested reader may subscribe the journal 'Technology, Pedagogy and Education' from Taylor and Francis Publication for regular updates in the field.

1.5 DIGITAL PEDAGOGY DEFINITION AND SIGNIFICANCE

It is established now that digital technologies (especially ICT) have numerous benefits in pedagogy (teaching–learning) as discussed above. So, it is high time to introduce the concept of digital pedagogy along with its significance in modern-day education.

Digital pedagogy is the art or science of teaching–learning using digital tools and technologies from pedagogical perspectives. The evolution of digital tools and technologies are the outcome of studying **information and communications technology (ICT)**. The mode (classrooms or face-to-face, distance or blended) of teaching–learning resource sharing varies with respect to the need of the target learners and availability of technological resources. It enables open education using **open educational resources** (OER, e.g. GitHub, Creative Commons, NPTEL, edX, Coursera) sharing syllabi and learning resources (or digital content). It allows self-directed interest-based learning and doing projects. The solutions of assignments may be published for peer or expert review in open access mode for critical analysis and enrichment.

Critical pedagogical perspectives may be addressed by digital pedagogy in addition to using digital technologies for teaching–learning. Thoughtful analysis of requirements of digital tools and its impact on learning normally considered under the purview of digital pedagogy. Digital pedagogy ensures collaborative learning much easier than what it was in traditional pedagogy. It deals with digital content for information and knowledge transfer along with traditional books and classrooms. The experimental nature of digital pedagogy seriously reflects its accomplishments and challenges through the study of the technologies in the different names such as **educational technologies**, ICT for education, digital technologies, etc. But this book encapsulates all these nomenclatures under the one umbrella which is **'learning technologies'**. The philosophies of digital pedagogy may emerge new debates, politics and ethics of technology towards technological malpractices like reducing human touch, less use of direct teaching which may have the possibilities of misguidance or diversion from actual objectives. Students have control over the pace and space of learning within the digital geography where new possibilities and platforms are offered like massive open online courses **(MOOCs)** to supplement physically located classrooms. School-level educations have also adopted digital pedagogy following hybrid or blended learning in the name of internationally acclaimed **K-12** (kindergarten to 12th grade) education. Controversies and debates on the efficacy of virtual school options are affecting largely on this domain. A large consensus on blended learning has been observed which advocated face-to-face instructions from teachers and learning from online content in partial time to overcome the infrastructural deficiencies.

There is much debate over the efficacy of virtual school options. The consensus on blended education, where students receive face-to-face instruction from teachers and the online portions are only conducted in partial time, is largely positive. The detailed discussion on this topic is addressed in chapter 3 of this book.

1.6 LEARNING TO TEACH AND TEACHING WITH TECHNOLOGY

Teaching is a creative work where the term 'design' reclaims the scholarship of teaching. This keyword reorganizes the pedagogy for the digital age. It bridges the gap between theory and practices. It includes both a systematic approach with rules based on evidence. Constantly adapting contextual practices create the evidence matching with the circumstances. This skillful activity can be improved with the manifestation of a scholarship of the designer.

In the new knowledge economy evolving in the digital age, design is considered as a highly valued activity. Knowledge is generated (appear) often from provisionally constructed, culturally specific and contextualized information. The process of design includes:

- *Investigation*: Here analyzing the users are required along with their needs. Identification of relevant principles and theories are also required in this step.
- *Application*: The next step is to understand how the identified principle will be applied in the relevant context.
- *Representation or modeling*: The next step is to design the solution which will meet the users need best. This step also includes communicating the design to developers and users.
- *Iteration*: The usefulness of the design is analysed with respect to the concerned practice in this step. A requirement of the changes in the design is also analysed and identified to meet the demands of developments.

The need for intentional design is a crucial part of the preparation and planning of e-learning. Immediate needs of the learners can be addressed in classroom teaching by the tutor in the following way.

- Swiftly finding out how learners are performing.
- Reorganize groups and reassign tasks along with activities.
- Express detailed justifications differently to assist learners to understand better.
- Supervise discussion and ask questions that test learners suitably.

All these pedagogical activities need prior thought and clear representation of what teachers and students will perform with the use of digital technologies. New technologies have the potential to make some of the pedagogical aspects visible that were previously taken for granted like how courses and learning activities are structured. Lesson plans, course diaries are routinely produced as evidence of reviewing quality teaching process and academic audit. Effective pedagogical approaches are highly essential in view of increasing class sizes and other economic burdens by reusing the investment of time and expertise. It still remains a question to be streamlined whether there exist general principles and universal patterns in all sorts of pedagogy.

Some generic principles and theories are presented in the following chapters of this book for understanding and applications by pedagogy practitioners and learning designers.

1.7 AFFORDANCES AND CONSTRAINTS IN TEACHING WITH TECHNOLOGY

Teaching with technology has a big question with respect to affordability since a country like has a huge number of student population and classrooms where new physical and technological infrastructures are required. The installation cost is not trivial and hence a huge investment is required by government-funded and self-financed institutions.

The major constrains in teaching with technology can be classified into the following.
- *Physical limitations*: Physical infrastructure (computing device and network connection) for learning technology implementation are initially high. It also includes maintenance and availability of those physical infrastructures irrespective of pace and space.
- *Semantic constraints*: The new technology may create a semantic burden for the developers and practitioners both. Sometimes the contents reach to a learner might appear as confusing with respect to his/her level of knowledge.
- *Cultural constraints*: New digital culture (information proficiency) needs to be evolved to realize its full potential even at remote countryside.
- *Logical constraints*: Losing human touch may suffer a logical burden for the learners. Shifting teachers' role as facilitators may create a logical hindrance for the old teachers to accept it in general.

1.8 INDIAN NATIONAL POLICY ON EDUCATION (NPE)

Since the dawn of human civilization, education systems are continuously evolving to address the diversified needs of all stakeholders by extending their reach and coverage. All developed and developing countries build-up their system of education to put across and uphold sociocultural identity and to convene the challenges of the times. After independence, Government of India envisaged a uniform educational system and central control over education throughout the country. Thus, University Education Commission (1948–1949), the Secondary Education Commission (1952–1953), National Council of Educational Research and Training (NCERT, an autonomous organization that would advise both the union and state governments on formulating and implementing education policies, 1961) and Indian Institute of Technology (1961), University Grants Commission (UGC) and the Kothari Commission (1964–66) were established to develop proposals for Indian education system and its modernization.

To promote education all over India, the government has formulated policy documents known as 'National Policy on Education (NPE)'. It covers elementary education to college-level education in both rural and urban India. The first NPE was published in 1968. It incorporates the acceptance of common structure (10 + 2 + 3) of education throughout the country. To meet the requirements of educated manpower, restructuring of courses at the undergraduate level was initiated and the centre of advanced studies was set-up for postgraduate education and research. The NPE was adopted by the parliament of India in 1986. Central Advisory Board of Education (CABE) was established in 1991 to make recommendations regarding modifications to be made in the NPE with respect to changing national and international needs.

Successful execution strategies of NPE involve the following.
- Greater accountability of both teachers and students obviously with a better deal.
- Opportunities to improve students' services with acceptable norms of behavior.
- Introduction of a system of performance assessment of institutions according to standard norms; and
- Provision of enhanced facilities (fund, training, and technology) to institutions.

The requirement of professional with technical, managerial and other type of expertises was found noteworthy to emerge India as a developing country. A number of commissions were established such as All Indian Council for Technical Education (AICTE), National Council for Teachers Education (NCTE), Bar Council of India (BCI), etc. for standardization and defining regulatory requirements of such different professional courses. Defining quality requirements with respect to international practices are very much essential as envisioned by different committees set-up for the purpose to see our country as a developed nation. National Assessment and Accreditation Council (NAAC) and the National Board of Accreditation (NBA) were two bodies set-up for higher education quality assurances under the preview of UGC and AICTE. Ministry of human resource development (MHRD) has also introduced the National Institute Ranking Framework (NIRF) for the same purpose with the added availability of ranking of the academic institutions for the stakeholders towards healthy competitions. With the present diversity, some initiatives were noticed from the government to bring all the regulatory bodies and commissions under one umbrella, Higher Educational Institutions (HEI) under MHRD. Stress is also observed in the skill development sectors along with innovation, incubations and entrepreneurship developments to promote self-employability.

The country has arrived at a stage in its technical development with necessary economic progress when a significant effort must be taken to obtain the full benefit from the assets already produced and to guarantee that the outcome of change reaches to all sections of people irrespective of economic, religious, gender and social status. The government of India has appointed a new committee under the chairmanship of space scientist Krishnaswamy Kasturirangan to prepare a draft for the new NPE in 2017. The committee has received thousands of suggestions, and proposals from teachers, expert educationists, students and other stakeholders. Consultations have also been made at district and state government level for consolidation of the proposals as state-level recommendations.

The people of the country have placed endless trust in the education system and corresponding policy formulation and execution. They have a right to expect tangible results. The execution of NPE can't be performed in a state of disorder. Highest intellectual rigor and purposeful attentions are required in the atmosphere of managing the policy execution. Freedom is also essential for innovations and creativity. The freedom may be offered in the present framework with the successful implementation of learning technologies to promote new age pedagogical practices.

The privatization of education and fast expansion of private institutions often resulted in deterioration of quality in education. This somehow led to review the policy so that private universities do not become a profit-making factories of producing useless human products. The policymakers have the responsibility of not only endorsing new technologies for augmenting pedagogical practices to compete with global challenges but also they should propose provisions to keep the education free from malpractices.

1.9 NATIONAL MISSION ON EDUCATION THROUGH ICT (NMEICT)

It is a central government-sponsored scheme which caters to the learning needs of more than 50 crores (learning and working) Indian population from all communities leveraging the great potential of ICT. There are three guiding philosophies in this mission:

- No talent in the country should be allowed to go waste.
- All the services offered through the content delivery portals (like Sakshat, NPTEL) should be free.
- The freely available portals are expected to be used to minimize the time for reinventing knowledge.

Objectives of the Mission

1. To develop rich knowledge modules to address the personalized needs of learners.
2. To make e-knowledge contents available to all Indians free of cost.
3. To spread digital literacy for teacher empowerment.
4. To identify and nurture talents.
5. To build inter- and intrainstitutes (of higher learning) knowledge network among researchers.
6. To provide support for the development of virtual technological universities.
7. To conduct research in the field of pedagogy of efficient learning to address the needs of an unequal group of learners.
8. To conduct field trials and experiments for performance optimization of devices (or tools) necessary for using ICT in education.
9. To offer certificates of competencies of the human resources acquired either through formal or non-formal means.
10. To standardize digital learning content for world-class quality assurance.

The mission has two major components, firstly content generation and secondly providing connectivity to learners along with a provision to access the tools and devices. It can bridge the gap between those who remained untouched by digital revolutions and mainstream users of the knowledge economy by the best use of ICT in teaching–learning. The mission has started creating high-quality e-content for the target groups. National Programme of Technology-enhanced Learning (NPTEL) was part of that initiative. It also plans to focus on appropriate pedagogy for technology enhanced learning, training, and empowerment of teachers for effective use of new methods of teaching–learning, providing the facility of conducting experiments through virtual laboratories, utilization of available education satellite (EduSAT) and direct to home (DTH) platforms, on-line testing, and certification.

A three-tier committee system was introduced to supervise and monitor the functioning of NMEICT. Hon'ble HRD minister is the chairperson of the 'National Apex Body'. This apex body takes all policy decisions and prescribes guidelines for the function of the other two committees, namely the 'empowered committee of experts (also known as 'project approval board') and 'core committees of domain experts'. 'Mission Director' act as secretary to National Apex Body and heads the mission secretariat. Agencies/individuals/institutions can submit proposals which come under the domain of the mission. Concerned core committee of domain experts scrutinizes the proposal and recommendations are sent to the project approval board for decision and sanctioning the projects. Various peer reviews are formed for monitoring of approved projects and concurrent evaluation.

1.10 EXPECTED OUTCOMES OF THIS BOOK

The expected outcomes of this book are building teachers competencies with digital pedagogy using learning technologies. Trainee teachers and professionals coming in the teaching profession need guidance and training on pedagogy and its modernization. After going through this book, learners will be able to:
- Know the concept of pedagogy in light of changing technological evolutions.
- Understand the concepts of digital pedagogy and its implementation issues.
- Apply the learning technologies for teaching practices.
- Analyse the necessity of learning technologies for pedagogical modernization.
- Evaluate the available technological tools and practices for their desired purpose.
- Design new personalized instructional materials at their field of teaching.
- Guide students in right direction according to national and global standards.
- Develop documentation for academic audit and regulatory purposes.

EXECUTIVE SUMMARY

- Pedagogy is the art or science of teaching whereas andragogy focuses on adult education.
- Information and knowledge society is continuously growing with the evolution of ICT literacy and corresponding tools and practices. Digital contents are developing for technology-enhanced learning with desired instructional goals.
- Technology helps pedagogy in various ways like improving knowledge retention, encouraging individual learning, improving engagement, encouraging collaboration, enhancing lifelong learning and benefiting teachers in various ways.
- Digital pedagogy is the art or science of teaching–learning using digital tools and technologies from pedagogical perspectives. Open educational resources (OER) like MOOCs are developed with the study of teaching–learning-related technologies (or learning technologies) where the use of digital pedagogy is earnestly essential.
- Teaching with technology requires the design of the teaching process which includes investigation, application, modeling and iteration. Teaching with technology has various constraints from the perspectives like physical, semantic, cultural, and logical.
- The Government of Indian have taken initiatives for educational policy formulation (NPE) over the years and moved forward towards implementation of learning technologies (ICT) in the name of NMEICT to bridge the gaps between having and have not with respect to the knowledge economy.

Review Questions

1. Define pedagogy and digital pedagogy and explain their importance with respect to modern age education.
2. What is Socratic method learning? How is andragogy different from pedagogy?
3. What is tacit knowledge? Differentiate between information and knowledge society.
4. What are the benefits of digital content? What are the key issues towards setting instructional goals and clear targets in digital learning content development?
5. Give the conceptual framework of knowledge potential with respect to learning activities.
6. How to carry out performance assessments of ICT tools for learning activities with knowledge potentials?
7. Illustrate the future of pedagogy with respect to evolving ICT. How can technology help in pedagogy?
8. Write the importance and processes of teaching design.
9. What are the major constraints in teaching with technologies?
10. Write a short note on Indian National Policy on Education.
11. Write the philosophy, objectives and functioning of NMEICT.

Chapter 2

Learning Theories

Objectives of this chapter

- To explain the educational philosophies.
- To present learning theories.
- To demonstrate educational psychology with respect to the learning theories.
- To illustrate taxonomy of educational objectives.
- To explain instructional theories.
- To present different instructional strategies.

Expected outcomes of this chapter

After going through this chapter learners will be able to:
- Understand various important educational philosophies.
- Demonstrate the concept of popular learning theories.
- Compare the learning theories from educational psychology.
- Understand and apply the revised taxonomy of educational objectives (Bloom's).
- Design instructional material according to instructional theories.
- Compare and contrast between old and new methods of instructional design and delivery.
- Apply the learning and instructional theories in the implementation of digital pedagogy.

2.1 INTRODUCTION TO LEARNING THEORIES AND EDUCATIONAL PHILOSOPHY

Learning theories demonstrate how knowledge is acquired, processed and retained by the learners. Understanding of the knowledge is dependent on cognitive, emotional and environmental factors along with prior experiences. Knowledge and skill are retained as it is understood. It changes with the situational demands. Pedagogical practices may be misleading without understanding learning theories.

Educational philosophy guides us to understand how an individual learns something when the topic is brand new. Two classical theorists, namely Plato (428–347 BC) and John Locke (1632–1704), have contributed much in educational philosophy. According to Plato, "knowledge is present at birth and all information learned by a person is merely a recollection of something the soul has already learned previously", which is called the Theory of Recollection' or 'Platonic epistemology'. A person cannot learn something if that was not known to him/her previously according to the theory. Over time, information and knowledge are ironed into the soul as a passive process while learning. Plato's theory seems complicated since it can't explain how our souls gained knowledge in the first place. This classical theory can still help us to understand how we expanded knowledge today.

Locke introduced a 'blank slate' theory to answer where human got initial knowledge. However, it assumed that something had to be present. That something is 'mental power' according to Locke's theory. Locke argued this power as a 'biological ability' with which the baby is born. This power is similar to the power of a baby function biologically entering the world. Immediately, from its surroundings, it takes experiences which are transcribed to the baby's 'slate'. Ultimately those experiences are converted into complex and abstract ideas.

2.2 EDUCATIONAL PSYCHOLOGY AND LEARNING THEORIES

In everyday teaching and learning, a teacher has to think about individual differences among students besides assessment, development, and the nature of a subject being taught. Teachers also need to focus on the transfer of learning and problem-solving skill development. Educational psychology emerged as a new and growing field of study to address the everyday psychological needs of teaching–learning though it can be date back to the days of Plato and Aristotle. This field of study helps to understand human cognition, learning, and social perception.

Following are the main categories of theories of learning.

1. Behaviorism Theory

Behaviorism considers knowledge as a compilation of behavioral reactions to various stimuli in the environment. Learning is facilitated here by optimistic reinforcement and recurrence. It advocates learning as an aspect of conditioning a system of rewards and targets to change the behavior of learners. Teachers take initiatives to alter student behavior by systematically rewarding students with stars or tokens redeemable for miscellaneous items while pursuing classroom practices. The theory is not free from criticism though it has shown the efficacy of awards in students' behavior change. There are evidence that rewards decrease inherent motivation in specific situations particularly when the students are already motivated at a high level to perform the tasks.

2. Cognitive Theory

Cognitive theory is more popular than the behavioral theory as current practices are concerned. It believes learning as a study of learners with respect to their convolution and memory. It considers related mental constructs such as motivation, memories, emotions, traits, and beliefs. How information is perceived, stored, processed, retrieved and forgotten, are determined by memory structure. Cognitive load theory and dual coding theory elucidate how people are trained through multimedia presentations. Psychology research has confirmed the applicability of spaced learning effect (i.e. students perform better after a second reading rather than first) using mnemonics for instantaneous and delayed retention of information.

According to cognitive psychologists, problem-solving is fundamental to learning. Longterm memory offers a schema to interpret a problem undertaken by a student. 'Activation' is the process, a student, runs into while reading. The student goes through the material without absorbing and retaining the information using working memory. 'Deactivation' occurs followed by understanding and retaining the information. Second reading helps readers to get a 'gist' by flashing their memory if deactivation takes place in the first reading. Analogical thinking to problem-solving occurs when the problem is mapped to a pre-existing schema. Student's attention is directed away from the features of the problem if the problem is assigned to a wrong or inconsistent schema. A cognitive view of intelligence believes that each person has an individual profile of characteristics, abilities, and challenges as an outcome of his/her inclination, learning and growth. Such profile differentiates them in intelligence, cognitive style, motivation, creativity, and the capacity to process information, communicate with others.

3. Constructivism Theory

The philosophy that explains the character of knowledge is constructivism. It believes the acquisition of knowledge should be a personalized tailored process of construction dependent on learners' ability and what they already understand. Thus it takes an epistemological stance. Interactions between human behavioral patterns and experiences develop the systems of knowledge called 'schemes'. Scheme and schema are not the same because the last one is inherited from schema theory dealing with information-processing angles of human cognition. The scheme is context-free whereas schema is a concept. This theory does not refer to a definite pedagogy and has the flavor of a mixture of practices. Here importance is given on the prior knowledge, experiences, activity of the learners along with sociocultural determinants of the learning process. Social constructivism includes sociocultural learning. It explains how cognitive tools are internalized to form mental constructs through interactions between adults, more capable peers, etc. According to the theory of instructional scaffolding, social (or information) environment provides supports for learning that are withdrawn step-by-step as they become internalized.

Constructivism suggests that learning is accomplished best using a hands-on approach. Learners do not learn by being told what will happen according to this theory. Learners learn by experimentation and subsequent inferences, discoveries, and conclusions. The success of this theory over traditional teaching methods is evident in problem and inquiry-based learning methods and may be proved by standardized tests. It is often noticed that students preferred student-centered constructivist methods over teacher-centered traditional ones for better retention of knowledge. Class discussions, wikis, and blogs are instances of constructivist teaching methods where learners need to remain active within a democratic classroom atmosphere.

Constructionism is a descendant educational method of constructivism. Learners need to construct physical artifacts to practice what they have learned to get the outcomes tangibly during the production of knowledge. Simply it is learning by making. Within constructionism, learners need more instructions to learn and design tangible products compared to constructivist approaches. Students are like blank slates where teachers need to put instructions to direct them in how to learn and perform in the constructionist approach. Instructors are facilitators and not explicitly teachers in constructivist approaches. Knowledge is not taught explicitly, but it is delivered as an accompaniment to learners' experiences. Constructivism gives more importance to learners' cognitive processes, whereas constructionism focuses more on tangible production. The interested reader may go through the Ackermann (2001) for further details.

4. Transformative Theory

It focuses on the change of learners' perception and views necessary with respect to environments and context. According to this theory, the perspective transformation has three angles: (1) Psychological—changes in the understanding of the self, (2) conviction—revision of belief systems, and (3) behavioral—changes in lifestyle. This learning is provided through consciously directed processes. Such a process includes enthusiastically accessing and getting the symbolic contents of the unconscious. This symbolic content is then critically analyzed to explore the underlying premises. Transformative learning is triggered by a life crisis or major life transition infrequently. Dramatic dilemmas created by teachers also promote transformation. Individuals change their frames of reference by critically reflecting their assumptions and beliefs as an important part of transformative learning. This process is essentially analytical and rational towards implementing plans for defining their worlds in new ways. Three ways in which experience is interpreted through reflection are:

- *Content reflection*: It is a study of the content. The question "What did I do that led to the outcome?" can help us to get this reflection.
- *Process reflection*: Problem-solving strategies are verified here. The question "Do I understand the needs of my students?" can help us to get this reflection.
- *Premise reflection*: It is the question of the problem itself. The question "Why do I feel responsible for this situation?" can help us to get this reflection.

Two visions of transformative learning are—(1) a rational approach that depends primarily on critical reflection; (2) relies more on intuition and emotion. Both make use of rational processes and include imagination as a part of the creative process. Teachers can only give an opportunity for transformative learning but it can't be guaranteed. The educator's task is to help learners in becoming aware of some critical assumptions in order to promote transformative learning. These critical assumptions include beliefs, habits of mind, or points of view, interpretations, as well as the assumptions of others. Creating an opportunity for effective (and equal) learners' participation is also under the educator's responsibility in discourses like assessing beliefs, feelings, and values. Metaphor analysis, consciousness-raising, concept mapping, repertory grids, life histories, and participation in social action are some of the methods by which educators can encourage implementation of critical reflection and experience. Educators also set objectives for autonomous thinking for adult learners to assess the assumptions critically, recognizing alternate perspectives better, collaborating with others effectively and arriving at judgments in regards to beliefs. Classroom methods such as group projects, learning contracts, case studies and simulations normally promote discovery learning. These transformative learning methods help learners to justify the new knowledge in their live context.

Applicability of transformative theory is evident in new professional education programs such as health, teachers' education, business, industry, law, engineering, and management, etc. Guiding principles for transformative professional development include action plans, case studies, curriculum development, reflective activities, and critical-theory discussions. Mentoring is another strategy for transformative professional, personal and organizational development by creating a supportive culture. A transformative learning framework is often used in a foundation or orientation course of new teachers. Participants build an individual and collective analysis of teaching experiences to help them reframe their practice when they find their expectations ambiguous and they lack the self-awareness to navigate in the educational setting. Transformative learning may not always be a goal of education, but its importance should not be overlooked.

5. Taxonomy of Educational Objectives or Bloom's Taxonomy (and Revised)

It is the classification of educational objectives into a set of three hierarchical models named after Benjamin Bloom who chaired the committee that formulated the taxonomy and edited the first volume Bloom et. al. (1956), as a standard text. Cognitive, affective and sensory domains are the components of the said model, where the cognitive domain has been used to structure curriculum learning objectives, assessments, and activities as the main focus of traditional education. The cognitive domain categorized and ordered thinking skills and objectives. Bloom's taxonomy pursues the thinking process. Normally, we understand a concept after remembering it; similarly, we can't apply a concept without understanding it. This thinking process is a continuum from lower-order thinking skills (LOTS) to higher-order thinking skills (HOTS) as knowledge, comprehension, application, analysis, synthesis, and evaluation. Bloom's taxonomy is revised (Anderson et.al., 2001) where the six levels of objectives are (from LOTS to HOTS)—remember, understand, apply, analyze, evaluate, create (rather than synthesize), a slightly different than the original (Fig. 2.1).

A statement of a learning objective, according to the Bloom's taxonomy, contains a verb (an action) and an object (usually a noun).

- The verb usually refers to (actions associated with) the intended cognitive process.
- The object usually depicts the knowledge students are likely to acquire or construct.

Anderson et. al. (2001) identified 19 specific cognitive processes presented in Table 2.1 that are further clarified the bounds of the six categories. On the other hand, knowledge dimension represents a range from concrete (factual) to abstract (metacognitive) presented in Table 2.2. Representing the knowledge dimension with a number of discrete steps may be misleading. For instance, all procedural knowledge may not be more abstract than all conceptual knowledge and metacognitive knowledge is a special case in which knowledge of cognition about oneself in relation to various subject matters.

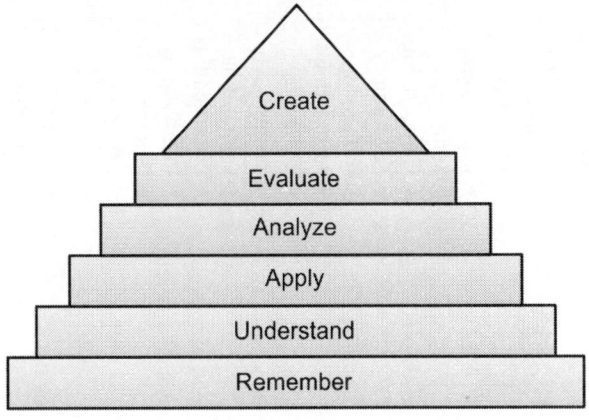

Fig. 2.1: Bloom's revised taxonomy

Table 2.1: The cognitive processes, dimension categories and alternative names [Anderson et. al. (2001)]

Lower-order thinking skills			Higher-order thinking skills		
Remember	Understand	Apply	Analyze	Evaluate	Create
Recognizing	Interpreting	Executing	Differentiating	Checking	Generating
• Identifying	• Clarifying	• Carrying out	• Discriminating	• Coordinating	• Hypothesizing
Recalling	• Paraphrasing	Implementing	• Distinguishing	• Detecting	Planning
• Retrieving	• Representing	Using	• Focusing	• Monitoring	• Designing
	• Translating		• Selecting	• Testing critiquing	Producing
	Exemplifying		Organizing	Judging	Constructing
	• Illustrating		• Finding coherence		
	• Instantiating		• Integrating		
	Classifying		• Outlining		
	• Categorizing		• Parsing		
	• Subsuming		• Structuring		
	Summarizing		Attributing		
	• Abstracting		• Deconstructing		
	• Generalizing				
	Inferring				
	• Concluding				
	• Extrapolating				
	• Interpolating				
	• Predicting				
	Comparing				
	• Contrasting				
	• Mapping				
	• Matching				
	Explaining				
	• Constructing models				

Table 2.2: Bloom's revised taxonomy model [Anderson et. al. (2001)]

The cognitive process dimension   *The knowledge dimension*

	Factual: The basic elements a student must know to be acquainted with a discipline or solve problems in it.	**Conceptual:** The interrelationships among the basic elements within a larger structure that enable them to function together.	**Procedural:** How to do something, methods of inquiry, and criteria for using skills, algorithms, techniques, and methods.	**Metacognitive:** Knowledge of cognition in general as well as awareness and knowledge of one's own cognition.
Remember: Retrieve relevant knowledge from long-term memory.	List primary and secondary colors.	Recognize the symptoms of exhaustion.	Recall how to perform CPR (coordinated program review).	Identify strategies for retaining information.
Understand: Construct meaning from instructional messages, including oral, written and graphic communication.	Summarize features of a new product.	Classify adhesives by toxicity.	Clarify assembly instructions.	Predict one's response to culture shock.
Apply: Carry out or use a procedure in a given situation.	Respond to frequently asked questions.	Provide advice to novices.	Carry out pH tests of water samples.	Use techniques that match one's strengths.
Analyze: Carry out or use a procedure in a given situation.	Select the most complete list of activities.	Differentiate high and low culture.	Integrate compliance with regulations.	Deconstruct one's biases.
Evaluate: Make judgments based on criteria and standards.	Select the most complete list of activities.	Determine the relevance of results.	Judge efficiency of sampling techniques.	Reflect on one's progress.
Create: Put elements together to form a coherent whole; reorganize into a new pattern or structure.	Generate a log of daily activities.	Assemble a team of experts.	Design an efficient project workflow.	Create a learning portfolio.

Bloom's taxonomy works as strength of teaching philosophies where focus is more on skills than content. This is used as a teaching tool to help balance the assessment of texts, assignments, evaluative questions, exercises, and information searching.

6. Gagne's Approach to Instruction Design

Robert Mills Gagne was an American educational psychologist best known for his theory on conditions of learning. Gagne's approach to instructional design is considered a semimodel that has influenced many other design approaches. Gagne proposed that events of learning and categories of learning outcome together provide a framework for an account of learning conditions. Gagne's model proposed nine events of learning. These events are specific functions of communication behaviors that he identified as components of instruction. Gagne divided these nine events into two groups—the first five represent communication behaviors that occur before the acquisition of information. They are:

- Level 1: Gaining attention (reception)—motivate the learners to learn. Start the learning experience by gaining the attention of the learner.
- Level 2: Informing learners of the objective (expectancy)—explain the objective of the course to the learners and what they will have learnt at the end of the course along with its organization.
- Level 3: Stimulating recall of prior learning (retrieval)—direct the learner's attention to the specified instructions and review previous learning experiences to be applied in the learner's present learning.
- Level 4: Presenting the stimulus (selective perception)—stimulate learners to recall information stored in the memory from previous instructions and organize the information in a logical and easy-to-understand manner.
- Level 5: Providing learning guidance (semantic encoding)—guide the learners through the course and help them by including examples.

The last four occur after acquisition have developed. They are:

- Level 6: Eliciting performance (responding)—enhance retention of the information provided through reinforcement. At this stage, it needs to be ensured that the learner demonstrates their knowledge acquired during learning process.
- Level 7: Providing feedback (reinforcement)—provide feedback to the learners to improve their performance based on the test results. This feedback and tips point out their mistakes so that they can correct them.
- Level 8: Assessing performance (retrieval)—apply tests to assess the performance of the learners. They should be able to complete a test to show that they've learned the material or skill effectively. They should complete this test independently, without any help or coaching.
- Level 9: Enhancing retention and transfer (generalization)—provide tasks to the learners for practice. Repeated practice is the best way to ensure that learners retain information and use it effectively.

In addition to the nine events of instruction, Gagne's instructional design theory proposed eight different conditions of learning. Gagne perceived learning conditions as building blocks for designing instruction. By categorizing each type of learning, the instructional designer is aware that each type of learning can potentially require a different event of instruction to optimize learning.

Gagne classified learning outcomes into five categories or taxonomies. These represent the variety of capabilities or outcomes in the form of performance categories that are possible as a result of the learning process. The different learning outcomes or performance categories not only differ in the human performances, but also differ in the conditions most favorable for their learning. The following are the different learning outcomes defined by Gagne

- Attitude is the experience of success following the choice of a personal action.
- Verbal information including facts, concepts, principles and procedures which exhibit declarative knowledge.
- Cognitive strategies aim at seeing problems in new and insightful ways.
- Psychomotor skills for executing required actions.
- Intellectual skills for discrimination between two objects, concrete concepts for classification, rules for demonstration, higher order rules for generating solutions.

To justify the effectiveness of the course or program regarding the student's performance, evaluation of instructions is required. Evaluation of instruction is conducted through the queries such as "Have the objectives been met?", is the new program better than the previous one, "What additional effects does the new program include?" Measures are taken based on the student's performance and analyzing the kind of student capabilities the program is planned to establish. The ultimate purpose is to supply data on feasibility and efficiency to develop and improve the course.

7. Learning by Teaching

The practices of students-teach-students have been there from ancient times. Learning by teaching is thus a method of teaching in the field of pedagogy theory. Students are asked to prepare lessons to teach it by learning the materials in this method. The acquisition of subject matter along with life skills is the emphasis of this theory. During the early 19th century, this practice became popular when initiatives were taken to spread education among masses of poor children with limited resources where older children used to teach younger children after learning the subject matter and life skills. Systematic research on how to develop this pedagogical method began in the middle of the 20th century.

Students become accountable for their own teaching and learning after guided preparation by the subject expert teacher. Students are divided into small groups of not more than three members. The course material is divided into units and distributed among the groups. Students are then asked to prepare a plan and develop the teaching material to teach others followed by learning the topic himself. Necessary content may be supplied or guidance may be provided to collect the materials. The student is then encouraged to present in the form of teaching the topic before other students in the presence of the expert teacher providing necessary corrections along with rectifications in the teaching presentation. The expert teacher also remains actively involved in the process by a further explanation if the learning students do not understand the material or teaching students commit mistakes in the teaching presentation. Several life skills like planning, problem-solving, respect for other people, taking chances in public speaking, identifying mistakes in understanding in real-time verbal and non-verbal communication among peers, etc. are automatically developed among the students going through these processes. These secondary goals of education are achieved in this way. This method is not the same as students teaching supported by the teacher as a part of teacher education.

There is another way of learning by teaching known as 'plastic platypus learning'. The method is inherited from the 'rubber duck debugging' concept by which the programmer can identify bugs in their code without the help of others in software engineering. Programmer just explains what the code does, line-by-line, to an inanimate object, namely, a rubber duck, in this process. Understanding and knowledge retention by the practitioners are found remarkable sometimes in this way. The benefit of this technique is that the learner does not call for the presence of a new person in order to teach the subject. This technique may work with any inanimate object obviously and not just plastic platypuses. The following may be adopted to increase the effectiveness of this 'plastic platypus learning' method.

- Prepare notes simultaneously while learning the subject.
- Prepare the lesson plan and filter material on the subject. These require huge time and energy, maybe omitted in some situation.
- Teach the subject without using notes al all assuming that the students aware about it beforehand.

8. Kinesthetic Learning

Kinesthetic learning is also known as tactile learning is a learning theory where learning takes place through physical activities carried out by the students, rather than simply listening to a lecture or watching demonstrations. Whole-body movements of the students accelerate to process new and difficult information while understanding. The VARK model proposed by Neil Fleming, a New Zealand educational theorist, emphasized hands-on experimental learning with the following categories.

- Visual learning
- Auditory learning
- Read/write learning
- Kinesthetic learning

The students shine through tangible learning such as work experience, on-the-job training, internships, simulations and so forth. Skill memory is developed easily while learning kinesthetically without much repetition and demonstration of the subject. Kinesthetic learning offers the best results when the learner uses their own words (or language) in order to define, explain and resolve how their body's movement reflects the concept studied.

The learning process is primarily affected by five stimuli, namely environmental, emotional, sociological, physiological and psychological variables according to the 'multiple intelligences and learning styles' theory. Perceptual element is one of the elements in physiological stimuli. This element depicts the auditory, visual, tactual and kinesthetic styles where students learn more effectively. Kinesthetic learners respond differently depending upon their memory systems. Kinesthetic learners have a variety such as whole-body learners, hands-on learners, doodlers and students learning through emotional experiences. The process of achieving long-term memory from short-term memory varies with learners' variety. Mind mapping, story mapping, webbing, drawing can be used for toddler whereas role play, clay building, and math manipulative can be used for hands-on learners. The whole body learner can learn better through role-playing, body mapping, puzzles and the use of computer technology. Students can be engaged in group activities that involve bodily movement such as dance, drama, sports, debate, charades, etc. for nurturing their learning. Educational institutes necessarily augment their curriculum with extracurricular and cocurricular activities to encourage kinesthetic learning among students. Some effective strategies used to involve unmotivated students during activities are:

- Option to choose activities for learning a particular concept
- Equal opportunity to every participant
- Attention and reward to students avoiding punishment
- Grading on participation by using score rubrics
- Encourage students to succeed and feel that they have accomplished learning through activity
- Organizing cooperative activities and positive feedback be given to encourage teamwork in a class.

The instructional strategies should include kinesthetic game-like format aligns with their lesson objectives. Technical colleges essentially include simulations, industrial visits, projects internship, role-playing, etc. towards fulfilling the same objective. Applied science, engineering and professional programs curriculums are equipped with corresponding laboratory subjects to visualize and to reason productively about these concepts.

The kinesthetic learning practice typically comes under threat due to its casual use in common vernacular and students misalignments to varying learning styles. All three parts of the brain, namely basal ganglia, cerebral cortex, and the cerebellum play equally important roles in the ability to learn new skills and master them in kinesthetic and skill learning. They work collectively for responding to sensory events, timing, controlling physical actions, and more. These parts of the brain won't help them get to their full potential unless a person is actively practicing the acquired skills. The interested reader may go through Favre (2009) for more detailed information regarding this learning theory.

Neuro-education also helps us to analyze biological changes in the brain from processing new information. It analyses the environmental, emotional, and social situations that best help the brain to store and retain new information via the linking of neurons as well as keeping the dendrites from being reabsorbed, losing the information. The three dominant methods for measuring brain activities are event-related potential, functional magnetic resonance imaging, and magneto-encephalography. The study of this field seems to have great potential to contribute to the field of learning theories. Researchers anticipated that new technologies and ways of observing will produce new scientific evidence that will refine the paradigms of what students need and how they learn best. Cognitive distortions like all-or-nothing thinking, magical thinking, overgeneralization, magnification, and emotional reasoning are typically taken care of by cognitive restructuring (a psychotherapeutic process) learning. On the other hand, intrinsic motivation is a natural motivational tendency where learning takes place by self-desire to seek out new things and new challenges, to analyze one's capacity, to observe and to gain knowledge. The two most important elements of intrinsic motivated learning are self-determination and an increase in perceived competence. It is a playful and curiosity-driven behavior even in the absence of reward. This intrinsically motivated learning often appears as a critical element in the cognitive, social, and physical development of learners.

Educational psychology heavily relies on a balance of empirical observations and quantitative methods. The study of education and child rearing generally unites the studies of history, sociology, and ethics with theoretical approaches. This has been emerging as a field of research study of social science due to additional quantitative emphasis of sociology and psychology on education. 'Common sense' approach of educational psychology research is now shifting to 'methodology' approach due to the encounter of independent and dependent variables through natural observation, experiments, or combinations of the two. The following list of technological resources incorporates computer-aided instruction and intelligence for educational psychologists and their students—intelligent tutoring system, cognitive tutor, cooperative learning, collaborative learning, problem-based learning, computer-supported collaborative learning, constructive alignment. These are addressed in other subsequent chapters.

2.3 INSTRUCTIONAL THEORY

Instructional theory (originated in 1970 in the USA) provides explicit guidance on how to help people during teaching–learning on a better way. Practitioners (instructional designers) focus on how to best structure material and instructional behavior to facilitate learning. Different actions with respect to different teaching–learning activities are designed and approaches of evaluation are given for help. This theory is influenced by four basic theories:

- Behaviorism—the theory that helps us understands how people conform to predetermined standards.
- Cognitivism—the theory that learning occurs through mental associations.
- Constructivism—the theory explores the value of human activity as a critical function of gaining knowledge.
- Bloom's taxonomy—taxonomy of education objectives—one of the first modern codifications of the learning process.

The instructional theory is not a learning theory since it describes how learning takes place where an instructional theory prescribes how to better help people learn. Learning theories are expected to direct how behaviorism (learning as response acquisition), cognitivism (learning as knowledge acquisition), constructivism (learning as knowledge construction), Bloom's taxonomy (classification of educational objectives and codification of learning process) will take part in instructional design. The ultimate goal of instructional theories is to understand the instructional systems to improve the process of instruction so that the probability of learning increases.

Instructional theories identify what instruction or teaching strategies that an educator may adopt to achieve learning objectives based on the learning style of the students. There are four tasks of instructional theory, namely knowledge selection, knowledge sequence, interaction management, a setting of interaction environment. It appears as a teaching tool consisting of methods, models, and strategies to facilitate learning. There are two primary methods of instructions, viz. universal and situational. Table 2.3 presents the principles of the universal methods of instructions whereas Table 2.4 presents the situational methods based on different approaches to instruction and different learning outcomes. Fundamental ideas for the post-industrial paradigm (new paradigm) of instructions are presented in the Table 2.5 with respect to the traditional paradigm.

Table 2.3: Universal methods of instructions

Principles	Details
Task-centered principle	Instruction should use a progression of increasingly complex whole tasks.
Demonstration principle	Instruction should guide learners through skill and engage in peer discussion/demonstration.
Application principle	Instruction should provide intrinsic or corrective feedback and engage peer-collaboration.
Activation principle	Instruction should build upon prior knowledge and encourage learners to acquire a structure for organizing new knowledge.
Integration principle	Instruction should engage learners in peer-critiques and synthesizing newly acquired knowledge.

Table 2.4: Situational methods based on different approaches to instructions and outcomes

Methods based on different approaches to instruction	Methods based on different learning outcomes
• Role play • Synectics • Mastery learning • Direct instruction • Discussion • Conflict resolution • Peer learning • Experiential learning • Problem-based learning • Simulation-based learning	• Knowledge • Comprehension • Application • Analysis • Synthesis • Evaluation • Affective development • Integrated learning

Table 2.5: Fundamental ideas for the post-industrial paradigm of instruction

S. No.	Ideas	Details
1.	Learner-centered *vs* teacher-centered instruction	With respect to the focus, instruction can be based on the capability and style of the learner or the teacher.
2.	Learning by doing *vs* teacher presenting	Students often learn more by doing rather than simply listening to instructions given by the teacher.
3.	Attainment based *vs* time-based progress	The instruction can either be based on the focus on the mastery of the concept or the time spent on learning the concept.
4.	Customized *vs* standardized instruction	The instruction can be different for different learners or the instruction can be given in general to the entire classroom
5.	Criterion-referenced *vs* norm-referenced instruction	Instruction related to different types of evaluations.
6.	Collaborative *vs* individual instruction	Instruction can be for a team of students or individual students.
7.	Enjoyable *vs* unpleasant instructions	Instructions can create a pleasant learning experience or a negative one (often to enforce discipline). Teachers must take care to ensure positive experiences.

Interested learners may go through Reigeluth (2013) for more understanding of instructional theory.

2.4 5E PEDAGOGICAL MODEL

5 Es of 5E pedagogical model are engage, explore, explain, elaborate, and evaluate. It is an instructional model with assumptions of constructivist approach to learning. It demonstrates that learners construct new ideas on top of their old ideas. This model can be used irrespective of the age of the learners. The 5 Es help learners as well as instructors to practice regular activities using prior knowledge and experiences towards meaning constructions through continuous assessments of their understanding of the concept.

Engage

Learners become mentally engaged in the concept, method and skill to be learned by connecting past and present learning experiences. It focuses learners' thinking of outcomes of the current learning activities and anticipates it.

Explore

Learners explore their surroundings and operate materials actively. They recognize and develop concepts, processes, and skills.

Explain

Learners explain the concept in this phase. They verbalize the understanding by demonstrating the new skills or behaviors. Instructors introduces the terms and definitions as well as explain the concept, processes, and behaviors or skills.

Elaborate

The learners build deeper and wider understanding of major concepts. They acquire more information to redefine their skills on the topic of interest.

Evaluate

The learners examine their understanding and abilities themselves in this phase. The teachers also assess the learners' skills development and understanding of the important concepts.

EXECUTIVE SUMMARY

- Learning theories demonstrate how knowledge is acquired, processed and retained. Pedagogical practices may be misleading without understanding learning theories.
- Educational philosophy guides us to understand how an individual learn something and those philosophies started to evolve from Plato.
- Educational psychology addresses the everyday psychological needs of teaching–learning and helps to understand human cognition, learning, and social perception.
- Behaviorism learning theory advocates learning as an aspect of conditioning a system of rewards and targets to change the behavior of learners through various stimuli in the environment.

- The cognitive theory believes learning as a study of learners with respect to their convolution and memory considering related mental constructs such as motivation, memories, emotions, traits, and beliefs.
- Constructivism theory believes acquisition of knowledge should be a personalized tailored process of construction dependent on learners' ability and what they already understand.
- Transformative theory focuses on the change (psychological, behavioral, and convictional) of learners' perception and view necessary with respect to environments and context.
- Remember, understand, apply, analyze, evaluate, and create are the six levels of Bloom's taxonomy of educational objectives. These help teachers to define learning outcomes and set assessment strategies of professional learners.
- Learning by teaching is a method of teaching where students are asked to prepare lessons to teach it by learning the materials in this method. Acquisition of subject matter along with the life skills is the emphasis of this theory.
- Kinesthetic learning takes place through physical activities carried out by the students, rather than simply listening to a lecture or watching demonstrations. VARK (visual, auditory, read-write and kinesthetic) model of kinesthetic learning emphasizes hands-on experimental learning.
- Instructional theory provides explicit guidance on how to help people during teaching learning on a better way. There are five principles (task-centered, demonstration, application, activation, and integration), by which instructional theory works.
- Instructional methods are basically of two types—based on different approaches to instruction and based on different learning outcomes.
- Instructional theories have observed a paradigm shift. Learner centered to teacher's centered, customized to standardized, collaborative to individual are few of these shifts.

Review Questions

1. What do you understand by learning theories? Differentiate between educational philosophy of Plato and Locke.
2. Describe the different learning theories with respect to educational psychology and compare them.
3. Compare and contrast between behaviorism and cognitive theory of learning. Which one is more modern?
4. Explain the constructivist theory of learning. How is it different from other learning theories?
5. Illustrate the transformative theory of learning. How is it different from other learning theories?
6. Describe the revised Bloom's taxonomy of educational objectives. Give its significance as a learning theory.
7. Write down the usefulness of learning by teaching. What is 'plastic platypus learning'?
8. Define kinesthetic learning. Explain the VARK model of kinesthetic learning.
9. What is the instructional theory? How does it influenced by learning theories? Briefly illustrate the universal methods of instructions.
10. Compare situational methods based on different approaches to instructions and outcomes.
11. Discuss the paradigm shift of instructional methods due to modernization.

Chapter 3

Pedagogical Practices

Objectives of this chapter
- To present different learning styles evolved in the field of education.
- To describe the teachers' role, duties and responsibilities.
- To illustrate the teaching styles and related issues.
- To explain some typical teaching rules.
- To discuss discipline- and degree-specific teaching effectiveness.

Expected outcomes of this chapter

After going through this chapter learners will be able to:
- Understand the different attributes and characteristics of different teaching styles.
- Apply suitable teaching styles for the case at his/her perusal.
- Evaluate different teaching styles with respect to his/her teaching domain.
- Formulate suitable (hybrid) teaching style necessary for his/her purpose.
- Perform the role, duties and responsibilities as a teacher as per standard.
- Maintain documentation of teaching practices for audit, corrective actions and improvements.
- Understand some role of technologies in teaching learning.
- Appreciate typical teaching rules.

3.1 LEARNING STYLES

We can teach students well if we know how they learn. We can improve the performance of our employees if we know how we ourselves learn or how to enhance their learning. Learning difficulties of so many students/employees are better understood as the teaching problems of tutors/workplace training managers. There is a strong intuitive appeal in the idea that teachers and course designers should pay closer attention to students' learning styles. Learning styles refer to a range of competing theories that intend to account for differences in individuals' learning, assuming individuals differ in how they learn. It is the way in which each learner begins to concentrate the process and retain new information. Researchers advocated that it is a biologically (genetically) imposed set of characteristics that make the same teaching method amazing for some and awful for others. Teachers assess the learning styles of their students and adapt their classroom methods to best fit each student's learning style. Individuals express preferences for how they prefer to receive information. A student will learn best if taught in a method deemed appropriate for the student's learning style. There are ample evidences that teachers couldn't assess the learning style of their students very accurately and hence the expected learning outcomes are not reached easily.

A. Visual, Auditory and Kinesthetic (VAK) Learning Style Categories

Learners may be categorized into the following three categories according to their preferred channel of perceptions. The following Table 3.1 provides the characteristics of the said learning styles and corresponding strategies suitable for them.

Table 3.1: Learning styles (of preferable channels of perception) and strategies

S. No.	Learning style	Characteristics	Strategies
1.	Visual learners	• Learn best from the information they can see or read. • Prefer written instructions as they remember the information they read. • Prefer visual aids to accompany verbal instructions. • Learn how something is done through the observation of others. • Enjoy information that is presented visually. • Visual learners encompass about 65% of all students.	• Provide a variety of visual materials to facilitate the learning process. • Visual learners will appreciate reading materials about the agency. • Demonstrate to students how something is done, rather than telling them. • Visual learners prefer to learn by observation before they feel comfortable performing the task independently. • Allow students many opportunities to observe others. • Provide written instructions and encourage students to take notes during supervision sessions. • Try to find a quiet environment during supervision sessions. • Visual learners are easily distracted by noise.
2.	Auditory learners	• Need to hear information to retain it • Prefer verbal instructions over written materials. • Remember information through verbal repetition. • Prefer to discuss ideas aloud in order to further process information. • Enjoy group discussions and activities. • About 30% of all students are auditory learners. • Sensitive to the speech quality, tone, and timbre of the voice, intonation, etc.	• Rephrase important points to increase understanding. • Ask students to discuss in their own words their understanding of the information being addressed. • Processing information and instructions aloud will increase the students' understanding and retention of the information. • Encourage discussion and invite questions. • Remember that students may not initially indicate that they do not understand. • Provide students with opportunities to talk to other social workers and staff members about their job functions and responsibilities.

(Contd.)

Table 3.1: Learning styles (of preferable channels of perception) and strategies *(Contd.)*

S. No.	Learning style	Characteristics	Strategies
3.	Kinesthetic (tactile) learners	• Prefer to learn through experience. • Obtain the greatest benefit by participation in an activity. • Remember information that they experience directly. • Enjoy acting out or recreating situations, such as role-playing. • Enjoy hands-on activities that involve active, practical participation.	• Provide opportunities for students to be involved in activities quickly. • Use role-plays to act out potential client scenarios. • Kinesthetic learners prefer to learn by doing and role-plays are an effective way to facilitate learning. • Provide early opportunities for students to have client contact. • Kinesthetic learners will be anxious to begin experiencing agency practice on their own and may become frustrated with continued observation. • Develop assignments that will be interactive.

B. Gregorc's Mind Styles Model

This model helps us to increase a better understanding of how we think and learn. It illustrates how our mind works. It depends on the measurement of how learners perceive and order new information. This style is a set of displayed behaviors that identifies individuals' mental strength and abilities. It recognizes our strength and weakness when comes to learning. This mind style model represents two continuums for individuals' preferences, namely perceptual preferences and ordering preferences to perceive and order new information. Perceptual preference is how we prefer to perceive information. It may be concrete or abstract. Ordering preference is how we arrange (or process) information. It may be sequential (linear) or random (non-linear) (Table 3.2).

Table 3.2: Perceptual preference of Gregorc's mind styles model

	Sequential	*Random*
Abstract	Abstract–Sequential	Abstract–Random
Concrete	Concrete–Sequential	Concrete–Random

Everybody exhibits each of the four styles, but we typically have one or two preferred way to think and learn. We all have the capability to perceive in concrete and abstract ways to some level. But we are more at ease using one more than others. The same is true with the order information.

C. Dunn and Dunn Model

According to the Dunn and Dunn model, learning style is not a single notion, but consists of related elements, that we call characteristics of the learning style. Strengths and preferences of each individual learner (learning characteristics) could be defined across the following five major categories of stimuli (Table 3.3).

Table 3.3: Dunn and Dunn Model's learning characteristics or stimuli

S. No.	Stimuli	Description
1.	Environmental	It incorporates individuals' preferences for the elements of sound, light, temperature including furniture and seating design.
2.	Emotional	It focuses on students' levels of motivation, responsibility, persistence, and need for structure.
3.	Sociological	It addresses students' preference for learning alone, with peers, in pairs, as part of a team, with either authoritative or collegial instructors.
4.	Physical	It incorporates the information-processing elements of global versus analytic and impulsive versus reflective behaviors.
5.	Psychological	It examines perceptual strengths (visual, auditory, kinesthetic or tactile), time-of-day energy levels, and the need for intake (food and drink) and mobility while learning.

Teachers need to adapt instruction and environmental conditions according to strong learners' preferences as far as possible. Learners' with minimum preferences can adapt more easily to different teaching styles and activities. Thus students can improve their achievement and motivation if teachers match preferences with individualized instruction, changes to environment, food and drink intake, time-of-day activities and opportunities to work alone or with others. The variance was also found in learning style preferences among males and females in different countries. Girl students often show stronger preferences in motivation, responsibility and working with others than boys whereas boys students show stronger preferences for kinesthetic learning.

D. Kolb's Flexibly Stable Learning Preferences Model

Kolb's model is based on experimental learning. This model has the following six characteristics.
1. Learning is best conceived as a process, not in terms of outcomes.
2. Learning is a continuous process grounded in experience.
3. Learning requires the resolution of conflicts between dialectically opposed modes of adaptation to the world.
4. Learning is a holistic process of adaptation to the world.
5. Learning involves transactions between the person and the environment.
6. Learning is the process of creating knowledge which is the result of the transaction between social knowledge and personal knowledge.

Effective learners need the following four kinds of ability to learn according to Kolb's model.
- From concrete experiences (CE);
- From reflective observations (RO);
- From abstract conceptualizations (AC);
- From active experimentations (AE).

The ideal learning process engages all four of these modes in response to situational demands. They form a learning cycle from experience to observation to conceptualization to experimentation and back to experience. These four capacities are structures along two independent axes—with the concrete-experiencing events at one end of the first axis and abstract conceptualization at the other. The second axis has active experimentation at one end and reflective observation at the other. The concern in the abstract–concrete dimension is between relying on conceptual interpretation (comprehension) or on immediate experience (apprehension) in order to grasp hold of experience. The concern in the active–reflective dimension is between relying on internal reflection (intention) or external manipulation (extension) in order to transform the experience. Individuals may exhibit a preference for one of the four styles—accommodating, converging, diverging and assimilating—depending on their approach to learning according to this model. Kolb's experience-transforming approach leading to prefer one of the following four learning styles (Table 3.4).

Table 3.4: Kolb's learning styles

S. No.	Learning styles	Combination	Strength and example
1.	Accommodator	Concrete experience + active experiment	Strong in 'hands-on' practical doing. (e.g. physical therapists)
2.	Converger	Abstract conceptualization + active experiment	Strong in practical 'hands-on' application of theories (e.g. engineers)
3.	Diverger	Concrete experience + reflective observation	Strong in imaginative ability and discussion (e.g. social workers)
4.	Assimilator	Abstract conceptualization + reflective observation	Strong in inductive reasoning and creation of theories (e.g. philosophers)

A learning style assessment method, namely learning style inventory has been evolved using Kolb's model. Though it is a widely accepted model with empirical support, it is not free from criticism like incorrectly dichotomizes individuals on the abstract/concrete and reflective/action dimensions of experiential learning.

E. Honey and Mumford Model

Honey and Mumford model adapted Kolb's experiential learning model and renamed the stages in the learning cycle to accord with managerial experiences such as having an experience, reviewing the experience, concluding from the experience and planning the next steps. They aligned these stages into four learning styles given in the following Table 3.5.

Table 3.5: Styles of Honey and Mumford Learning model

S. No.	Styles	Preferences
1.	Activist	Want to learn by dividing straight into new experiences and do not particularly like theory.
2.	Reflector	Like to stand back and gather information before coming to a conclusion.
3.	Theorist	Wants to fully understand the theory behind a subject before they feel comfortable with it.
4.	Pragmatist	Want to see the practical use of what they are learning and want practical techniques.

These learning styles are fixed personality characteristics and expected to acquire adaptable preferences either at will or through changed circumstances. Honey and Mumford's learning styles questionnaire (differs from Kolb's learning style inventory) often works as a self-development tool for managers where they can perform self-assessment and focus on strengthening under-utilized styles in order to learn better from a wide range of everyday experiences.

F. Allinson and Hayes' Cognitive Style Index (CSI)

Allinson and Hayes' cognitive style assumes intuition and analysis as the primary elements. Intuition refers to immediate judgment based on feeling and the adoption of a global perspective based on the characteristics of our right-brain orientation. Analysis refers to judgment based on mental reasoning and a focus on detail based on the characteristics of our left-brain orientation. Right-brained intuition power is required while managers to make quick decisions on the basis of soft information. On the other hand, left-brained analysis is witnessed as the kind of rational information processing that makes for good planning. A left-brain oriented learner (tends to be compliant) prefers structure and is most effective when handling problems that require a step-by-step solution while a right-brain oriented learner (tends to be non-conformist), prefers open-ended tasks and works best on problems favoring a holistic approach. The following table summarizes analysis–intuition (cognitive) styles model of Allinson and Hayes (Table 3.6).

Table 3.6: Allinson and Hayes' style attributes

Styles	Attributes
Analysis	• Detailed methodological work satisfies. • Careful to follow rules and regulations at work. • Take time and thoroughly consider all relevant factors while taking a decision. • Feel better to be safe than being sorry.
Intuition	• Make decisions and get on with things rather than analyse every last detail. • Find too much analysis results in paralysis. • Gut-feeling is just as good a basis for decision making as careful analysis. • Make many decisions on the basis of intuition.

Intuition rather than analysis would be more strongly associated with seniority in business organizations according to this model. Hence senior managers and directors appear as more intuitive than lower-level managers and supervisors.

G. 4MAT Learning Style

There are 4 major learning styles each of which portrays different strengths during the learning process (Table 3.7).

Different ideas about learning styles create distinct approaches to identify the specific attitudes and skills that characterize styles with respect to learning contexts and types of learners. The notion of reliability to identify learning styles is very much dependent on context and the type of students. Observation and interviews may be more likely and often practiced methods than learning styles instruments to capture some of the broad learning strategies that learners adopt.

Educational researchers are in favor of the opinion that learning styles are not fixed and that they are dependent on circumstance, purpose, and conditions. Interested readers may go through Coffield et al. (2004) for understanding more details on learning styles—theories and practices.

Table 3.7: 4MAT learning style preferences

S. No.	Styles	Description	Preferences
1.	Innovative/imaginative learners (feeling and reflecting)	S/he perceives with sensing and feeling and process reflectively. They need to answer the question, 'why?'	Interested in personal meaning and making connections. They prefer to have reasons for learning. Ideally, reasons that connect new information with personal experience and establish that information's usefulness in daily life.
2.	Analytic learners (reflecting and thinking)	S/he perceives with thinking and process reflectively. They need the facts and answer the question, 'what?'	Interested in acquiring facts in order to deepen their understanding of concepts and processes. Prefer to listen to and think about information, seek facts, and think things through.
3.	Common sense learners (thinking and doing)	S/he perceives with thinking and processes actively. They need to see real world relevance and answer the question, 'how?'	Interested in how things work. They want to 'get in and try it'.
4.	Dynamic learners (creating and acting)	S/he perceives with senses and feeling and processes actively. The need to answer the question, 'if?'	Interested in self-directed discovery. Prefer to seek hidden possibilities, explore, and learn by trial and error.

H. Felder-Silverman Learning Style Model

Richard Felder and Linda Silverman developed a learning style model to capture learning style differences among engineering students and to offer a strong base for instructors in technical education to design a teaching approach. The objective is to address the learning requirements of all the students. Though it is based on technical students, it may be useful to understand other learning models (Table 3.8).

Table 3.8: Felder-Silverman learning style model attributes

Active or reflective	Visual or verbal
Sensing or intuitive	Sequential or global

This model recognizes four traits or dimensions of personality that contribute to learning. These dimensions are active or reflective, sensing or intuitive, visual or verbal and sequential or global. Individual learning preferences are based on the combination of these styles.

- *Active or reflective*: It determines how we prefer to process information.
- *Sensing or intuitive*: It determines how we perceive information.
- *Visual or verbal*: It determines how we prefer information to be presented.
- *Sequential or global*: It determines how we prefer to arrange and move towards understanding information.

According to this model learning preferences are given in Table 3.9.

Table 3.9: Felder-Silverman learners' preferences

Type of learners	Preferences
Active	Prefers working with others in groups and try things out.
Reflective	Prefers working alone or with familiar partners.
Sensing	Prefers practical concerned with facts and procedures (concrete thinking).
Intuitive	Prefers innovative concerned with theories and meanings (conceptual thinking).
Visual	Prefers picture, diagram and flowcharts (visual representation).
Verbal	Prefers spoken and written explanations.
Sequential	Prefers learning in small incremental steps (linear thinking).
Global	Prefers learning in large steps (holistic thinking).

I. Personalized Instruction Model

According to this model, learning styles are based on the basic component in their personalized instruction model of schooling. Six such basic elements constitute the culture and context of personalized instruction. These are given in Table 3.10.

Table 3.10: Personalized instruction model elements

Category	Basic elements	Functions
Cultural components	Teacher role, student learning characteristics, and collegial relationships	It establishes the foundation of personalization and ensures that the school prizes a caring and collaborative environment.
Contextual factors	Interactivity, flexible scheduling, and authentic assessment	It establishes the structure of personalization.

Technology can help us to provide learning personalization and adaptation. This has gained prime focus in this digital age since a lot of facilities may be offered through technological innovations to fulfill the demands of fast and efficient learners. The details of the models and technology enhanced practices are illustrated in a separate chapter.

J. Technology Enabled Learning Style

Instructions through the computer or the web can be beneficial not only to some students but also to most of the students in this recent time. Although there are not many studies done comparing learning styles to web-based learning, the result of these studies can help instructors develop effective instructional methods based on students learning. Giving instruction through the use of technology is considered to be a new trend in the environment of education. Using computers in teaching–learning has received more attention during the past two decades. Computer-assisted instruction (CAI) has the potential to facilitate and supplement individual learning in a manner, unlike any other educational media. The research done on CAI programs has established that learning styles play a key role in any student's achievement. Recognizing that individuals have a unique learning style has become a very important factor in the future creation and usage of the CAI programs. The use of the CAI programs appeared to be helpful all year round due to the fact that pictures of say plants that only grow in the summer are able to be seen during winter months. The role of simple computers in CAI has been shifted to many other portable handheld devices like mobile phones. The total broad domain of education has been revolutionized by digital evolution. The pedagogical theories and practices must take new dimensions to fit into these evolutions. These have been explored in the coming chapters, especially in the next chapter.

3.2 TEACHERS' ROLE

Expectations from teachers are enormous to fulfill the demand of all stakeholders of the educational institutions and program of teaching with respect to existing curriculum and curriculum changes. The demands may vary with respect to subject or course. Documenting evidence of pedagogical practices in the classroom discourse appeared as the primary educational needs of outcome-based education. There are several common practices teachers must adhere in the classroom to promote students engagement in thoughtful and sustained discourse as generic pedagogical requirements. Teachers normally ask students—write or present explanation, guess or predict answers, debate alternative approach to problem, clarify or justify their assertions, understanding big ideas of curriculum along with appreciation of its value, capability and disposition to apply in future life, identifying effective discursive practices in domain-specific areas, recent research trends and practices in the topic.

Effective teaching includes observing students (and), listening carefully to their ideas and explanations. Teacher's responsibility also includes identifying major and minor competencies of individual learners besides pointing their pedagogical weaknesses and threats. Many students may not succeed in a course failing to engage in a particular course of study. It will be the joint responsibility of teachers, institutions and policymakers catering to the diverse group of learners. Characterizing effective and equitable pedagogy is not simply a matter of applying generic approaches, but expected to vary over courses and programs. Enhancing the competencies and identities of all learners rests with how teachers operationalize the core dimensions of pedagogy to a large extent. Teachers' themselves reiterate this by taking it as a challenge. In relation to classroom discourse, teachers must focus on developing a community to support and nurture each other's learning. A literature search is also required to focus attention on different contexts, different communities, and multiple ways of thinking and working to do the best possible job for their students. Literature search and community development will help them to develop knowledge and pedagogical competencies suited for multicultural societies, cosmopolitan citizenship, and educational change. Theorizing classrooms as activity systems will help them to do the best possible job for students. Within the collective activity system, the subject is the teacher, and the student is the object of pedagogical work. Classroom discourse is not a dialogue between equals no matter how equitable the goals of classroom community might be and no matter how skillful the teacher is at exploiting and scaffolding the pedagogy during knowledge construction.

The pedagogical practice is general with regards to generic motives and individual, with respect to unique imperatives. Contingent cultural scripts and imperatives build the students outcomes along with the teaching–learning of subject content. To the wider network of pedagogical activity systems, each classroom context brings its own characteristics. There is a strong cohesion between all the various elements and interrelated contingencies of a teacher's work while positive classroom discourse is in focus to develop a habit of mind to engage productively to support students understanding. Teaching is influenced by adaptive and interactive factors rather than additive and isolated variables, respectively. This indicates outcomes of teaching are contingent on a network of interrelated factors, conditions, and environments. Teachers modify and transform (i.e. adapt) their pedagogical practices in relation to their personal understandings and to the system level processes of the institution's concern.

Some significant issues follow from the above:
- Quality teaching is not simply the fact of 'knowing your subject' or the condition of 'being born a teacher.' Creating discourse opportunities in the classroom is a complex activity.
- We can't claim that teaching causes student outcomes by nesting teaching within a system's network. Understanding this prevents us from romanticizing the teaching. They can at least be occasioned by those practices if student outcomes are not caused by teaching practices.

Taking all these aspects together allows us to envisage what quality classroom discourse might look like. Facilitating courteous and purposeful interactions in the classroom contributes to the improvement of students' attitudes, aspirations and achievements. Students' sense of control is developed on the subject concern if the teachers are able to provide such context. Subject-specific research into classroom pedagogy is still in its initial stages, but we are gradually developing a teachers' sensibility from these researches. Experienced and new teachers, policy-makers and other educators often fail to appreciate the full potentials of pedagogical practice. We expect, teachers and policy-makers are now enlightened on the role of teachers and these discussions will assist all stakeholders towards realizing the teachers' role in a comprehensive way.

3.3 DUTIES AND RESPONSIBILITIES OF A TEACHER

1. **Subject knowledge**
   - To have expert knowledge of the subject area.
   - To pursue relevant opportunities to grow professionally and keep up-to-date about the current knowledge and research in the subject area.
2. **Teaching practices**
   - To plan and prepare appropriately the assigned courses and lectures.
   - To conduct assigned classes at the scheduled times.
   - To demonstrate competency in classroom instruction.
   - To implement the designated curriculum completely and in due time to plan and implement effective classroom management practices.
   - To design and implement effective strategies to develop self-responsible/independent learners.
   - To promote students' intrinsic motivation by providing meaningful and progressively challenging learning experiences which include, but are not limited to self-exploration, questioning, making choices, setting goals, planning and organizing, implementing, self-evaluating and demonstrating initiative in tasks and projects.
   - To engage students in active, hands-on, creative problem-based learning.

- To provide opportunities for students to access and use current technology, resources and information to solve problems.
- To provide opportunities for students to apply and practice what is learned.
- To engage students in creative thinking and integrated or interdisciplinary learning experiences.
- To build students' ability to work collaboratively with others.
- To adapt instruction/support to students' differences in development, learning styles, strengths and needs.
- To vary instructional roles (e.g. instructor, coach, facilitator, co-learner, audience) in relation to content and purpose of instruction and students' needs.
- To maintain a safe, orderly environment conducive to learning.
- To comply with requirements for the safety and supervision of students inside and outside the classroom.

3. **Assessment and/or evaluation**
   - To define and communicate learning expectations to students.
   - To apply appropriate multiple assessment tools and strategies to evaluate and promote the continuous intellectual development of the students.
   - To assign reasonable assignments and homework to students as per university rules.
   - To evaluate students' performances in an objective, fair and timely manner.
   - To record and report timely the results of quizzes, assignments, mid- and final semester exams.
   - To use student assessment data to guide changes in instruction and practice, and to improve student learning.

4. **Professionalism attitudes**
   - To be punctual and be available in the university during official working hours.
   - To comply with policies, standards, rules, regulations and procedures of the university.
   - To prepare and maintain course files.
   - To take precautions to protect university records, equipment, materials, and facilities.
   - To participate responsibly in university improvement initiatives.
   - To attend and participate in faculty meetings and other assigned meetings and activities according to university policy.
   - To demonstrate timeliness and attendance for assigned responsibilities.
   - To work collaboratively with other professionals and staff.
   - To participate in partnerships with other members of the university's community to support student learning and university-related activities.
   - To demonstrate the ability to perform teaching or other responsibilities, including good work habits, reliability, punctuality and follow-through on commitments.
   - To provide and accept evaluative feedback in a professional manner.
   - To create and maintain a positive and safe learning environment.
   - To carry out any other related duties assigned by the chairman of department.

5. **Behavioral attitudes**
   - To model honesty, fairness and ethical conduct.
   - To model a caring attitude and promote positive inter-personal relationships.
   - To model correct use of language, oral and written.

- To foster student self-control, self-discipline and responsibility to others.
- To model and promote empathy, compassion and respect for the gender, ethnic, religious, cultural and learning diversity of students.
- To demonstrate skill when managing student behavior, intervening and resolving discipline problems.
- To model good social skills, leadership and civic responsibility.

6. **Specific targets** (Table 3.11)

Table 3.11: Specific targets of teachers

S. No.	Task	Targets
1.	Course specifications	During the introductory lecture of the course, course specifications and evaluation strategies should be shared with the students: • Prerequisite • Objectives • Syllabus • Outcomes • Lesson plan
2.	Class activity report	Class activity report must be prepared for each class lecture and placed in the course file: • Topic covered • Attendance and absentees (for multiple consecutive classes) • Theory and problems discussed • Pedagogical classifications or taxonomy with respect to the topics covered, mentioning books, class notes, handouts, web references, etc. • Discussion of related important topics beyond syllabus and cocurricular activities (if any).
3.	Attendance	A copy of the attendance summary sheet must be displayed on notice board after every 4 weeks of the semester and a copy should be placed in the course file.
4.	Quizzes	Quiz contest must be conducted at least once in a week and a copy of the result (weekly) must be displayed on notice board and a copy should be placed in the course file. Quizzes/assignments should be equally distributed before and after the mid examination.
5.	Assignments	Within 1 week of receiving every assignment, a copy of the result must be displayed on notice board and a copy should be placed in the course file.
6.	Mid-semester exam	Within 2 weeks of the examination, a copy of the result must be displayed on notice board and a copy should be placed in the course file.
7.	Final attendance report	A copy of the final student attendance report must be submitted to COE/HOD office before the end-semester examination.
8.	Setting of mid and final papers	All examination papers should be set within the prescribed course made known to the students by the teacher following COs and taxonomy.

(Contd.)

Table 3.11: Specific targets of teachers *(Contd.)*

S. No.	Task	Targets
9.	End-semester exam	Within 2 weeks of the examination, submit the comprehensive results to the controller of examination along with answer-sheets of mid- and end-semester exams.
10.	Course file	Course file for each course must be kept updated all the time for periodic review by the chairman/principal/director or dean (academics)/HOD/course director and random checks by the quality assurance director (QAD) having the following components • Course details (name, code, contact hours, credits, etc.) • Faculty profile (short biography with teaching and research experiences) • Institute and departmental mission, vision • Program educational objectives (PEOs) • Program outcomes (POs) • Program specific outcomes (PSOs) • Course objectives, course prerequisite, syllabus, textbooks, reference books, web references • Course outcomes (COs) statements • Mapping/correlations between COs and POs with justifications • Mapping/correlations between COs and PSOs with justifications • Lecture/lesson plan with CO and taxonomy mapping with justifications • Gaps in the syllabus to meet industry/professional requirements • Topics beyond syllabus/advanced topics • List of assignments and quiz questions • Quizzes performance reports • Class timetable • Students' attendance • Course diary (day-wise topics covered, teaching aids used, difficulty faced and corresponding actions taken reports). • Unit test (UT) questions papers with COs and taxonomy mappings. • Unit tests marks, attainments and students performance analysis, action taken reports (if any) • Question banks (MCQ and descriptive with marks allocations) • Semester question (previous and current) papers. • Semester-wise students marks/grades, attainments and performance analysis. • Rubrics for evaluation of unit test answer scripts, semester examination answer scripts, assignments, quizzes. • Students' feedback, analysis of students' feedback and action taken reports. • Sample UT answer scripts, assignments answer with evaluation and allocating negative marks of mistakes.

3.4 TEACHING STYLES

Teaching style is a collection of special behaviors including actions, interactions, and communications exhibited in persistent and dependable way the teacher approaches the learners across techniques of teaching. It is perceived during conducting classes. Teachers' educational philosophy is manifested through the practice of teaching styles. The said style shows the balance between the guiding vision (beliefs, values) and attitudes towards all the elements of teaching–learning through practical aspects of teaching. It integrates the following.

- Different content needs with respect to professional needs.
- The ways in which one accumulates, systematizes, and alters information.
- The way of using media during interactions (viz. conveying information, interacting with learners, managing tasks, supervising work in progress) and socializing learners to the field.

Teaching style plays important role for quality teaching and fruitful students' outcomes. Understanding and measuring (valid and reliable) the same gain growing significance for practicing teachers and teacher educators as well as researchers of education. Due to paradigm shift from behaviorist to constructivist, many practicing teachers are facing real world difficulties in changing their teaching behavior. Policy makers and curriculum planners need to identify what teaching style will best suit for the envisaged curriculum for implementation. Teachers also need to identify best suited teaching style to cater the needs of the target learners in curriculum framework in force. Teacher educators must also be aware of teaching style preferences of trainee teachers to provide them individualized experience affecting healthy style-profile shifts among them. Teaching styles are greatly influenced by the following array of personality factors.

- Cognitive factors,
- Experiences during own schooling,
- Learning styles,
- Institutional factors and
- Curricular factors.

We also need to gauge how and to what extent such factors influence the preferred teaching style for students' outcomes needs to be exposed further. A refined version of the list of teaching styles is presented in the Table 3.12 taken from Gafoor (2016) with respect to their chronological development.

Expert, formal authority, personal model, facilitator, and delegator are the five styles cluster identified by Grasha (2002) focusing on different outcomes in childhood. The expert-style teachers have the information, knowledge and skills essentially required by the students. S/he keeps up the position as an expert by exhibiting detailed knowledge with frequent references to information and facts. It may lead to students becoming anxious by the teacher's rich knowledge if it is over-used in the classroom. Formal authority style teachers emphasize on a clear and systematic way of conducting class in line with institutional expectations. S/he earns status among learners because of her/his knowledge, position and formal organizations roles as a senior person in the field. A personal model style teacher teaches by encouraging students as a role model to observe and follow the teacher's approach through personal examples. The facilitator style teachers incorporate an open and flexible approach to lesson delivery

Table 3.12: Summary of categories of teaching styles [Gafoor (2016)]

Year	Scholar	Types of teaching styles
1940	Corey	Direct, indirect
1951	Wispe	Directive, permissive
1959	Anderson	Authoritarian, democratic, laissez-faire
1968	Soar	Direct, mixed, indirect
1970	Flanders	Direct, indirect, discipline centered
1970	Axelrod	Intellect-centered, instructor-centered, drill-centered, person-centered, content-centered
1974	Berger	Teacher-centered, student-centered, student–teacher cooperation centered
1976	Bennet	Formal, informal
1977	Dunn and Dunn	Individualizing, somewhat individualizing, transitional, somewhat traditional, traditional
1982	Lenz	Proactive, reactive
1982	Dressel and Marcus	Teacher-centered, student-centered, discipline-centered
1983	Weinberg	Direct, peer, problem-solving, group approach
1984	Henson and Borthwick	Task-oriented, cooperative planner, child-centered, subject-centered, learning-centered, emotionally exciting
1985	Jarvis	Socratic, didactic, facilitative, student reactive
1986	Robinson	Lecturing/charismatic, teacher-centered, child-centered
1993	Grigorenko and Sternberg	Legislative, executive, judicial, global, local, liberal, conservative
1994	Oi and Stimpson	Guided learning, exposition, inquiry
1994	Heimlich and Norland	Expert, provider, facilitator, enabler
1994	Quirk	Assertive, suggestive, collaborative, facilitative
1996	Grasha	Expert, formal authority, personal, facilitator, delegator
1996	Singer	Content-oriented, process-oriented, motivation-oriented, student involvement behavior, discipline-centered behavior, management of feedback behavior, professor involvement behavior
2002	Mosston and Ashworth	Command, practice, reciprocal, self-check, inclusion, guided discovery, convergent discovery, divergent discovery, learner-designed, learner-initiated.

by student–teacher interactions. This style is more prone to a 'student-centered' approach coupled with enthusiasm to explore alternate ways of completing tasks. The teachers supervise learners by suggesting alternatives, exploring options, asking questions in this facilitator style. This style may emerge students discomfort in response to the open atmosphere when practicing teacher is not executing the style in a positive and affirming manner. The delegator style uses a full student-centered approach where students are delegated to take responsibility while developing their competence to function in an independent mode. The style can be time consuming and may misread students' readiness to take on independent work before they are ready to take it on. Researchers in this field recommended blending of styles that can dominate the teaching since almost all styles are not free from obstacles.

Singer (1996) advocated some styles cluster for adults and college teaching. Summary of the styles and their corresponding attributes are presented below in Table 3.13.

Table 3.13: Summary of the attributes of college-teaching styles

S. No.	Styles	Attributes
1.	Content-oriented	• Teaching primarily involves imparting facts, principles, and concepts related to an organized body of knowledge. • Knowledge is a commodity that is transferred from teachers to students. • Student mastery of course subject matter is the primary goal of teaching. • The instructor is the primary source of knowledge and authority in the classroom.
2.	Process-oriented	• Education should involve students in a series of personally meaningful experiences. • It is important for students to learn to make quantitative and qualitative judgments about the extent to which course content and instructors' methods satisfy personal and predetermined criteria. • Students' reactions and feelings about the subject matter represent a significant part of their learning experience. • The most important teaching goal is to motivate students.
3.	Motivation-oriented	• Class participation is considered in awarding the final course grade. • Student attendance is weighted in determining the final course grade. • Individual students are responsible for the presentation of course content. • Class discussion is used for disseminating course content. • Learning activities emphasize peer interaction and collaboration. • Students are encouraged to express individual viewpoints.
4.	Student-involvement centered	• Class participation is considered in awarding the final course grade. • Student attendance is weighted in determining the final course grade. • Individual students are responsible for the presentation of course content. • Class discussion is used for disseminating course content. • Learning activities emphasize peer interaction and collaboration. • Students are encouraged to express individual viewpoints.
5.	Discipline-centered	• Examination questions require the retention and memorization of principles, facts, and concepts. • The class format is structured and formal. • Course content is presented using the lecture method. • Objective tests are the primary means for assessing performance.
6.	Management of feedback centered	• Papers and assignments are promptly returned to students. • Graded tests are promptly returned to students.
7.	Professor involvement centered	• Student learning is assessed using essay examinations. • Reading assignments and in-class activities are updated and revised to reflect advancements in the field. • The course is amended to incorporate feedback of students who have previously taken the course. • Assignments are especially designed to foster critical thinking.

3.5 TYPICAL TEACHING RULES TO REMEMBER

The '20-40 Rule'

Talk for 20 minutes out of every hour and use the rest of the time for reinforcement, skills practice or discussion.

The '15-85 Rule'

Devote 15% of your time to lecture or presentation, 85% of the time should be devoted to small-group activities and large-group sharing exploration.

The '90-20-8 Rule'

Adults can listen with understanding for 90 minutes. They only listen with retention for 20 minutes. They need to be involved every 8 minutes. So, break your content into chunks that are 20 minutes or less in length, and involve people in those chunks at least once every 8 minutes.

3.6 DISCUSSIONS

Research found that disciplinary perspectives greatly influence cognitive and behavioral aspects of teaching and learning. Content-teaching paradigms and some instructional behaviors are at least partly shaped by the disciplinary affiliations of faculty. The academic discipline is the natural focal point of teaching paradigms and the behaviors associated with them when teaching and learning center on subject matter. The composition of the knowledge itself facilitates conformity relating to the content to be taught and the accompanying teaching methods. Contextual factors, such as class size and class level, sometimes necessitate temporary paradigm shifts and behavioral realignments from faculty. Essential factors, such as motivation and job satisfaction, force the growth needs of faculty over the entire career span.

Teaching effectiveness and faculty vitality are either enhanced or weaken in differing degrees with respect to developmental context. Cognitive theories of motivation may provide an appropriate direction for future faculty development in this regard. Faculty cognitions and behavioral responses greatly influence effective teaching-learning. It may be evident that content, process, and motivation are equally considerable elements of teaching. However, the interplay between these components and their complex relationship to behavioral and situational factors is often less prominent or overlooked. A belief in the hypothesis that there is no one best way to teach and/or learn is the key to effective teaching-learning. This idea offers a visionary approach that promotes 'multiframe thinking'.

Lots of researches are conducted and are still going on to find the effectiveness of learning styles and teaching styles independently as well as to match them together. This effectiveness is subject to learners' specifications, demography, facilities available, national and institutional mission-visions. Technologies are taking crucial role and observed to be used very frequently to bridge the gaps in the effective teaching-learning system development. This technology enhanced pedagogical practicing initiatives, are cultivated and nurtured in the coming chapter in this book.

EXECUTIVE SUMMARY

- Learning styles refer to the ways in which each learner begins to concentrate process and retain new information during learning.
- VAK model of learning style categorizes learners into visual, auditory and kinesthetic learners according to their preferred channel of perceptions.
- Gregoric's mind styles model depends on the measurement of how learners perceive and order new information based on the mind works.
- Dunn and Dunn learning style model demonstrates learning characteristics using five major categories of stimuli—environmental, emotional, sociological, physical, and psychological.
- Honey and Mumford learning model renamed the Kolb's stages in the learning cycle as activist, reflector, theorist and pragmatist to accord with managerial experiences.
- Allinson and Hayes cognitive style assumes intuition-analysis to immediate judgment based on feeling and the adoption of a global perspective based on the characteristics of our right-brain orientation.
- 4MAT learning style adopts 4 major learning styles, namely innovative, analytic, common sense and dynamic, each of which portrays different strengths during the learning process.
- Personalized instruction model works on personal references of learners based on their cultural components and contextual factors.
- Technology enabled learning style is based on the instructional delivery through computers, web, mobiles and other PDAs where learner's have the liberty to learn at his/her best preferences.
- Teachers play most crucial role to fulfill the requirements of all stakeholders as far as pedagogic practices is concern.
- Teachers must be an expert in subject knowledge, meticulous in teaching practices, serious in learner's assessment and/or evaluations, maintain behavioral and professional attitudes, and achieve specific targets with documentation as their duties and responsibilities of pedagogic practices.
- Teaching styles are greatly influenced by cognitive factors, experiences during own schooling, learning styles, institutional factors and curricular factors. Teachers as to choose a teaching style according to his/her teaching environments and factors. For example, teaching styles of school level will not be the same as college level.

Review Questions

1. What do you understand by learning styles? Write the names of learning styles useful for present day learners.
2. Explain the characteristics and strategies of VAK learning styles.
3. Why are Gregorc's learning styles called mind style model? Briefly explain the perceptual preferences of this model.
4. Describe the different stimuli of Dunn and Dunn learning style. How learners' preferences affect learning in this style?
5. Write down the characteristics of Kolb's flexibly stable learning preferences model. Describe the attributes of the same with their strength and example.

6. Write the attributes and preferences of Honey and Mumford learning style model. How is it different from Kolb's model?
7. What is cognitive style index? How it works? Briefly explain the attributes of 4MAT learning style.
8. What is technology-enhanced learning style? What are different elements of personalized instructional learning style model?
9. What role does a teacher play in pedagogical practices?
10. Write down the duties and responsibilities of a teacher in the teaching–learning process.
11. Write down the specific targets that a teacher has to achieve during pedagogic practices.
12. Illustrate the different teaching styles existing in modern pedagogical practices. How is college teaching style different from school teaching style?
13. Briefly explain '20–40 rule', '15–85 rule', and '90–20–8 rule' of teaching to enhance remembering.
14. How do discipline and degree level affect the pedagogical practices?

Chapter 4

Digital Pedagogy

Objectives of this chapter

- Introduce the characteristics of the digital age.
- Explain the components, processes, and performances of innovations in pedagogy.
- Present the activity system of digital pedagogy.
- Explain the principles of digital pedagogy.
- Present the new pedagogies in the digital age.
- Explain the theories of instructional technologies with respect to digital pedagogy.
- Present the taxonomy of digital tools and learning resources of digital pedagogy.
- Address the debates emerging in this new field of study.

Expected outcomes of this chapter

After going through this chapter learners will be able to:
- Understand the basic principles and applications of digital pedagogy.
- Explain the characteristics and importance of innovations in digital pedagogy.
- Advocate the implementations of digital pedagogy across all educational systems.
- Analyze the taxonomy of digital tools and learning resources in digital pedagogy.
- Analyze the theories of instructional technologies with respect to digital pedagogy.
- Assess a given pedagogical system towards digital pedagogy.
- Modify the instructional designs incorporating digital tools and learning resources.

4.1 THE DIGITAL AGE

The digital age is the historic period accompanied by a revolution in the society, industry, and economy with modern digital technologies. This is also known as 'information age' or 'computer age' or 'media age'. New technologies, user devices, methods of interaction with other humans and devices enter the domain to characterize the term digital. The digital age set in motion with the widespread use of the internet is intense. The democratization of information evolution and usage has come with personal web pages, social networks, blogs, podcasts, wikis and other applications of ICTs/digital technologies. All these together ensure public participation in online communities. Mobiles and other wireless handheld devices are assimilated with global computer networks to provide location-independent access to information services. The contexts of education are changing with a social and cultural reorganization that took place with this information revolutions. Academic, scientific, research and commercial enterprises are now heavily dependent on data being shared on the internet almost instantaneously. These are important for the development of a knowledge economy simplifying the way of making decisions for transactions and significantly lowering costs both for producers and for buyers. Academic institutions have a central role to play to resolve the dispute between digital commons and digital consumerism. Less thought has been observed in the knowledge that is forgotten during digitization, practical skills that are intensely rooted in its use and other implicit knowledge coupled with the behavior of practice. Incidentally, exactly this kind of knowledge is being practiced by effective teachers and by effective learners too. Following are some characteristics which define learning in the digital age.

1. **Engaging in learning experience:** The learning experience must be attractive, relevant and meaningful both for the learner and for the organization to sustain the engagement. This is facilitated by learner-centric instructional design towards business allied objectives.
2. **Empowering, personalizing and self-directed:** Learners are empowered to choose what, how and when they learn using learning technologies. Learners' individual preferences and needs are satisfied in this era besides individuals directing themselves towards which learning to follow.
3. **Just-in-time, on-demand, in context:** Specific skill or knowledge gap encountered by digital learners are bridged at the time of occurrence to achieve the desired goal. The learning facilities must be available in the real world and on-the-job in spite of teaching knowledge and theories beforehand.
4. **Right blend of social, formal, informal and experiential learning:** Technology supports the right blending of accessible internal and external information through the interaction with networks of experts and peers. The right mixing and right format for the right purpose ensures learning more effective.
5. **Hyper-connected with analytics:** To enhance the effectiveness of learning, learners require connecting with learning resources, peers and experts through ICT. The institutions involved must ensure simple tools of learning analytics for different activities like understanding learners' insights, learning-need analysis, learning-assets analysis, learning-usability analysis, learning-improvements and effectiveness analysis.
6. **Continuous learning based on inquiry, exploring and doing:** Learning must be continuous, may be on the job, based on collective experiences and existing knowledge. The instructional design is expected to promote search, exploring and doing for finding research solutions to a particular state of affairs.

4.2 COMPONENTS, PROCESSES AND PERFORMANCES OF INNOVATIONS IN PEDAGOGY

Components

Digital pedagogy sometimes known as technopedagogy has three essential components:
1. Content
2. Pedagogy
3. Technology

Content is the subject matter or materials to be taught. Pedagogy presents the accumulated processes, practices, procedures, strategies, and methods of teaching–learning.

It also encompasses knowledge about the aims of instruction, student learning, and assessment. The technology consists of latest machinery such as the internet, computer, mobiles, e-books, digital video, open educational resources (OER) and commonplace technologies including blackboards, overhead projectors, and books.

Technology has the potential and inherent abilities to change the social and educational environment of classrooms by helping learners to learn and teachers to teach. The value of technological innovations must be judged with respect to pedagogical goals and pedagogical assessments. It is also not easy to judge the goodness of technology outside the rationale for which it was produced. For example, a screwdriver is a superior innovation in some cases and would be bad at times when a wrench is required. Technological innovations can provide good performance with the availability of good pedagogy and good people. The performances are realized through outcomes and implementations where pedagogy and technology are closely linked to getting the best results. Innovations are expected to be steeped in all academic theories and practices. This includes tying the innovation in learning theories to establish realistically and involving activities for students.

The building blocks of the innovations are normally designed from a social constructivist perspective. The following are the important issues of the building blocks of innovations.

- To engage students more, the innovations must include interesting and challenging content designed from authentic, meaningful and real-world problems.
- To ensure the self-regulating role of learners, students should have the opportunity to take control of their learning offering ownership of the solution design of the project or problem.
- To adopt social constructivist learning theories, an active student's participation must be guaranteed steeped with good pedagogy.
- To create a variety of artifacts, students must learn the concept, apply those concepts and represent knowledge reflecting their understanding and resulting solution of the problems.
- To realize the manifestation and feedback of their learning tasks, publications of their learning outcomes are the way out because of the following:
  - Teachers and researchers can infer from their study by transforming meaning and strategies relevant to the social domain.
  - The materials become accessible for subsequent reflection and analysis by which the students can revisit and revise their artifacts for learning enrichment.
  - Knowledge construction, knowledge integration, self-regulatory behavior and higher-order thinking outcomes of learning are realized through feedbacks and scaffolding the outcomes thereof.

Process

A pedagogically sound innovation process includes creation (or design), implementation and use by innovator, teacher, and students. It often acts as a cognitive learning tool. Following are four important concepts related to the people in innovation implementation.

- Technology implementation may be bidirectional dialogic interaction between innovation and established practice. Innovations and established practices are dependent on one another and changes in each other simultaneously.

- The innovator may be the class teacher, technology expert (developer), technology coordinators, and volunteers from local businesses or educational researchers. External specialists are often highly essential to the success of innovations particularly if the teacher is not feeling comfortable with technology to start with.
- Innovations are realized through the flexible nature of both teaching and technology. According to the social constructivist theory, learning requires continuous improvisations, adaptation and decision making in fluctuating circumstances. Teachers must require innovations to supports all these. Developers can help teachers through technology innovations to reach the desired outcomes of modern age education.
- Good innovations require legitimate participation and coparticipate in the practices. This legitimate participation allows learners to practice the tasks for which they are enrolled to become a master practitioner.

Performance

Technology innovation must be judged with pedagogy and people from two angles, namely what they were and how they were implemented. We may also be interested to judge an innovation by the question 'Is this innovation good?' or 'Is this a good innovation?' The first one is evaluating the goodness of innovation outside the world (to appeal to some external standard for goodness), whereas last one is judging within the world of innovations.

Innovation will be treated as successful if the pedagogical goal is attained. There should have appropriate tools to measuring the student's performance with respect to the pedagogical design to ensure the quality of the innovation. The following three criteria are essential to measure the performance of the pedagogical innovations.

- *Appropriate use of technology*: Technologies are not good or bad inherently, but it is the pedagogy and people, they determine the quality impact of creations, implementation and subsequent use of technology. A technology innovation may have failed only because of the reason that the school not having enough computers to use by the students. On the other hand, the good performance makes certain technologies conducive to teaching–learning environments.
- *Assessing learning outcomes through cognitive tools*: A successful innovation by teachers or researchers should meet the pedagogical goals evidenced by cognitive measured through standardized tests. Assessment of the cognitive outcomes of technology uses has two important aspects. (1) First relates to having good innovation realized by both the pedagogy and dialogic relationships among the innovator, teacher, and students. (2) Second is a very difficult endeavor that measures student-learning gains made with technology.
- *Diverse method of more complex analysis*: Evaluating the gains in the cognitive domain is a vital component of technology research as emotional and social development (affective gains) often drive it. Teachers should be awarded for innovations implementation technology in their curriculum delivery. Individuals' interaction with computers, handheld devices, television, and new media now became social and natural like real life. Success and failure of technology innovations might depend on implicit assumptions and expectations of our students on technology rather than the pedagogy we put up into those technologies.

A good innovation involves people, pedagogy and performance. This can be brought into existence through appreciate the use of technology to provide desired learning outcomes. Technological pedagogical content knowledge (teaching how to teach rather than teaching the subject), are the key elements for desired innovation performances through technology. With the advancement of the World Wide Web, it has become easier to focus on the impact of technology in education without focusing on curriculum, pedagogy, and instructions. The practitioners must be careful about the emotional, psychological and social development of students during educational technology integration approaches.

4.3 ACTIVITY SYSTEM FOR BALANCE IN DIGITAL PEDAGOGY

The technical mastery is not the only implementation issues faced by academics. Robust and friendly technologies are available to create technology-mediated learning environments. Researchers have established an activity system, a cross-disciplinary framework, for the analysis of data associated with human practices. This represents a mapping of how individuals interact within a given environment over the years. The elements of this activity system are subject, rules, tools (technical, operational, process), community and object with each being sloping to an outcome (Fig. 4.1).

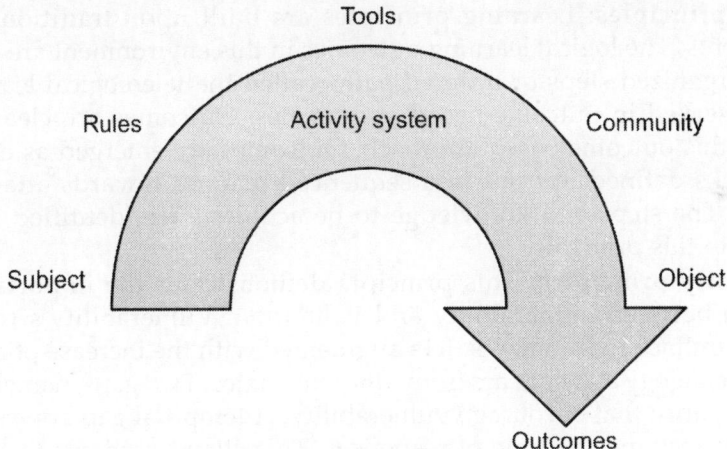

Fig. 4.1: Activity system

Developing an activity system using mediated learning environments is a multifaceted challenging and continuing process. Redefinition of rules and roles drive the technical mastery over the domain. To achieve learning goals, a balance between human elements and technical mastery issues need to be combined as they come with emergent digital pedagogy maintaining dependability issues. Immediate technical support and altered work practices have been emerging as the fundamental factors for the success of effective mediated learning environments.

4.4 NEW PRINCIPLES OF DIGITAL PEDAGOGY

With respect to digital revolutions, silicon coating on pedagogy by copy–paste operations may not be sufficient in technology-mediated online teaching–learning.

New principals are required to structure the practices of digital pedagogy and proceed further with reduced pressures. For this purpose, the principles of digital pedagogy may be classified from the following four perspectives.

1. **Power principles:** Primarily, these principles govern the pedagogy towards learner-centric approach from teacher-centric approach by moving away towards homeocracy from autocracy.
   - *Old principle autocracy*: Appropriate governance model for tradition pedagogy was autocratically driven by teachers. Content is designed from single user or group perspectives. Here the content is not a result of the normal voting process. Small changes are either accepted or rejected by users groups. Online digital environments have the flexibility to move beyond this autocratic model. A new form of decision making in collaborative environments is empowered by individuals making changes.
   - *New principle homeocracy*: Homeocracy is governed by gradual evolutionary changes towards a comparatively steady equilibrium between interdependent elements. It is a mechanistic control and structure that drive the said change. These principles are dependent on the internal conditions of the system and feedback control mechanisms. If accepted, small incremental fine-tuning are tested and inculcated into the new space. The environment is changed by the power of small incremental decision making.

2. **Learning principles:** Learning principles are built upon traditional learning environments. The logical learning outcomes in this environment are driven by a series of organized steps or ordered paths called the teleological learning path. This is observed in outcome-based approaches. Outcomes are clearly defined lucidly in this outcome-based approach. Outcomes are emerged as execution of several tasks defined upfront in a sequenced manner towards attaining these outcomes. The steps and knowledge to be acquired are identified in advance according to this principle.

3. **Vulnerability principles:** This principle demonstrates the importance of the interaction between vulnerability and validation. Vulnerability's role is quite implicit in online environments. It is augmented with the increase of affordances of digital pedagogy and appears from different angles. Two gaps, namely temporal and spatial, arise that encourage vulnerability. A temporal gap appears between the time of post and the time of responses. This allows students to think about their responses to the question posted for which response they are shouted. In addition, a spatial gap arises due to differences in the actual physical location of the students.

4. **Validation principles:** Online spaces offer a variety of facilities and mechanisms through which validation is enacted. These include likes, dislikes, agreements, disagreements, replies to comments, hash-tags such as #nice, #like, #great, and shares of posts. Validation takes place through all these mechanisms. All of these help to validate the content of the post. These are not only a mental validation but also a technological validation. Posts becoming even more visible that attract more responses, though these may be negative responses or rising debate in the content stream. These types of validation are missing in traditional face-to-face learning environments where validation is typically conducted by the teacher.

There are several principles for the effective incorporation of digital pedagogy. These are given below.
1. **Focus on collaboration:** Focus on collaboration is truly beneficial since it facilitates skill development necessary for working in a team during future employment. It appends a dimension to group work towards soft skill development through the appropriate choice of technologies.
2. **Design for inclusion:** It is true that all students are not technology savvy. There are issues of the digital divide with the technology use. So, it is very important to ensure everyone's participation through the inclusion of the right instructional design.
3. **Work towards class participation or learner engagement:** The design of digital pedagogy must be such that there should have suitable tools for engaging students in class activities. To fulfill these requirements, proper considerations of learner's prior knowledge, desires and expectations must be analysed.
4. **Acknowledgement of the learning context:** The design should consider positional indications within the broader program of study for the learner. The system must implement such learning design with those indications and linear and non-linear navigation facilities.
5. **Learner challenge:** To ensure active learners' participation, the design should include student's encouragements through tests, challenges and being self-critical. Frequent such facilities should be offered in the effective digital pedagogy design.
6. **Provision of practice:** The design must include facilities to practice acquired skills during learning. These also include encouraging students to articulate and demonstrate to their peers what they are learning.
7. **Communities:** There are advantages to working within the existing communities and networks with which practitioners are affiliated beforehand. This put forward another issue of authenticity and ownership. Practitioners should experience interventions as genuinely sharing their concerns and being supported by people with whom they can recognize.
8. **Professional learning:** Digital pedagogy practice requires practitioners to alter their conceptions of teaching and learning through opportunities to construct their own meanings, learning from experience, informal learning, action learning, problem-based learning and peer-supported learning.

The following are the key attributes to be verified while designing digital pedagogy for ensuring its quality issues. Description of these attributes is given in a tabular form in Table 4.1.

Following are nine principles of designing digital pedagogy.
1. The design should be activity-focused rather than content.
2. The design should be a community focus rather than repository focus.
3. Search design should be based on free-text, not metadata.
4. The design should include automated usage tracking and rating systems.
5. The design should include a small set of simple authorization.
6. Learning software and learning content should be made freely available.
7. Resources should be easily personalized by others.
8. The design should facilitate integration with learning platforms and communities for sharing.
9. The design should offer options to share all facilities easily.

Table 4.1: Attributes for designing digital pedagogy

S. No.	Attributes	Descriptions
1.	Adaptivity	Does the tool accommodate non-linear learning?
2.	Complexity	Does the tool address language complexity on multiple levels?
3.	Input	Is there rich, comprehensible input?
4.	Noticing	Are users directed to notice useful elements of input?
5.	Output	Are there regular opportunities for language production?
6.	Scaffolding	Are learning tasks modeled and mediated?
7.	Feedback	Do users get focused and informative feedback?
8.	Interaction	Is there a way for users to interact and work together?
9.	Automaticity	Are there opportunities for practice?
10.	Chunks	Do the tool help with learning the formulaic language?
11.	Personalisation	Does the tool encourage personal relationships with the material?
12.	Flow	Is the tool engaging, challenging, with clear benefits?

4.5 NEW PEDAGOGIES

There are four new pedagogic approaches that are appropriate to a digital world. They interplay among themselves. The intensity of the interplay depends on the teacher's adherence to the digital principles. These new pedagogies are discussed below.

1. **Consumption to creation:** From the perspective of digital pedagogy, the first pedagogic alteration is consumption (pedagogic) to the creation (pedagogic) of content. A large chunk of content is distributed to students and they are asked to understand that content together with its reproduction in a test or examination. This is known as the consumption of content. This focuses on the transfer of facts, understanding, and remembering. These are according to the core concept of earlier theories of pedagogy. On the other hand, digital pedagogy offers multiple opportunities to create content besides consuming it. It supports teaching and learning through creation. Teachers and learners users are easily able to create content through video creation, wikis, animation software and simply content curation through social networks. This ensures the pedagogic shifts from consumptions to creations in line with the power principle focusing the swing from teacher-centric to learner-centric learning. Students turn out to be a cocreator of the content besides being a passive consumer of teachers curated content.

2. **Correct to correcting:** The traditional teaching approaches are based on the a priori correctness of the content. The second pedagogic swing is correct to correcting. A correcting pedagogy is not a priori focused on the correct answer. In spite, it accentuates a process whereby content is in a state of correcting. This is evident in the wikis space where content is the negotiated outcome of many contributing individuals. Everybody can take part to continually improve and correct the content. The vulnerability principle is closely associated with this pedagogic change. Learners are ready to make themselves vulnerable to learning opportunities during the correcting state.

3. **Content to conversation:** Learning began to center gradually more around the content and content consumption with the introduction of the printing press. This has dominated teaching and learning for over 500 years. Technological innovations are influencing teaching and learning in a great manner. The development around social media is causing a shift from content-based pedagogies to conversation-based

approaches. Fundamentally learning took place here through conversation, in what was termed the Socratic method. Conversation-based methods focus on learning through discourse. These methods are reliant on the key underlying principles of validation, vulnerability and correcting. Multiple streams of content weave together in the learning process and microchunking of content takes place during the practice of conversation pedagogies.

4. **Control to chaos:** Traditional learning aligns to focus on order, sequence, and control driven by teachers. Teachers make the decisions regarding contentment selection to learners' engagements in controlled pedagogy. Learners are given a set of facts and are controlled in how they solve the problems. Digital pedagogies encourage a shift away from control towards chaos. Often the teachers intentionally cause adequate chaos to motivate the student to reorganize. Modern learning environments are built around 'noise' and chaos shifting from the realm of the ordered, understood, controlled, to the realm of the unordered, confusing and laissez-faire to offer more challenges to teacher and students alike. Chaotic learning is not learning without order but the patterns and paths cannot be predetermined. This promotes pedagogy where learning cannot be reduced to simple practices (behaviorism) or to models (cognitivism) or to motivations (humanism) or to activities (constructivism). Learning takes place in an emergent sense in this new pedagogy. Here, learning is the process born of connections (connectivism) between human and non-human actants, unfolded in a plethora of ways where each path creates an array of opportunities for new connections, and new learning encounters.

4.6 INSTRUCTIONAL TECHNOLOGIES

The design of digital pedagogy depends on instructional technologies. The following table gives the issues that need to be addressed while designing instructional technologies (Table 4.2).

Educational ICT based on instructional technologies does not clearly cluster into distinct categories. Specific instantiations of instructional technologies are represented in the multidimensional design space with given pedagogical tools, applications, media, or environments with different intellectual positions and perspectives. These correspond to the schools of thought sketched below.

1. **Behaviorism/objectivism:** Students attain skills of recognizing (i.e. recalling facts), simplification (i.e. defining and illustrating concepts), linking (i.e. applying

Table 4.2: Questions to be addressed while designing instructional technologies

S. No.	Issues	Questions to be addressed
1.	Investigation	Who are my users and what do they need? What principles and theories are relevant?
2.	Application	How should these principles be applied in this case?
3.	Representation or modeling	What solution will best meet users' needs? How can this be communicated to developers and/or directly to users?
4.	Iteration	How does the design stand up to the demands of development? How useful is it in practice? What are the changes needed?

explanation) and sequencing (i.e. automatically performing a specified procedure) during learning. Knowledge and skills are relocated as scholarly behaviors to fulfill the educational objectives. Internal mental processing is not well-thought-out as part of instructional design in classical behaviorism. Behaviorist design includes two types of instructional technologies, namely computer-assisted instruction (CAI) and learner management systems (LMS). Instructional designers have been utilizing this educational philosophy to create huge amounts of educational software for content and skill training. CAI emphasizes factual knowledge and recipe (correct ways) like procedures. On the other hand, LMS includes more detailed forms of behaviorist instructions based on web and multimedia presentations, alternative elucidation for struggling students, various types of extrinsic engagement, comprehensive record keeping that presents analytic summaries. Only some forms of content and skills are efficiently mastered by behaviorist instructional methods and not all modern curriculum lie within the domain of these pedagogical media. No complex knowledge or skill is learnable until the student has mastered every simple underlying subskill as a limitation of behaviorist instructional design with real-world utility.

2. **Cognitivism/pragmatism:** Instruction characteristic of the cognitivist school of thought include
   - Offering a deep foundation of factual knowledge and procedural skills.
   - Connecting facts, skills, and ideas via conceptual frameworks.
   - Arranging domain knowledge in ways that facilitate retrieval and application as experts in that field perform.
   - Assisting students to develop skills that engage improving their own thinking processes, such as setting their own learning objectives and monitoring progress towards reaching these objectives.

   The cognitivist theories of learning presume realism as a mental construct symbolically. Already existing relationships among content and skills are the building block of knowledge acquisition where optimal mental processing takes place through the organization and sequencing by instructors. Such acquisition also demands internal coding and structuring by the student. Learning success reliant on three aspects—(1) students activity (to process input, storing and retrieving information in memory), (2) teachers or instructors, and (3) pedagogical medium. Instructional design strategies based on cognitivism fundamentally help students to acquire the disciplinary knowledge. Following are the cognitive processes to acquire knowledge through multimedia.
   - *Selecting*: It is applied to inward verbal information to yield a text base and is applied to inward visual information to yield an image base.
   - *Organizing*: It is applied to the word base to create a verbally-based model of the to-be-explained system and is applied to the image base to create a visually-based model of the to-be-explained system.
   - *Integrating*: It occurs when the learner builds connections between corresponding events (or states or parts) in the verbally-based model and the visually-based model.

   A variety of intrinsic and extrinsic factors are responsible for student's motivation towards achieving these goals. These factors include satisfaction from achievement, challenge, curiosity and contributing to others. Intelligent tutoring systems (ITS) are among those wide varieties of instructional technologies which adopt some principles from cognitivism school of thought for illustrating pedagogical media. ITSs offer two loops by which it guides learning activities. The outer loop executes once for each task. A task usually consists of solving a complex multistep problem. Given the student's past performance, its purpose is to select an appropriate task for the learner. On the other hand, the inner loop is executed once for each step taken by the student in the solution of a task. Its purpose is to supply hints and feedback on that specific step. It also updates the model of what the student is evolving competence at this point in the instructional sequence. That model of student's knowledge is used by the outer loop to select a next task appropriate for the student. Cognitivist approaches assume that ITS-like educational tools will teach most of the curriculum coupled with human instructors including fuzzy skills such as the rhetoric of writing an evocative essay. Limited progress toward this ambitious goal is noticed till date in spite of three decades of work.

3. **Constructivism/interpretivism:** This school of thought is characterized by goals for instruction that include:
   - Instruction is a method of supporting knowledge construction rather than transmitting knowledge.
   - The role of the teacher is a guide, rather than an expert transferring knowledge to novice's 'blank slates'.
   - Learning activities are authentic and center on learners' confusion as their incomplete knowledge and skills fail to predict what they are experiencing.
   - Teachers persuade students in reflecting on experiences, seeking alternative opinions, and testing feasibility of ideas.

   People create new knowledge and develop understandings based on what they already know and believe, which is shaped by their developmental level, their prior experiences, and their sociocultural background and context. Constructivist theories assume that meaning is imposed by the individual rather than existing in the world independently. Learning involves mastering authentic tasks in meaningful, realistic situations. Instruction can promote learning by providing rich, loosely structured experiences and guidance (like coaching, apprenticeships and mentoring) that support meaning-making without imposing a fixed set of knowledge and skills. Constructivist theories-based instructional design approaches include cognitive flexibility theory, case-based learning, anchored instruction, micro-worlds and simulations, mind tools, collaborative learning, and situated learning in communities of practice. Student motivation is determined by factors such as curiosity, challenge, fantasy, choice, and social recognition. Constructivist approach can teach a very broad spectrum of knowledge and skills, in contrast to behaviorist and cognitivist instructional designs. High-quality constructivist curricula can ensure solid learning through high engagement towards metacognitive outcomes.

4.7 TAXONOMY OF DIGITAL TOOLS AND LEARNING RESOURCES

The digital multimedia tools are the basic components of digital pedagogy practices and these are used as the fundamental learning resources as far as the packaging of content is concerned. The following are the six classes of media according to their representation.

1. **Narrative:** Narrative tools are those which perform the tasks that include representations. Formal learning depends on representations and interactions instead of the real world. Narrative systems are used for assimilation and reproduction of images, sound, text, etc. Learners should not be on the receiving end for a long time without involving into some activities like notes, mind maps, answering to comprehensions questions, etc. Narrative tools like electronic whiteboards, wikis can be shared between teachers and students to enable group representation and collaborations. Examples of digital narrative tools have two classes. Assimilative class includes on-screen text, image, video files, PowerPoint slides, DVDs, web pages, animations, etc. Productive class includes web and multimedia authoring tools, word and image processing tools, PowerPoint, audio and video capturing and editing tools. Electronic whiteboards, wikis, shared write/show systems may be included in both the classes.

    Narrative media are accessible in place to suit the learner overcoming the physical access problems. Information presented through multimedia is better recalled by the learners. Multiple access paths (serial, historical, visual, or textual) and preferences provide greater autonomy into their learning process. Moreover, the problem of information overload takes place here, easy production and distribution often affect the loss of quality control. Some media encourages passive (cut–paste) rather than active (note-taking) reception.

2. **Communicative:** Communicative tools are those which perform the tasks of communication between individual and groups. These tools are valuable because dialogue is essential to learning and takes place through writing, speaking, gesture, drawing, or other channels. Asynchronous communication can be used to encourage reflective learning and allow thoughts to be built collaboratively over time. The synchronous communication has the advantage of immediacy and high motivation. Learners experience these communication tools easy to adopt and use. Examples of synchronous tools are chat, video conferencing, mobile phones, and instant messaging, etc. Asynchronous tools include a text discussion board, email, blogs, wikis, video, and audio messages.

    While practicing through these synchronous tools, learners have to communicate and take explicit moves. They have to responding swiftly standing on their own feet. Immediate feedback is motivational in this case. Demand for rapid responses often become intimidating to some learners in this synchronous case. Asynchronous tools have access at a time to suit the learners. Communication problems can be overcome with adaptive technologies here and dialogues are easily recorded for later review and reflection. Lack of immediacy is often demoralizing for many learners in these asynchronous tools.

3. **Interactive:** The interactive tools perform the tasks that return information based on user input. Interactive tools are important for supporting research tasks and developing information skills. These tools make learners more active with respect to narrative tools because learners require seeking and selecting content and activities. Examples of interactive tools include computer-assisted assessment (CAA) tools (quizzes) where student's answers and appropriate feedback are the inputs. Another interactive emerging tool is position awareness systems (GPS).

4. **Productive:** The productive tools perform the tasks that involve the exploitation of data. Productive tools are valuable because they support the skill of application and analysis. In digital pedagogy practice, productive data-driven engines are used in several interactive interfaces. Parameters and protocols of productive technologies allow learners to manipulate data explicitly and consciously. Examples of productive tools include spreadsheets, statistical tools, databases, qualitative analysis tools, calculators, etc.
5. **Adaptive:** Adaptive tools depend on continuous adaptation to user inputs. These tools are valuable because learners receive essential feedback in reply to their actions. Complex productive and interactive systems will be experienced as adaptive if they have some elements of sensory realism. These environments may support experiential along with experimental learning and higher-order learning skills (evaluation, research, problem-solving), with low risk and cost. Examples of adaptive tools include computer games, virtual world simulations, models, and interactive tutorials. Learners practicing these tools acquire information handling and management skills. If the routine tasks are found automated in these tools, we may focus on higher-order tasks. The experiential and experimental tasks (fieldwork, laboratory simulations), can be performed in a reliable, safe, and supportive environment. Real-world complexities can be modeled in the classrooms using these tools. The experience of data analysis and modeling will help learners in a wide range of their future occupations.
6. **Integrative:** Integrative tools help learners in the management of learning activities. These tools allow the recording of achievements, reviewing their progress and take actions accordingly. Integrative technologies help the learning activities to more easily be managed, organized, captured and presented for review. Complex assessment systems are often best regarded as integrative in spite of simple interactive tools. Examples of integrative tools are virtual learning environments, task and time management software, learning design systems, assessment management systems, learning record systems. These tools help learners towards tasks and time management. These tools promote a sense of belongingness to the institution when learners sign in. Learners monitoring can be improved in difficult situations of learning through these tools. These tools offer enhanced fairness and reliability of learner's assessment systems. Basic ICT skills are required by the learners for accessing core facilities and services of these integrative tools. They often focus on administrative efficiency and system integration at the cost of pedagogical considerations.

Learning design works as crucial learning resources especially in digital learning, may be analysed from four perspectives—incident, strategy, rule, and role. These four perspectives have specific learning outcomes focus. These are given in Table 4.3, as a typological framework of learning design.

4.8 HYBRID PEDAGOGY AND BLENDED LEARNING

Networked and open learning environments must functions as platform for engaging teachers and students besides working as a content repositories to fulfill the following objectives of critical digital pedagogy.
- It must be open to heterogeneous global voices for communication and collaboration across cultural boundaries.

Table 4.3: A taxonomical framework for learning design

S. No.	Learning design focus	Outcomes	Description
1.	Incident-based	Applying the knowledge and understand the roles and procedures.	The learners have to participate in authentic and real incidents to reflect and take decisions.
2.	Strategy-based on	Applying knowledge in real-life situations meaningfully.	The learning is driven by tasks that include strategic planning and actions.
3.	Rule-based	Applying processes and procedures meaningfully and reflectively	The learners have to apply standard procedures and rules (algorithms) in the solutions.
4.	Role-based	Understanding of processes and interactions in situations with multivariables	The learners have to participate as players in real-world applications and apply judgments to make decisions based on understanding.

- Its practice focuses on digital community development.
- Its usage and applications must reach beyond traditional institutions of education.

Critical digital pedagogy is practiced through two approaches, namely hybrid pedagogy and blended learning. Hybrid pedagogy refers to the learning that takes place both in a classroom, online space and other overlapping situations. It is often used synonymously with the concept of blended learning. But they have some conceptual distinctions. Hybrid pedagogy is a procedural and strategic approach which facilitates defining a series of processes and practices. But blended learning directly describes a process or practices tactically. When we think about blended learning, it actually indicates the place where learning takes place. On the other hand, hybrid pedagogy not only concerns the place of learning but also fundamentally rethinks our conception of place. It combines the learning in virtual place and learning in a physical place (mixing of on-ground and online learning) into a more engaged and dynamic conversation. Hybrid pedagogy encourages virtual learning, online classrooms, informal education, collaborative communities, critical engagement with tools, and experiential learning.

4.9 REMARKABLE DEBATES

1. Does Learning via Media Inherently Inferior to Learning Face-to-face?

Historically, technology-enhanced education have suffered from common misconceptions that these forms of learning are inferior to the traditional of face-to-face instructions. Such misconception has delayed the adoption of powerful models for teaching based on sophisticated ICT. Many levels of education are now recognizing the value of ICT to support learning, whether applied as a complement to face-to-face instruction (termed hybrid, blended, or distributed approaches) or as a resources of instruction without the personal presence (distance education). Usage of media can change the processes by which people receive, create, and share knowledge. Hence, the learning styles, strengths, and preferences for students of all ages are changing. Many research studies show that the use of asynchronous learning environments certainly affected their involvement and their cognitive processes for engaging with the content. Students have also reported that online threaded discussions often encouraged better quality conversations than they had experienced in traditional classrooms. Use of synchronous media also enhanced their learning experience and complemented other delivery modes including face-to-face. Synchronous media also offers a clear advantage over asynchronous media in facilitating the work of small groups and interact within a classroom setting. Unfortunately, most teachers mistakenly assume that their students must be similar in their learning preferences and styles because face-to-face is the form of teaching–learning with which they are most comfortable and proficient.

2. Do Media Influence Learning?

Historically, controversies have also come up about the relationship between ICT and pedagogy. Researcher like Clark [Clark, (1994)] has found that no single media feature serves a unique cognitive effect for some learning task because the same effect can be accomplished via various types of media. The use of ICT attributes must be proxies for some other variables that are instrumental in learning gains. Clark also found that media not only fail to influence learning, they are also not directly accountable for motivating learning. Students' beliefs about their likelihood to learn from any given media are different for different students. These beliefs also vary with time. The researcher also noticed that innovative applications of new media can improve learning outcomes. They have argued that teachers could present mathematics via engaging story lines based in real world circumstances without using a visual medium. Screwdrivers are particularly designed to facilitate torque and hence from an instrumental point of view to argue that the screwdriver cannot influence construction seems an overly narrow point of view about cause and effect. ICT can be comparable to fire, but one has to stand near the fire to get the benefit from it. Similarly, knowledge does not fundamentally radiate from computers, blending students with learning as fires infuse their bystander with heat. Media can be proficient to support various aspects of learning, such as student engagement, visual representation and the collection of assessment data. Identifying whether and how each instructional technology can best enhance some aspect of a specific pedagogy is as reasonable instrumentally as developing tools that support a carpenter's ability to construct artifacts. Nonetheless, there may have some media which can oppose learning the objectives of education.

3. Do Some Media Weaken the Purpose of Education?

Few researchers like Seymour Papert [Papert, (1980)] argued that some instructional technologies are harmful to education because they promote a pedagogy that is detrimental to 'true' learning. Teaches should emphasis on reading as the essential route to knowledge, but assimilation, presentation and testing of information can also contribute to overall success irrespective of age and level. Since the use of ICT for CAI and ITSs are treated at the emphasis on behaviorist and cognitivist views of learning, these may be looked down if we want to focus on constructionist (a variant of constructivist approaches) perspective. Various media types are used to develop learner's knowledge through constructing some external, sharable artifact (i.e. a computer program) rather than assimilating content and skills from a teacher. Some media are fundamentally better for learning and teaching because instructionist (behaviorist or cognitivist) media control children's learning, while constructionist media allow students to control their own education. Since constructionism pedagogy cannot work as a perfect solution for all types of learning, the instructionist model definitely has a bright future in the long run towards promoting flexibility in learning avoiding dogmatic approaches.

4. Reconceiving Media as Empowering Diversity in Learning

Learning is an activity quite diverse in its manifestations from person to person. Individual's learning is as diverse as complex as bonding according to the latest educational research. Philosophies of learning and theories about how to use ICT for instruction treat learning like a simple sleeping activity relatively invariant across subject areas, learners, and educational objectives. Latest instructional technology implementations have a few varieties in approach. Instructional designers also search for the single best medium for learning often assuming about the existence of such a universal tool. Many researchers suggest that instructional ICT moves toward embodying the universally finest way of learning. On the other hand, other gurus aggressively oppose pedagogical approach towards incorporating a new type of instructional ICT with the apprehension of undercutting both the ways students can best learn and the true objectives of education. Politicians and guardians are criticizing the use of smart phones and e-gazettes in schools and they are also advocating for banning social networking sites despite its widespread use in social life of everybody. General public is very much confused about the use of ICT infrastructure and its diversified nature. It remains another issue about how much to invest in instructional technologies towards offering effective education to learners.

5. Do Investments in Instructional ICT Infrastructures Worth?

Many people argue that investment in instructional ICT is less useful than in any other forms of educational investments. They have also shown that learning technologies are often utilized ineffectively and may appear contradictory from teachers' current pedagogies. One of the reasons behind these is the lack of availability of 'one size fits all' solution of instructional media. To overcome these weaknesses, ICT industry have already evolved some tools like LMS and strengthening them to satisfy the varied requirements of the educational industry. Variety of specialized tools may also cater to the needs instead of a single device that attempts to accomplish everything. Literature also shows that no single instructional medium can offer optimal pedagogy regardless of the subject matter. Thus, the character of the content and skills to be learned shapes the type of instruction to use. Developmental level of the students influences what teaching methods will work best for the set environment. The best approach to invest in learning technologies is an instrumental approach that analyzes the natures of the students, curriculum, and teachers to identify the appropriate applications, tools, environments, and media as no educational ICT is universally good.

4.10 WHAT DIGITAL PEDAGOGY IS NOT?

Experts have emphasized that the mere use of technological components in the classroom does not equate to digital pedagogy. If we use digital technologies in our teaching that does not imply that we are practicing digital pedagogy. To guarantee digital pedagogy, we have to reproduce pedagogical changes. Simple incorporation of tools like PowerPoint in a lecture may not assure us the implementation of digital pedagogy unless we think about changing the pedagogical approach to the lecture as an outcome. Digital pedagogy is an orientation towards a pedagogy that does not fetishize digital tools. Digital pedagogy should focus on how instructors' interaction through machines could influence teaching and learning. It emphasizes processes and elements of instructional technology in practice. Technology cannot revolutionize the classroom without first altering the pedagogy. Technologies are not the only elements that make the lecture more meaningful or enjoying from a pedagogical point of view. New tools (electronic tools or computers) are not that much difficult, but a rethinking of how to use them in social and institutional conditions are the main milestones to overcome by the practitioners of digital pedagogy. Because of these reasons, many researchers have advocated the use of digital resources outside the classroom while class time may be used for questions and discussions.

EXECUTIVE SUMMARY

- Digital age is characterized by revolutionizing digital technologies along with some other attributes and benefits.
- Innovations in pedagogy are the basic building blocks of digital pedagogy accompanied by some processes to provide the expected performances in its implementation.
- Subject, rules, pedagogic tools, community interactions, learning objects all together emerge provide the outcome the learning and hence they all are essential components of the activity system of digital pedagogy.
- Four new principles, namely power, learning, vulnerability and validation, govern the digital pedagogy. Collaboration, inclusion, participation, acknowledgement, challenge, practice, communities, professionalism all are essentially required for effective incorporation of digital pedagogy.
- There are 12 attributes and 9 principles for designing digital pedagogy. These required to be incorporated to the existing designs of pedagogy.
- Four new pedagogies have been emerged in light of practicing attributes and principles of digital pedagogies. They are consumption to creation, correct to correcting, content to conversation and control to chaos.
- Design of instructional technologies addresses the basic design issues of digital pedagogy. Behaviorism, cognitivism, and constructivism are three basic schools of thought which control the instructional design issues.
- We must analyze the digital tools and learning resources for digital pedagogy implementation from a taxonomical point of view with respect to their usage. The taxonomy includes narrative, communicative, interactive, productive, adaptive, and integrative quality classes of digital tools and resources. On the other hand, learning designs have four basis, namely incident, strategy, rule and role.
- Learner must be aware and resolve the existing controversies or debates towards the introduction and effective practices of digital pedagogy.
- All implementations of digital aids in pedagogy are not treated as digital pedagogy. Digital pedagogy must have pedagogical focus.

Review Questions

1. Define the digital age. Write down the characteristics that define learning in digital age.
2. Describe the important components, processes and performance criteria of innovations in pedagogy.
3. Discuss the activity system for balancing digital pedagogy.
4. How homeocracy is different from autocracy power principles? Describe four new principles of digital pedagogy.
5. Write down the principles of effective implementation of digital pedagogy.
6. What are the different attributes and principles of designing digital pedagogy?
7. What are the new pedagogies emerged in this digital age?
8. How do instructional technologies affect the digital pedagogical practices?
9. Illustrate the taxonomy of digital tools and learning resources of digital pedagogy.
10. Explain how will you characterize a given pedagogical practices to be digital pedagogy.
11. Does learning via media inherently inferior to learning face-to-face?
12. Do the media influence learning?
13. Do some media weaken the purpose of education?
14. How do media empower diversity in learning?

Chapter 5

Critical Understanding of ICT

Objectives of this chapter

- To acquire the critical understandings of ICT for digital pedagogy practice.
- To understand the social, economic, security and ethical issues ICT use.
- To identify the policy concerns for ICT.
- To describe a computer system and operate the Windows operating systems.
- To use Word processing, spread sheets and presentation software.
- To operate on internet with safety, antivirus and other tools.
- To elucidate the application of ICT for teaching–learning.
- To develop various skills to use computer technology for sharing the information and ideas through the blogs, groups, etc.
- To understand the aspects of learning design with digital pedagogy.

Expected outcomes of this chapter

After going through this chapter learners will be able to:
- Understand various issues concerned with the use of ICT and practically use them in their daily teaching–learning activities along with content identification.
- Understand the difficulties that are faced while incorporating ICT in regular curriculum.
- Have an idea of the different ways to help masses imbibe ICT in daily learning.
- Have an idea of all the basic softwares that come along with the operating system of the computer. Learn the proper use of internet and to use it safely.
- Have an idea about the different types of learning in contemporary learning methodology.
- Understand the essence of the intersection of technology and education and practice different effective technopedagogic skills in teaching.
- Design learning activities (lesson/lecture/delivery plan) using digital pedagogy.

5.1 DIGITAL TECHNOLOGY AND SOCIOECONOMIC CONTEXT

ICT is an acronym for Information and Communications Technology. ICT is being hailed as the most indispensable weapon of progress nowadays. It is very much evident that in the current century, media has been strongly influenced by the vast changes in ICT. ICT is playing a major role in transforming the socioeconomic conditions of India as well as the entire world. It allows users to actively contribute to the transformative world where there is a paradigm shift in varied types of technologies. It is a cover underneath which various audio–visual and telephonic networks are converged through a single cabling or link system. In the recent past, there has been a humongous rise in the number of mobile networks, and since then, people all over the world are trying to extend the exposure and span of ICT to enhance development in all sectors.

ICT finds its usage focus in the fields of education and healthcare for nearly two decades. It is responsible for the employment of a huge number of professionals worldwide. ICT should be used openly, tactically and internally to help organizations adapt to the latest tools in order to ensure development. Efficient collection, communication and storing of relevant data and information are the main reasons why ICT should be adapted to progress towards development goals.

To acquire information or expertise, every student must be occupied in learning. ICT is considered as one of the major means for improving the quality of education in today's society. It is anticipated that if ICT is implemented effectively, then it can pave a way for redesigning the entire education system which will ultimately lead to quality education for one and all. The quality enhancement occurs through many processes like bridging the digital divide gap between the classes of people who have proper access to ICT resources and who does not, by broadening the limited educational prospects to underserved categories based on cost and time constraints. Teachers and learners are the main stakeholders in this entire teaching–learning process. The biggest advantage of this type of learning is that users can access these resources anywhere and at any preferred time. There is no need for the instructor and the learner to be in the same geographical location. Both the teachers and students can get access to remote learning materials in the digital medium apart from the physical medium for their relevant educational requirements. Summarizing it all, it can be said that with the recent surge of the internet, there is a plethora of online resources in almost all subjects and in all possible media forms which can be accessed from any platform and at any suitable time by an infinite number of people. Appropriate use of ICT can act as a catalyst being responsible for the paradigm shift in content and pedagogy which is the main factor of the vast education reform in this 21st century.

Universal Access *vs* Digital Divide: Issues and Initiatives

The concepts for universal accessibility or design for all aims to conquer all hurdles and provide accessibility to disabled people based on the conjecture that considerable amounts of resources are available to the user. Unfortunately, this concept stands true for a very little area of the world population. Difficulties in access to computer parts, usage of outdated machinery, illiteracy and language barrier are the many factors which act as a hindrance to providing universal access to users.

The digital divide is considered as one of the main problems of developing countries like India, where due to the lack of proper technological and monetary resources, ICT cannot reach all people. The digital divide is the split caused among people on the basis of having access to the internet or ICT. While access to the internet is one of the main issues, other factors like quality of the internet connection should also seek attention causing the digital divide. One of the methods that can help to reduce the extent of the digital divide is literacy. Irrespective of the rise of technologies, a human being needs to be able to think good of one, help shape a fruitful career by learning new things through self-motivation and self-guidance, make important decisions and use the internet appropriately. It is anticipated that eliminating the digital divide may bring in financial growth and stability in the society, communal mobility and may result in increased involvement in democratic decisions.

5.2 CHALLENGES OF INTEGRATION OF ICT IN SCHOOL

It is widely accepted nowadays that incorporating ICT in the curriculum can make students more competitive globally and help them to be a part of a skilled workforce. This feat can be achieved by pursuing the following.
- Enriching the familiarity in learning and present innovative sets of skills.
- Enroll more students to massive open online courses (MOOCs).
- Arrange proper training for faculties.
- Reduce cost and time regarding the delivery of resources and automating the daily tasks.
- Improving the management of the institute to augment the value and competence of service delivery.

Overall, practicing ICT-based innovations in classrooms are many-a-times hindered by the impact factor, economic investment, impartiality and sustainability issues. Lack of awareness of ICT-based education, absence of dynamically trained teachers, no urge for proper skill development trainings imparted to teachers to help practice ICT-based education on regular basis, unsuitable organizational culture and orthodox approach and values against adaptation to latest trends in technologies, shortage of time due to multiple tasks assigned to the teachers, absence of precise perception about the importance of ICT-based education, proper maintenance and upgradation of ICT equipments due to limited financial resources, insufficient funds allocated for procurement of latest digital technologies, proficiency in English language being a obstruction in rural areas and lack of technical help are the factors which leads to the rendering of the entire ICT experience meaningless. Paying heed to these internal and external factors in curriculum and aiming to improve the access, usage, social and economic impact may help ICTs more effective.

5.3 AIMS AND OBJECTIVES OF INDIAN NATIONAL POLICY ON ICT IN SCHOOL EDUCATION

The National Policy on Education 1986, as modified in 1992, stressed the need to employ educational technology to improve the quality of education. The significant role ICT can play in school education has also been highlighted in the National Curriculum Framework 2005 (NCF) 2005. The initiative of ICT policy in school education is encouraged by the remarkable potential of ICT for augmenting outreach and enhancing the quality of teaching. This policy ensures providing guidelines to assist the states in optimizing the use of ICT in school education within a national policy framework.

Vision of the Policy

"The ICT policy in school education aims at preparing youth to participate creatively in the establishment, sustenance and growth of a knowledge society leading to all round socioeconomic development of the nation and global competitiveness."

Mission of the Policy

"To devise, catalyse, support and sustain ICT and ICT enabled activities and processes in order to improve access, quality and efficiency in the school system."

Policy Goals

The ICT policy in school education attempts to meet the vision and mission through the following methods. It endeavors to generate an ambience to develop a society that will have knowledge about ICT. This society, in turn, will help to organize, utilise and make a profit from ICT and help in the betterment of the country. The ICT literates will work together, help each other and distribute ideas in order to yield the maximum benefits regarding the prospective of imbibing ICT in education.

It endorses worldwide, impartial, open and complimentary access to ICT resources to all students and teachers. It supports the creation of materials at the local centers with standard quality to help teachers and students involved as a contributor to the sharing of digitized resources. This policy aims to enhance the standard of the schooling process as a whole; it plans to incorporate ICT to help form a professional community of teachers, provide a platform to facilitate resource sharing, an improved connection between the authorities of the schools which eventually will lead to the effective teaching–learning environment in schools. Supporting research, assessment and testing to judge the prospective of ICT and its effectiveness is also a prerogative of this policy along with understanding its advantages and disadvantages that can cause a major impact on the society. Finally, the aim of this policy is to inspire a huge number of people to enhance the quality of school education procedure through proper exploitation of ICT.

5.4 IT @ SCHOOL PROJECT

IT @ School Project is an information technology project formulated under the Department of General Education, Government of Kerala in India. This project was launched in 2001 since which it has been solely responsible for converting the traditional scenario of teaching–learning and is currently deployed in over 12,000 schools in Kerala. One of the greatest achievements of this project, which operates on an open source software platform, is that it provides training for visually impaired teachers of Kerala. Training is imparted on various programmes like ICT, hardware, internet, camera handling and ICT permissible substance.

This project claims to deploy the largest free and open source software (FOSS)-based ICT education in the world, provides excellent infrastructure to promote schools, provide access to high speed internet to all the schools in Kerala, allows the setup of hardware labs to repair hardware parts of a non-functional computer, helps provide electricity to all schools to initiate ICT-based education, promotes e-governance initiatives and helps prepare School-Wiki to encourage combined resource creation. Around 1.2 lakh teachers and 30 lakh students have been benefitted from this project until now.

5.5 COMPONENTS AND OBJECTIVES OF NATIONAL MISSION ON EDUCATION THROUGH ICT

The National Mission on Education through ICT (NMEICT) has been visualized as a centrally sponsored scheme to influence the potential of ICT, in teaching–learning process for the gain of all the learners in higher education institutions in 'any time anywhere' mode. The objectives of NMEICT are:

a. To create innovative and informative associations within organizations with a view to acquiring a huge number of scholars in all possible domains.
b. To increase digital literacy for the empowerment of instructors.
c. To prepare informative modules containing appropriate content and also to cater to the individual needs of the learners.
d. To standardize the quality of the e-resources to be able to recognize them globally.
e. To devise effective teaching–learning methods to prepare appropriate content for specific learner types.
f. To make resources freely accessible to Indians.
g. To formulate cost-effective methods to incorporate ICT in regular learning.
h. To help the formation of an efficient virtual technological university.
i. To discover and cultivate talents among students.
j. To be able to certify competencies of the resources through a properly authorized structure.
k. To efficiently create and preserve databases with the summaries of human resources.

Following are the initiatives for appropriate implementation of NMEICT.

Spoken Tutorials: The Spoken Tutorial project is the proposal of the 'Talk to a Teacher' activity of the NMEICT, initiated by the Ministry of Human Resources and Development (MHRD), Government of India. Learners can learn from a varied list of FOSS by himself, from any place, at any convenient time and in any language. All details regarding these courses are available on https://spoken-tutorial.org/.

Gyan Darshan: DD Gyan Darshan 1 is a state-owned television channel telecasting from Doordarshan Kendra, IGNOU.

Gyan Vani: Gyan Vani is an educational FM radio station broadcasted in several cities of India.

Sakshat portal: Sakshat portal is a one-stop education portal that encompasses the learning requirements of learners from the kindergarten level to post-graduation level. This free-to-use portal was prepared by eGyanKosh of IGNOU, and was launched by the then President of India Dr APJ Abdul Kalam in October 2006. The portal has five modules which comprise educational materials, scholarship opportunities, testing, super achiever and interaction platforms.

eGyanKosh: eGyanKosh is a national digital repository to accumulate, index, conserve, allocate and disseminate the digital learning resources developed by the open and distance learning institutions in the country. Items in eGyanKosh are protected by copyright laws, with all rights reserved by IGNOU.

Virtual Laboratory: Virtual Labs project is an initiative of MHRD, Government of India under the aegis of NMEICT. Twelve educational organizations participate in creating this conglomerate of resources headed by IIT Delhi as the coordinator. Under the Virtual Labs project, over 100 Virtual Labs consisting of approximately 700+ web-enabled experiments were designed for remote-operation and viewing.

Haptic Technology: Of late, virtual reality systems are being furnished with haptic gadgets, to help in the learning process. The main advantage of incorporating haptic technology is thorough understanding the simulations generated by providing power or perceptible response to the learner. It is not far when tactile senses will rule over intelligent learning systems implemented with upgraded e-learning systems.

5.6 MICROSOFT WINDOWS AND OFFICE SOFTWARE

Microsoft Windows is the most used GUI OS in our laptops and PCs developed by Microsoft Corporation. It can install and run the necessary software for all ICT implementation.

Installation of Operating Systems (Case Study: Windows 10)

The operating system (OS) helps the user to exploit the functions of a computer by managing the hardware and software in it. The software that acts as a media between the hardware and software is known as the operating system. Here the installation process of the Operating System: Windows 10 has been provided.

To begin with, the disc or external drive containing the installation file must be inserted into the computer. The OS may be installed through pen drives, bootable CD/DVD and external hard disks. Let us assume that a drive is being used to install the OS. The machine then needs to be restarted. Booting is a process where the OS has to be loaded into the main memory or random access machine (RAM). To boot the system, the user needs to press DELETE and F2 to enter the BIOS for booting. Next, the location is to be selected from which the booting is to be done. In this case, the booting will be done from the pen drive. An option will come to save the settings and we should wait until the machine restarts again. For the final installation, the language, time format, currency format and keyboard input method is to be selected and 'Next' to be pressed. Then the installation is initiated by clicking 'Install Now'. For authentication of the OS, the key is to be entered and the terms and conditions of Microsoft License are to be accepted. Finally, after the installation process will be completed and the on-screen setup settings are to be customized as per need. The above procedure is summarized below stepwise.

1. The disc or external drive containing the installation file must be inserted into the computer.
2. Restart the machine.
3. Press 'DELETE' and 'F2' to enter BIOS.
4. Steer to the BOOT tab and select the device from which the machine is to be booted.
5. The settings should be saved.
6. The machine should be waited to restart once again.
7. The preferred language is to be selected.
8. 'Install Now' is to be clicked.
9. The Windows 10 key is to be inserted.
10. The acceptance option of the Microsoft License terms is to be selected.
11. Then we need to wait for the installation process.
12. Finally, the on-screen setup settings are to be customized as per need.

Microsoft Office

Microsoft Office is a group of desktop applications that has been built-up by Microsoft Corporation and was initially released in 1990. It is widely used for office and business purposes and is offered in 35 languages supported by Windows, Mac and Linux alternatives. This software claims to be one of the most widely used software in the entire world. Microsoft Word, Excel, Access, Publisher, PowerPoint and Outlook are some of the applications having a specific purpose of its own and each of them is attuned with the other programs included in the package.

MS Word

MS Word is an application program that allows input, formatting, editing and output texts along with supplementary features. Word 6 for Windows NT was the first 32-bit version of this application. The extension of Word files is denoted by .doc or .docx and comes with the latest features in its 2010 version onwards.

Basic Functions of MS WORD

1. Performing basic editing functions, formatting text, copy and moving objects and text.
2. Learning the formatting skills in paragraphs, tables, lists, and pages.
3. Knowledge of navigating the Word Ribbon Interface.
4. Understanding the process of inserting graphics, pictures, and table of contents, Drop Cap.
5. Learning the utilities of Auto text, AutoCorrect, Footnotes and Bookmark.
6. Demonstrate the mechanics and uses of Word tables to organize and present data.
7. Working knowledge of using Word's themes and clip art to create a variety of visual effects.
8. Word's advanced formatting techniques and presentation styles.
9. Applicable knowledge and uses of accepted business style formatting conventions.
10. Creating and producing a mail merge.

Typical Features of Microsoft Word

Typical features of Microsoft Word (Fig. 5.1) are as following:

1. Commands comprising all features required to work in Word are accumulated as a menu on the Microsoft Office button.
2. The Quick Access Toolbar contains the Save, Undo and Repeat buttons.
3. The title bar shows the name of the document.
4. The Ribbon allows a common space where all the facilities are presented in a single area for ease of the users.
5. In every tab, buttons are structured into groups.
6. Some of the buttons have their names displayed while others don't.
7. For any sort of assistance, the Help button is present at the right end of the ribbon.

MS PowerPoint

This is the most influential presentation software presented by Microsoft. Slides are used to express information affluent with multimedia. It was developed by Dennis Austin and Robert Gaskins at Forethought Inc. and was released in 1987. It was initially made to present visuals for business purposes but later gained momentum in various

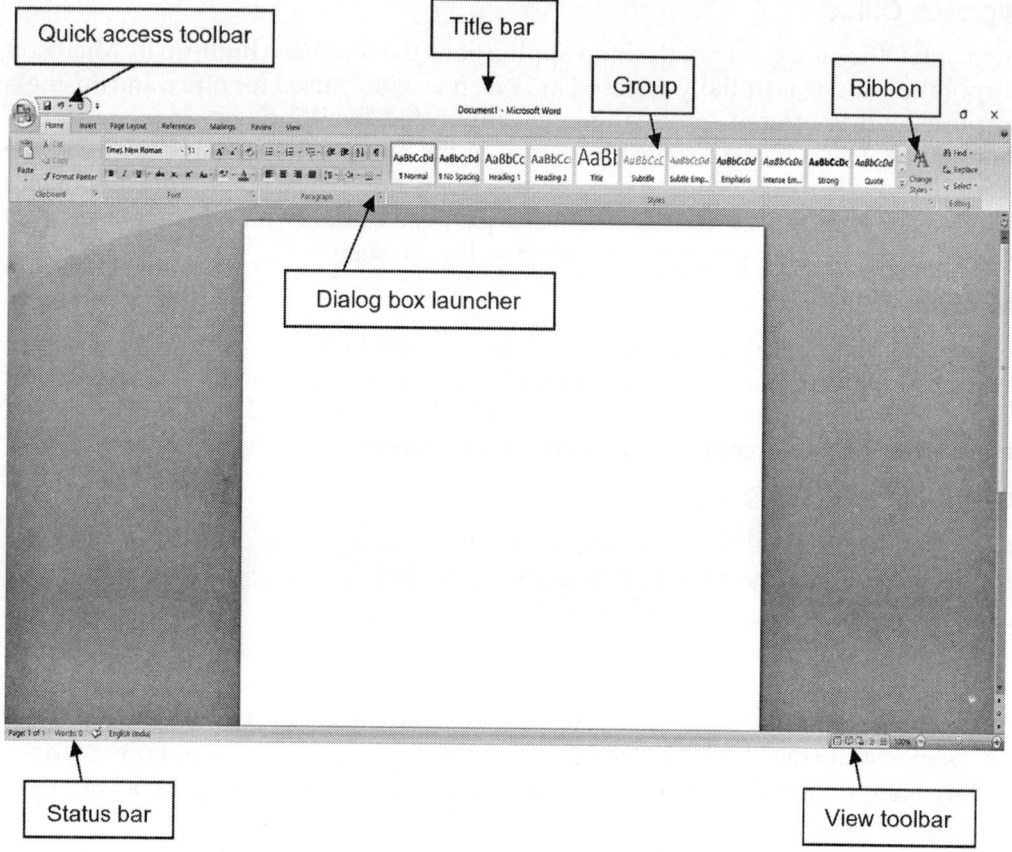

Fig. 5.1: Basic functionalities of MS Word application software

applications in daily use. The extension .ppt or .pptx is used for saving PowerPoint presentations. Basic functions of MS PowerPoint are:
1. Learning to modify presentation themes.
2. Analyzing formatting techniques and presentation styles.
3. Integrating information from other Microsoft programs into a PowerPoint presentation.
4. Working with text, themes, and styles.
5. Creating charts, grants, and tables.
6. Inserting media clips and animation.
7. Learning use macros, customize, package and publish your presentation.
8. Creating and manipulating simple slide shows with outlines and notes.
9. Create slide presentations that include text, graphics, animation, and transitions.
10. Use design layouts and templates for presentations.
11. Add special effects to slide transitions to spice-up your presentations.
12. Work with Master Slides to make editing your presentation easy.
13. Set-up slide shows and rehearse timings for your slides.
14. Collaborate using social media and PowerPoint together.

Features of Microsoft PowerPoint (Fig 5.2)

Microsoft PowerPoint features (Fig. 5.2) are as following:
1. The Outline tab is required to prioritize the content of the presentation.
2. The Slides tab shows the miniature versions of the slides in a single pane. The positions of the slides can be interchanged through this tab.
3. The title bar shows the name of the presentation above all other bars.
4. All menus available for making the presentation are available in Menu Bar.
5. The Standard toolbar comprises most frequently required functions to create presentations.
6. View Buttons provides options to swiftly shift different views of the presentation for the ease of the user.
7. Slide Pane helps to view one slide at a time and its format when it will be printed.
8. Notes Pane provides options to insert notes to the presentation.
9. Status Bar shows specific messages.
10. Task Pane makes a list of the operations that are of most significance for the presentation.

MS Excel

Microsoft Excel is a spreadsheet program contained in the Microsoft Office set of applications. Here, work is done on spreadsheets, which comprises of values arranged in rows and columns. Most of the work done is based on simple and complex mathematical concepts. The extensions for these types of files were earlier .xls which later changed to .xlsx (Fig. 5.3).

Basic Functions of MS EXCEL

Following are the basic functions of Microsoft Excel:
1. Demonstrating the basic mechanics and navigation of an Excel spreadsheet.
2. Formatting techniques and presentation styles.
3. Learning the use and utility of functions and formulas on excel spreadsheet.
4. Working knowledge of organizing and displaying large amounts and complex data.

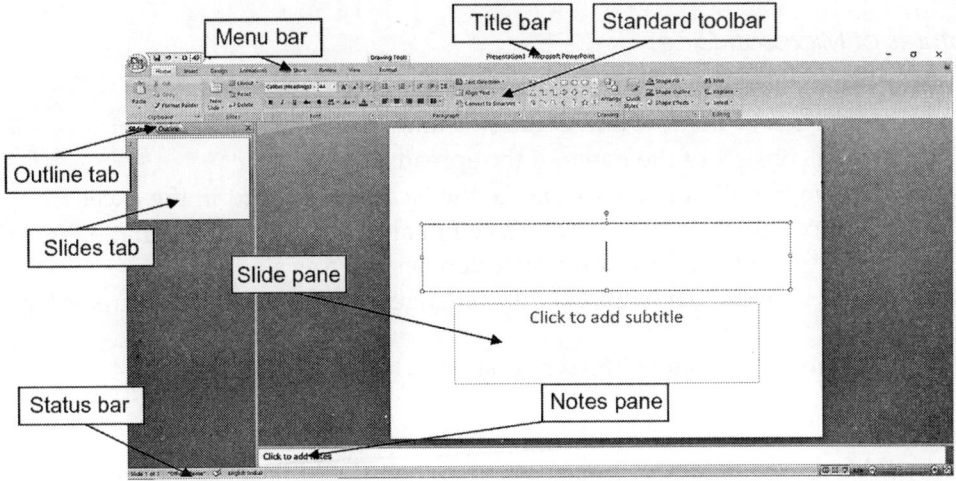

Fig. 5.2: Basic functionalities of MS PowerPoint application software

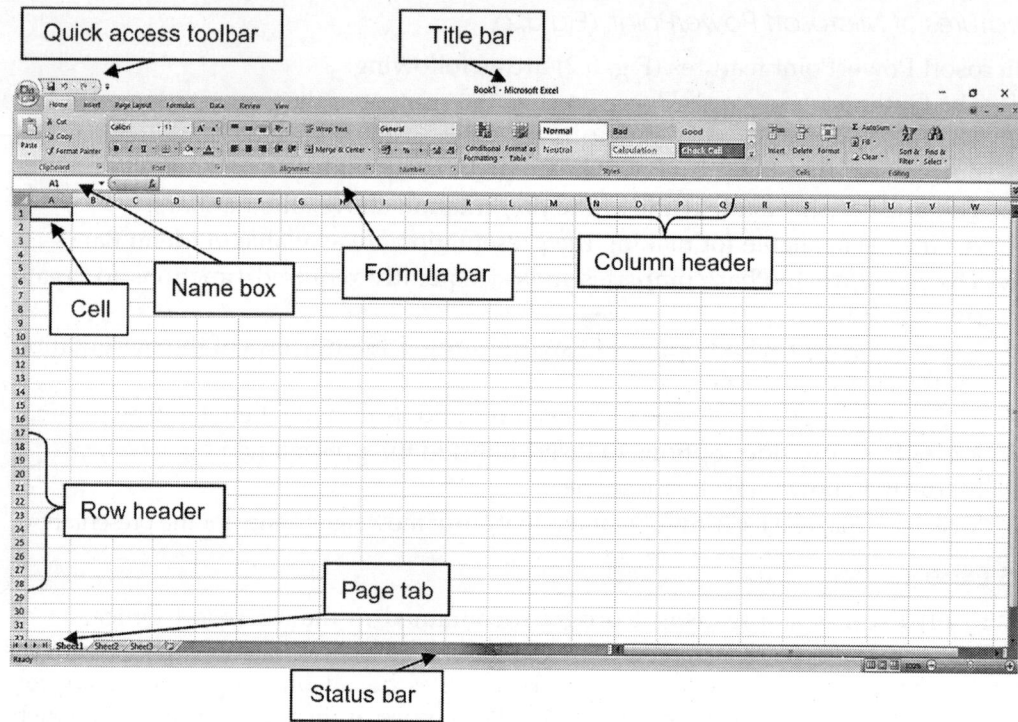

Fig. 5.3: Basic functionalities of MS Excel application software

5. Using clip art to enhance ideas and information in Excel worksheets.
6. Understanding the need and use of Excel templates.
7. Securing information in an Excel workbook.
8. Manipulate data using data names and ranges, filters and sort, and validation lists.
9. Learning formulas, creating charts and graphs that can easily explain or simplify complex information or data.
10. Analyzing data using Pivot Tables and Pivot Charts.

Features of Microsoft Excel

Following are the features of Microsoft Excel:
1. Each intersection of the row and column is known as a cell.
2. The Title Bar consists of the name of the spreadsheet.
3. The Formatting Toolbar helps to change the facade of the text in the excel.
4. The Name Box indicates the name of a cell in an alpha numeric format, where the letter indicates the column and number denotes the row.
5. Editor Bar or Formula Bar helps to edit or change information and also create logical formula.
6. The scroll bars help to move the worksheets in specific directions.

MS Access

Microsoft Access is a database management system (DBMS) developed by Microsoft which stores data with the help of Access Jet Database Engine and provides a graphical user interface. Data from other sources can be imported and correlated directly to be used in other applications. It helps to connect interrelated data effortlessly. Usage of MS Access requires creating a database, entering data into the database, retrieving information from the database and presenting the queried information in a report format. Basic functions of MS Access are:

1. Examine database concepts and explore the Microsoft Office Access environment.
2. Designing and building database with related tables in datasheet view or by using the table wizard.
3. Managing data in tables.
4. Develop simple, multiple-criteria, calculated fields, parameter, totaling and action-based queries.
5. Designing Forms build complex forms in design view using different form elements. Build forms of the type: Main/Sub form and query-based.
6. Learning the advanced form design features such as use of the toolbox, command buttons, option groups, combo-boxes, lines or rectangles, or designing a form from scratch in Design view.
7. Generating reports and creating report based application.
8. Import and export data.
9. Sorting, retrieving and analyzing data (Fig. 5.4).

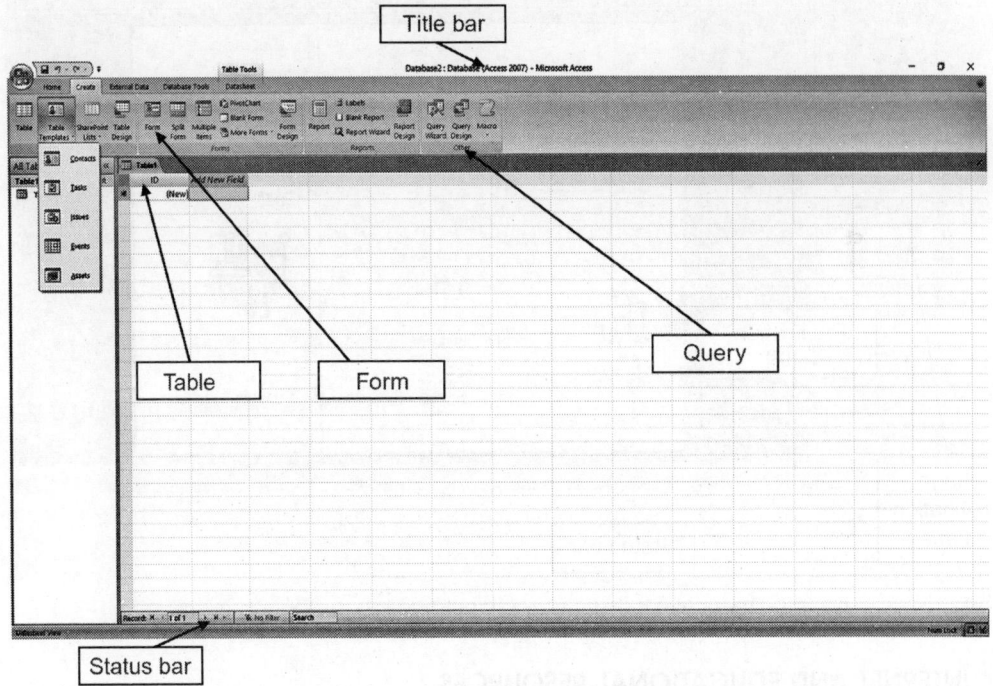

Fig. 5.4: Basic functionalities of MS Access application software

MS Publisher

This application is similar to Microsoft Word except for the fact that Microsoft Publisher concentrates more on the design and layout of the page. It is flexible and inexpensive for making designs and logos for small enterprises. Templates of business cards, brochures, address labels and calendars are few of the available applications of MS Publisher. Basic functions of MS Publisher are:

1. Looking at the Publisher Interface, its layout, commands and creating a basic Publication.
2. Learning to import text and organize the layout of text boxes and placeholders within a publication and other related features.
3. Formatting text and paragraphs as well as applying Microsoft's supplied styles and themes to enhance the overall look of your publication.
4. Introducing tools and features to edit/review your text as well as using tables for a more organized layout.
5. Adding pictures and images to your Publication and using various tools to format and fine tune their appearance.
6. Using Publisher's tools to check your design, preview, print and sent by email (Fig. 5.5).

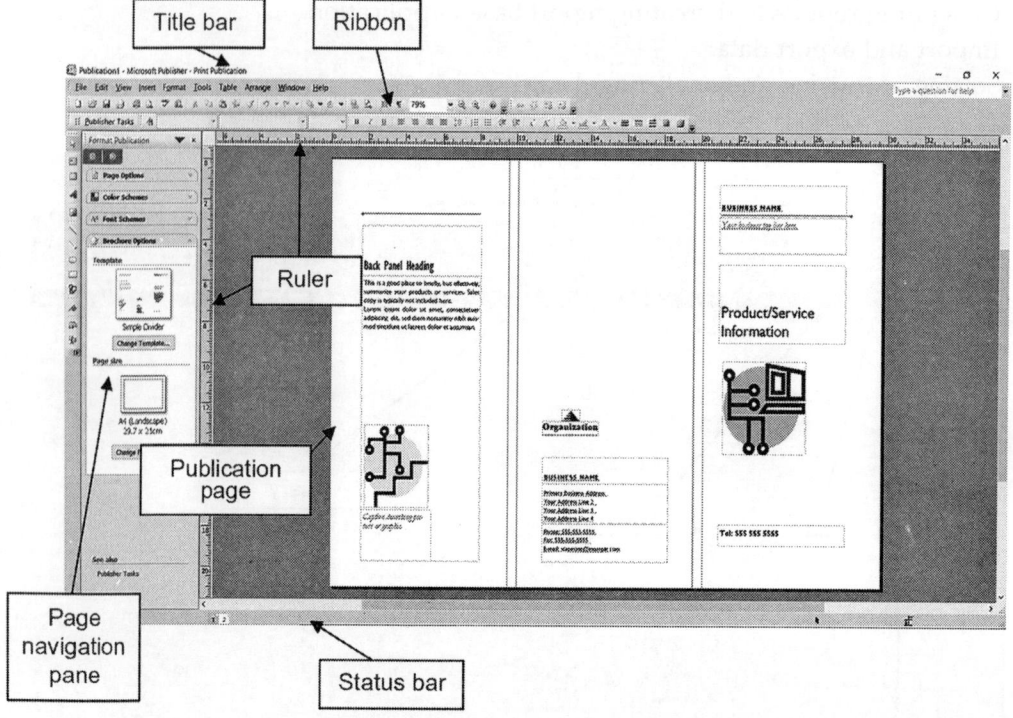

Fig. 5.5: Basic functionalities of MS Publisher application software

5.7 INTERNET AND EDUCATIONAL RESOURCES

Every individual has the right to education (as envisaged in the Constitution of India) which is important for self development as well as to sustain in the society. Education is the main factor that is responsible for uplifting the socio-economic condition of society. One of the key factors that can help reach education to one and all is the internet.

Introduction to Internet

In almost all aspects of life, the influence of internet is always on in this digital age. For a bigger part of the population, internet is a basic entity of life much like oxygen and water. Internet has already emerged as an integral part of modern education. It is anticipated that the influence of internet will gradually increase in the upcoming times. Internet provides a plethora of knowledge in various fields and is instrumental in transforming the traditional teaching methods from within the classroom and beyond. Teachers are able to prepare their teaching materials with the help of internet and students can extend their learning range other than their textbooks. One of the major boons of internet is that the teaching can be more personalized than the conventional generalized approach. Individual's requirements can be addressed and collaborative learning is possible using the different services offered through the internet.

Five factors are needed to be kept in mind to help internet and education intertwine to produce a sustainable development model. They are:

1. Investment in internet infrastructure and equal distribution of internet access.
2. Adoption of practical policies for using the internet that will do good to the students and lead to the development of the nation.
3. Authorities should ensure comprehensive and impartial education for one and all to endorse lifelong learning prospects.
4. There should be an urge to learn and imbibe the latest technologies so that the internet and its resources are fully utilized.
5. Improve the quality of content available on the internet so that it can act as a valuable alternative to the textbooks which are primarily used for learning purposes.

Email

Email is the abbreviation for Electronic Mail. Similar to the concept of sending letters in person through post offices, emails are letters sent to addressee via the internet. To receive emails, a unique email address is required. Emails can be sent instantly, in a protected manner, without spending huge money, by attaching multiple formats of documents, photos and other files and can be sent to multiple persons concurrently. In the present time, many web portals like Google, Rediff, Yahoo, etc. are offering mail services almost free of cost. Benchmark technologies and protocols are still evolving to provide such services in a secure way. Even a company can access services from Google mail server with the company domain names as part of the email address of their employees without any cost.

Search Engines

A search engine is a pathway to access content from the internet. Relevant keywords are typed into the search engine which in turn returns a list of web content in various formats like websites, images, videos or other forms of online data. A search that is returned as a result works in two stages, initially, a web crawler searches for resources that are listed in the search index. Then as per the retrieval query, the pertinent results are provided based on a specific algorithm. Google and Microsoft's Bing are the two most widely used search engines available free of cost. Search engine tasks may be optimized using different techniques to get fast results may be with respect to or in favor of some desired goals. Learners today often do not remember even the web addresses of their intended learning resources. They initiate their learning often from a search engine.

Info-savvy Skills

There is a huge amount of data available on the internet, and to aptly integrate ICT in education, the basic perception of the proper usage of internet is required. Many schools are introducing ICT courses in its curriculum to help the students, as well as teachers, acquire the basic information as they have less or no knowledge about computers. Along with computers, the basics of internet are also taught in these courses. Learners are taught both theoretically and practically including various teaching–learning techniques. Information is available in huge quantities and extracting the precise data requires expertise. This efficiency is known as an info-savvy skill which is the art of collecting and fitting information from the internet. It is extremely crucial for a teacher to learn info-savvy skills to gather desired data from internet.

Digital Age Skills

In today's digital world, acquiring knowledge comprises two powerful intertwined components, namely content and skill. As it is evident that maximum knowledge-based activities are entirely technology dependant, the skills pertinent to a specific knowledge base needs to be acquired. Few digital age skills that should be acquired by modern day learner's are branding of personal profile, creating an effective portfolio, enhance searching skills, appropriately citing the work performed by others in your own work, editing videos and images, converting files to required formats, writing codes and blogs, make an impactful presentation and constructing a website.

Safe Surfing Mode

Safe surfing is the exercise of maintaining security measures while surfing the internet. Issues like cyber-bullying are one of the common incidents faced by the young generation nowadays. To prevent such traumatic situations, certain tips must be followed while surfing the net. Parents should also make their children aware of such incidents and make certain that they stay protected online. Both children and adults should be barred from spilling-out personal information, privacy settings must be checked while posting details online, sharing of password should be a big no-no and security should be ensured while using mobile phones by locking personal information through 4-digit pin numbers or thumb impression. It is advisable not to make more virtual friends and spill all information without having the authenticity of the person on the other side. Removing all egos aside, children must pay attention to adults who warn about such dangers, be careful of malicious websites and links that they are visiting and keep the security software updated.

Firewall and Antivirus

Firewall is a software program that prevents unauthorized access to or from a private network. Often firewall service is found as a special service of modern operating systems. Some organizations can separately install firewall system at the gateway of the network. It is a tool that can be used to enhance the security of computers connected to a network, such as LAN or the internet. On the other hand, antivirus protects users from lingering and predictable-yet-still-dangerous malware. Its main job is to watch and screen all incoming files (through downloads from the internet, email attachments, files copied over through USB or Bluetooth, etc.) looking for malware like a virus, spoofing attacks, Trojan horse, etc. embedded in those files. Both firewall and antivirus softwares may be used simultaneously within the computer system to manage security risks. Windows OS is more vulnerable with respect to security attacks than Linux and Macintosh systems.

E-learning

E-learning is the type of learning which uses electronic devices and special methods to teach and learn courses in contrast to conventional learning methods. The objective of digital pedagogy is to fulfill the ever expanding demands of e-learning. E-learning operates on the foundation of ICT. Critical understanding of ICT has the potential to uplift the power of e-learning to support the society as a whole by disseminating educational media content to the intended recipient. Most often, e-learning refers to a course or program in which the degree or certificate is presented completely online. The students are allowed to cooperate along with the course content and this type of learning has proved to be more attractive and appealing in nature. Students are made to learn through a wide variety of methods like power point presentations, discussions within groups, video lectures, impromptu quizzes, game strategies and through surveys. Advantages of e-learning compared to the traditional learning techniques are cheaper to implement, consumes less time, yields best results for concise topics, students can avail the courses at their flexible time and pace and takes less time than implementing traditional classes.

M-learning

M-learning or mobile learning is a subset of e-learning as both of them require the help of digital means to impart education. Mobile-learning is the method of sharing knowledge through handheld or movable devices. This type of learning is more apt for acquiring knowledge at a fast pace and can be helpful in motivating students when they are made to learn boring things in a more interesting and interactive manner. More details on these are covered in Chapter 9 on emerging learning technologies.

Distance Learning

Distance learning is concerned about learning from a distance. This type of learning is applicable for students who are situated at geographically dispersed locations. The content for these courses are provided online and their maybe few face-to-face interactions with the instructors to assess the status of the learner. In India, distance education can be pursued through Indira Gandhi National Open University (IGNOU), where in contrast to an earlier time, distance learning now involves more of e-learning techniques. More details regarding these are discussed in Chapter 9 on emerging learning technologies.

Online Learning Content

Online learning is one of the greatest reasons for causing the huge paradigm shift in the contemporary education scenario. It aims to provide learning scope to every individual who wants to learn, not in a traditional way, due to some irresolvable problems. Online learning provides the flexibility to the learners to learn as per their needs, at their convenient time, makes an impact on the resume and comes across to recruiters as someone who has the urge to learn something extra outside the intended syllabus, makes provision for learning at the suitable speed of the learner and incurs minimum cost. The details regarding learning content and content management system are explained in Chapter 7 on the learning management system.

Virtual University

As the name suggests, virtual university is the method of teaching where education degrees are conferred online, specifically through the internet. It is an online learning organization that makes use of the internet to conduct classes and seminars. Students will acquire the degree on completion of the course and require a working computer with standard internet connection as per the requirements of the particular virtual university. Tough this method of learning is widely accepted worldwide, but still, the question arises on maintaining the value of the evaluation.

Wikipedia

Wikipedia is one of the widely used educational resources which is supported by Wikimedia Foundation and allows editing its content without any restrictions. Content in Wikipedia is available online in multiple languages with the advantage of providing links to interrelated pages to easily track co-related knowledge. Wikipedia had its first release in 2001, and is continuously proving to be one of the best reference sites that people look up to for appropriate information. Compared to other informative sites, Wikipedia is continuously involved in updating its contents to improve the magnitude as well as the superiority of the resources. Huge number of resources in Wikipedia are licensed under the Creative Commons Attribution-Sharealike 3.0 Unported License (CC-BY-SA) and the GNU Free Documentation License (GFDL) to ensure the sharing and imitation of the contents.

Massive Open Online Courses (MOOCs)

Massive open online courses (MOOC's) is a web-based platform that allows innumerable learners the chance to acquire education in a distance mode from the great universities of the world. Instructors and learners collaborate to create an online pool of resources that can be utilized by the common people. Few of the MOOC providers are—NPTEL (India), WizIQ (India and USA), Open2Study (Australia), edX (USA) and Udemy (USA). More details on the MOOCs are illustrated in Chapter 6 on open educational resources.

Social Networking

Social Networking is the habit of staying connected socially through internet-based social media sites. Friends, family, colleagues, customers, or clients may connect to each other through these sites for personal, professional and entertainment purposes. Some of the widely used social media sites are Facebook, Twitter, LinkedIn, and Instagram. Social media sites are widely used to promote business among social circles and help increase the brand value of the company but fake profiles and excess time consumption are still the major drawbacks of such sites. The flexibility of using social media sites can lead to a fruitful distribution of educational resources amongst students as well but the negative impact of social media on teenagers is a matter of great concern, which can be eliminated through proper counseling at school and home levels. As per statistics, the most used social media in 2019 is Facebook and studies reveal that social media is continuously developing, and to be at par with the daily changes are quite challenging. Social networking sites have the great potential of content distribution to a group of learners and management of their activities. This concept of social networking site to function as learning management system is explained in Chapter 7 on learning management system.

5.8 TECHNOPEDAGOGIC SKILLS

ICT training helps using and integrating correct technology in correct place. Teachers should know how to combine technology, pedagogy and subject area content effectively in their classroom practice. Merely introducing ICT in education is not enough and teachers must ensure technological integration to uphold the teaching quality in parallel with ICT evolutions. The teachers' training on ICT should not emerge as a separate and unrelated body of knowledge. Teachers should be enriched with self-confidence and new attitudes to serve best for their students in the ICT enabled classrooms.

Technopedagogic skill is the blending of effective teaching processes through the appropriate use of technology. Competencies should be identified to increase interaction in teaching–learning methods by mixing of technology and pedagogy. Incorporating technopedagogic skills helps in transforming the boring classes into more interactive ones with a lot of involvement from the students. The ease and clarity with which information is imparted to the students serve as a blessing to the education system, but lack of proper ICT facilities, lack of time and interest devoted by teachers to gain more experiences using ICT are the major causes that are acting as a hurdle to imply effective technopedagogic skills in today's education.

Media Message Compatibility

Communication is always a two-way process. Communication between the sender and recipient happens through a dedicated communication channel. The data sent by a sender become message for the intended recipient. In a classroom, the teacher is the source or creator of the message that is projected for the receiver, who is the student. The format of the message may vary in different cases. The medium which is appropriate for the spoken or written message is selected for transmission of the data from the sender to the receiver. The format of the message is prioritized while its compatibility with the media is considered.

Contiguity of Various Message Forms

The principle of contiguity states that people tend to understand graphical images better when they are explained with appropriate words in their vicinity. The words should be aligned with the graphics to ensure the appropriate implementation of the contiguity principles. If the explanation is verbal in nature, then it should be narrated concurrently when the images are being displayed. The audio should also be aligned with graphics and texts. Printed words should be represented along with graphics so that users do not have to scroll back and forth to understand a picture.

Message Credibility and Media Fidelity

Message credibility is termed as the authenticity of the message received from a source. It comprises the objective and subjective aspects of the validity of a message. To validate the message, factual data and emotions are considered in detail. Media fidelity is the way in which the media manipulates the way at which we look at an event. High fidelity media send messages which are easily interpretable and have a high impact on the users. For example, movies block out external images and sounds as well as involve the audience in submerging them into reality. Contrarily, low fidelity media transmit incomplete messages. For example, cartoons portray events eliminating a lot of details.

Message Currency, Communication Speed and Control

Messages are used as the major means of exchange system similar to the currency system used to exchange goods and services. To fulfill the demand of currency system and message exchange systems new currency systems (digital currency) like cryptocurrency is evolving where encryption techniques are used to regulate the generation of units of currency and verify the transfer of funds, operating independently of a central bank. Decentralized cryptocurrencies such as bitcoin now provide an outlet for personal wealth that is beyond restriction and confiscation. Information is the main item that is exchanged between two parties in both these cases. The pace at which information is disseminating is alarming and it requires high degree of adoption capability to be at par with the evolving changes in technology. Speed in communication can be achieved through partnering with the recruiters, applying teaching skills that motivates and changes the already built mindsets, give emphasis on practical-based learning that helps earn experience, update curriculum regularly keeping at par with the evolving trends in that specific knowledge domain and finally unearth more of technologies, study their potential and incorporate them in regular curriculum.

Sender-message-medium-receiver Correspondence

The sender-message-medium-receiver is also known as the Berlo's model of communication which was initially developed to augment the communication between two parties. Here, the sender is the source that generates the information, a message is the information that is shared between both the parties, medium is the mode in which the message is broadcasted and receiver is the recipient towards whom the message was being directed. While teachers are the senders, students are the receivers, the content delivered is the message and the method in which the content is delivered is the medium. The disadvantages of this model are that there is no scope of handling feedback, no method to combat errors during communication, this is the simplest way of communicating, both the parties need to be the same in nature and no scope of adding the feature of perception of humans. Hence, this model doesn't seem to be practically feasible.

5.9 PRACTICAL ICT TOOLS

It is an established fact that ICT can enhance the learning potential and outcome of students as well as teaching potential and teaching performances of teachers. As far as higher education is concerned, the professors bring their students to the seashore of the knowledge corpus and it is the student who decides whether the content at his/her reach will be imbibed or throw it away given that they often focus on self-learning. While practicing digital pedagogies through teaching–learning, both students and teachers have to take help of ICT tools to fulfill the requirements of the digital pedagogy. The tools are of two types, namely hardware tools and software tools. Basic ICT tools from both these categories are explained below as a brief introduction.

1. LCD/LED Projector

An LCD Projector works on the principle of transmission technology and is capable of displaying information in the form of images and videos. They project the images through LCDs and are cheaper to manufacture. Recent technology offers LED for the manufacturing of these devices instead of LCD to offer the product at less cost with more durability.

2. Digital Camera

A digital camera stores pictures as images in digitized format. Still images, sound and video can also be captured through the modern age digital cameras. The cost of the device varies with quality of output images. The quality depends on the quality of the used lens and computing resources such as speed, memory, resolutions of capturing.

3. Camcorder

A camcorder or a digital camcorder is a device that captures videos at a higher resolution. It originally combines a video camera and a videocassette recorder. The earlier camcorders were tape-based. It records analog signals onto videotape cassettes. Digital recording became the norm in 2006 with tape replaced by storage media such as mini-HD, micro-DVD, internal flash memory and SD cards.

4. Scanner

Scanner (device) scans texts and images and transforms them into digitized formats. Nowadays, other than the normal scanners, barcode and CT scanners are also widely used. It uses reflected light to capture images and translate them into computer readable files. It comes in high and low resolution and can scan images in both BW and color.

5. Printer

A printer is an output device that helps transforming the soft copy document into the hard copy. Printers may vary in types such as 3D printer, AIO (all-in-one) printer, dot matrix printer, inkjet printer, laser printer, LED printer, MFP (multifunction printer), plotter, and thermal printer. They vary with respect to functions, technology and quality of output produced.

6. Interactive Whiteboard

A whiteboard that connects a computer and a projector are collectively known as an interactive whiteboard. It is also known as interactive board or smart whiteboard. It can be used as a standalone board or can be used as an interactive board in the form of a touchpad to control computers from projectors. The user can conduct a presentation almost exclusively from the whiteboard.

7. Word Processors (MS Word/Libre Office)

These are computer programs that are used widely for the input, edit and format of texts. Graphics can also be included in modern age word processors. Microsoft word is an example of word processor already presented before. Writer is word processor comes with Libre Office available free of cost (open source). Libre Office is available for a variety of computing platforms, including Microsoft Windows, macOS, and Linux, and Android as well as in the form of an online office suite.

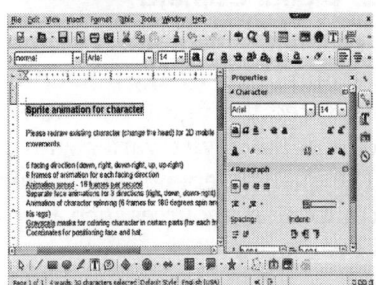

8. Slide Presentation (PPT/Impress)

A ppt is a slide show which can contain various forms of texts, images, audio and video. The slides are presented using animation to increase the look of the topic being explained through the ppt. Microsoft PowerPoint is already presented before. Impress is a slide presentation tool that comes with Libre Office available free of cost (open source).

9. Blogs

A blog is a platform where information is shared with the world online. To create a blog, a name has to be decided, the page has to be hosted, necessary customization made in the blogs, content created and necessary promotions made for the job. There are various content management systems (explained in Chapter 7) available almost freely for creating and maintenance of blogs.

10. Google Groups

Google Groups is a service from Google that provides discussion groups for people sharing common interests. The Groups service also provides a gateway to Usenet newsgroups via a shared user interface. It helps us to build a community online. Through this, the users can create communities where information is shared which help in the decision making process. This application is mobile friendly.

11. Google Docs

Google Docs is a word processor included as part of a free, web-based software office suite offered by Google within its Google Drive service. This service also includes Google Sheets and Google Slides, a spreadsheet and presentation program respectively. It allows editing access to all the members to whom the document has been shared.

5.10 USING ICT TOOLS (FOR CONTENT PREPARATION)

There are four approaches to using ICT tools given below.

- **ICT skills development approach:** Learners are required to be a skilled ICT user for their common activities. Training is offered on how to use hardware and software tools in regular academics.
- **ICT pedagogy approach:** This approach will empower learners focusing on constructivism principles towards the practice of digital pedagogy. Learners develop skills on how to use ICT literacy in designing classroom resources like learning design with digital pedagogy.
- **Subject-specific approach:** Here ICT is not an 'add on' but embedded into one's subject area as an integral tool to be accessed by practitioners in a wide range of curricular.
- **Practice driven approach:** It addresses the practical aspects of the training. Here learners get opportunities to evaluate the ICT facilities at their institution and efficiently use their skills.

Here is a case study of demonstrating the process of navigating, searching, selecting, saving and evaluating the authenticity of the material.

To search for a topic on the internet, a web browser is required. A web browser is a software that helps to search and find information from the websites. Google Chrome, Internet Explorer, Mozilla Firefox and Safari are examples of widely used browsers. The address of the web server where the website is hosted is known as the Uniform Resource Locator (URL). URL helps us to reach a specific website in the internet. We have to type the address in the URL bar of the web browser to go to a specific page. In cases, when the text or the name of a website appears to be underlined in blue, it has to be a hyperlink, which will navigate to a different webpage. Links also allow the direct downloading of files with the option 'Save link as' within the browser. Other than this, the forward and backward navigation buttons help us to visit the pages that we had recently traversed. Links may be opened in the same browser windows or in more than one window (Figs 5.6 to 5.8).

Fig. 5.6: URL for Google homepage

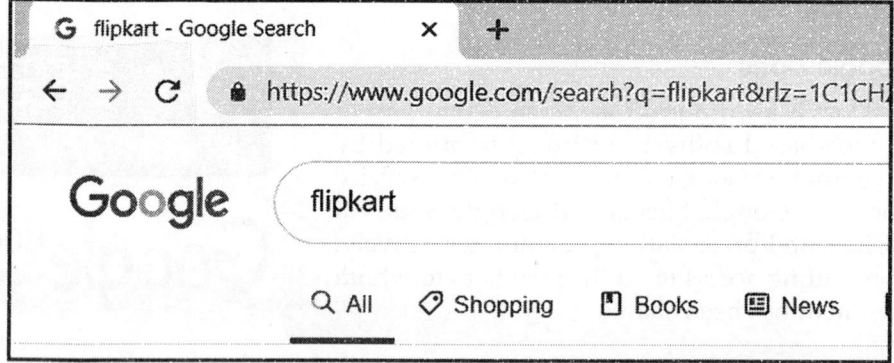

Fig. 5.7: Navigation buttons → ← (forward, backward and refresh)

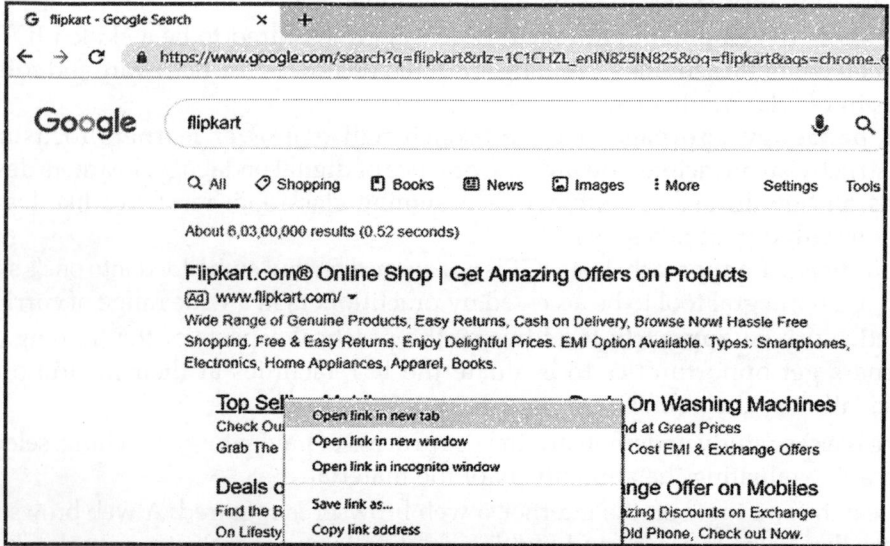

Fig. 5.8: Opening link in the same window

Bookmarks help to save the address of a website so that they can be visited in future. Bookmarks are done by clicking on the star sign available in the right upper end of the browser (Fig. 5.9).

Images can be saved by right clicking the mouse and selecting 'Save image as' (Fig. 5.10).

To check the authenticity of material, plagiarism can be checked through open source software or through online. Even the grammatical errors can be checked from many available websites to enrich the quality of the document (Figs 5.11 and 5.12).

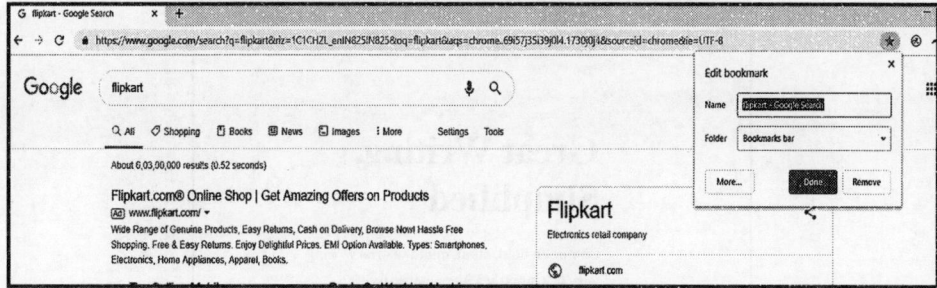

Fig. 5.9: Bookmarks

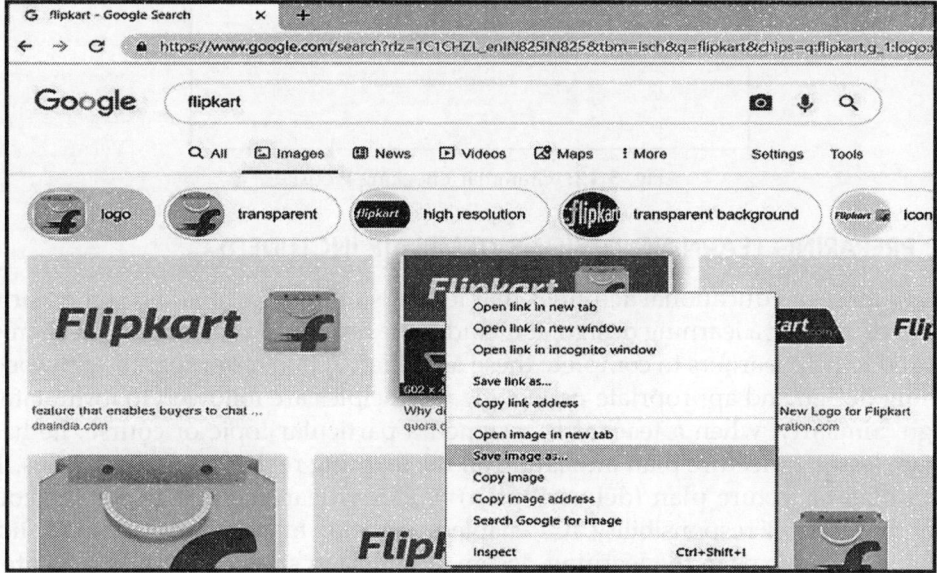

Fig. 5.10: Saving images from browser

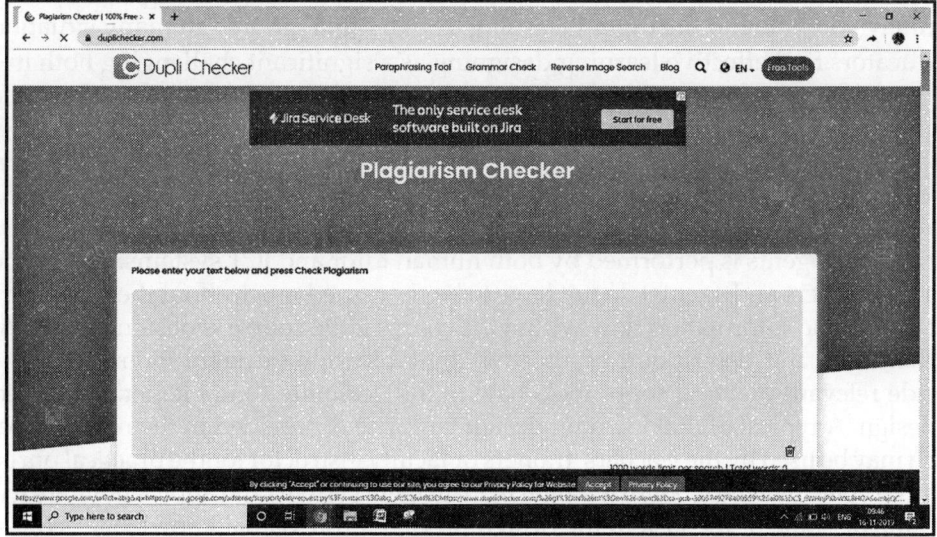

Fig. 5.11: Plagiarism checker website

Fig. 5.12: Grammar checking website

5.11 PREPARING LEARNING DESIGNS (TEMPLATE INCLUDED)

The sequence of educational activities that learners undertake to attain some learning objectives is called a learning design. It includes the resources and support mechanisms required to help learners to complete these activities. A book is prepared with specific learning design and appropriate pedagogical principles are followed to formulate the design. Similarly, when a teacher is assigned a particular topic or course, he has to prepare lesson or lecture plan indicating all the learning resources and activities. This lesson plan or lecture plan (delivery plan) works as learning design for the course under the teachers' responsibility. ICT enabled education must be formulated including all the ICT resources in the learning design. The design should not only indicate the digital resources but also elucidate how to utilize these resources and appropriate evaluation strategy. Technological characterization of the learning resources will definitely add value to the digital learning design often ignored in many situations.

Educators find effective learning designing as a significant challenging both in ICT and Non-ICT paradigm. Activities like reading, thinking, discussing, exploring and problem solving drive the learning process. The crucial role of learning design is to make the learner more active through different activities. ICT has the potential to augment the learning outcomes by its proper usage in the learning design and implementation of the design inside and outside the classrooms. The role of instructional designers and instructional agents is performed by both human tutor and ICT systems. The different actors (designers and agents) do not have to be concerned much about the management of activities and information flow within the course if the course is designed well. After the definition and description of effective digital learning design, the next task is to provide relevant practical set of tools having the flexibility to implement and execute the design. A typical digital learning design template is provided in the next few pages which may be used by the teachers, trainers or faculty instructor for the practical purpose. It may be noted that the modern learning management systems and applications are trying to automate some of the task in the design process. Professional knowledge, skills and judgment powers enable a teacher or faculty instructor to be a good learning designer.

Critical Understanding of ICT 89

Name of the institution	**Learning Design with Digital Pedagogy**	Logo

Name of the teacher	
Name of the school/college	
Name of the course	
Course code	
Standard/semester	
Year of study	

Date:		Lesson No.:	1	Period:	1
Topic Name:	Parts of a computer			Duration:	1 hour

1. Teaching Objectives

Objective of the topic	Students will be able to acquire the knowledge about the different parts of computer.
Objective of ICT skills	Students will be able to browse the internet, download audio, video and images and be able to handle hardware aspects while preparing a presentation on different parts of a computer.
Prerequisite of the topic	Idea about the generation of Computers and knowledge of electronic devices.
Mode of teaching	Online/offline/both

2. Digital Means Required for Conducting the Class

Software used to make the lesson plan	Microsoft Word (*application software*) and Windows 10 OS (*system software*)
Hardware used to make the lesson plan and take the class	Computer, LCD projector, projector screen, laser pointer

3. Learning Objectives

Content analysis	*Check whether there is any previous knowledge about the topic.*
Teacher activities	*Video showing the parts of a computer are displayed. Questions asked.* • *What did you see in the video?* • *What is a computer?* • *What are the different parts of a computer?* • *What is the difference between hardware and software?*
Student activities	*Students view the video displayed. Students answer all the questions except the last one as that had not been told.*
Digital domains used	*Video displayed from YouTube in LCD projector screen.* *PPT displayed to make understand the different parts of a computer.*
Learning activities	• *Students should go through the video that was referred to for the basic knowledge.* • *The class be divided into teams and discuss the problems raised.* • *Students should prepare and submit their assignments through LMS.*

(Contd.)

Learning Design with Digital Pedagogy (Contd.)

4. Doubt Clearance and Evaluation

Content analysis	Clarify about the difference between hardware and software.
Teacher activities	Teacher explains about the difference between hardware and software to the students. Teacher gives certain examples of hardware and software and asks the class to reply with the correct option.
Student activities	Students respond to the teacher stating that they have understood the difference properly. Students respond accordingly.
Digital domains used	Hyperlink in the PPT clicked for difference between hardware and software. Images from Google are shown for the students to identify.
Test on the topic taught in the class through LMS	Ref. Chapter 7
Assignments to be done, which are to be submitted through LMS	Ref. Chapter 7

5. Sources Collected and Referred From

Free resources	https://www.informationq.com/about-the-basic-parts-of-a-computer-with-devices/
Open educational resources	Ref. Chapter 6
MOOCS courses relevant to the topic	Ref. Chapter 6
Videos and PPTs on different parts of a computer system provided as supplementary resources	YouTube Refs.(may be)

6. Activity Planning

Recap of previous class	5 minutes
Discussion on topic	20 minutes
Group work	10 minutes
Discuss on the results of the group work	10 minutes
Test in LMS	5 minutes
Discussion on the answers of the test	5 minutes
On demand miscellaneous ICT activities	5 minutes

Total no. of students		Absent		Present	

Special remarks by teacher (if any)

Signature of the Teacher

(Contd.)

Learning Design with Digital Pedagogy (Contd.)				
7. Teacher Performance Evaluation				
Criteria	*Excellent*	*Good*	*Average*	*Poor*
Digital classroom organization				
Digital lesson plan creation				
Content quality				
Efficiency in handling of digital media				
Communication with students				
Clarity of content				
Effectiveness of topic taught				
Presentation quality				
Incorporation of ICT in teaching–learning				
Overall performance				

Special comments (if any) by evaluator

Signature of the HOD/In-Charge/Course Director

EXECUTIVE SUMMARY

- ICT is playing a major role in socioeconomic transformations by making information available at the right place, right time and in the right manner whenever required.
- Organizations should imbibe evolving ICT to broadcast, divide, accumulate and replace resources after eliminating all types of constraints.
- E-learning should be a mandate at the school level itself to sharpen their learning skills through ICT enabled education according to national ICT policy and IT @ school project. The ICT policy encourages learning through internet and television-based broadcasting like spoken tutorials, Gyan Darshan, Gyan Vani, Sakshat portal, eGyanKosh, haptic technology and virtual laboratories.
- Proper infrastructure should be present in all institutions to implement ICT education in regular activities other than regular teaching–learning. Internet tools like emails, social media, social networks, blogs, etc. must be utilized to aide information exchange within students.
- Though the academic institutions are encouraging the use of free and open source software tools for content development and distributions, the role and benefits of Microsoft Windows and Office tools cannot be neglected. Experiments should be made in classroom practice through PowerPoint presentations and interactive boards.
- Practicing ICT ensures a variety of services, reliable learning experiences, flexible learning formats, motivation for students to learn and grow together, enhances

communication amongst introvert learners, and provides a plethora of resources in all possible subjects.
- ICT has added the previously unavailable dimension of learning that motivates, stimulates and engages students in a far more effective and efficient way. Parents should aware students about the shortfalls of engaging themselves in technology.
- Technopedagogic skill is the blending of effective teaching processes through the appropriate use of technology. This must be developed across all academic communities for effective learning outcomes by analyzing media message compatibility, contiguity of various message forms, message credibility and media fidelity, message currency, communication speed and control, and sender-message-medium-receiver correspondence.
- Practicing digital pedagogy depends on both hardware and software tools including LCD/LED projector, digital camera, camcorder, scanner, printers, interactive whiteboard, word processors, slide presentations, blogs, Google groups, Google docs etc.
- There are four approaches to using ICT tools, namely ICT skills development approach, ICT pedagogy approach, subject-specific approach, and practice driven approach. A reader must understand the process of navigating, searching, selecting, saving and evaluating the authenticity of the material.
- The sequence of educational activities that learners undertake to attain some learning objectives is called a learning design. It includes the resources and support mechanisms required to help learners to complete these activities. A template of digital learning design is given here for practitioners to implement digital pedagogy.

Review Questions

1. What is the role of digital technologies in Indian socioeconomic context?
2. How to provide universal access to educational resources against the digital divide of educational resources and technologies?
3. Write down the challenges of integration of ICT in schools.
4. What are the aims and objectives of NMEICT in school education?
5. Write down the objectives of NMEICT. Explain the initiatives for appropriate implementation of NMEICT.
6. Write the process of installing Windows 10 operating system. Discuss briefly about Microsoft Office.
7. Write the functions and features of
    a. MS Word,
    b. MS PowerPoint,
    c. MS Excel,
    d. MS Publisher and
    e. MS Access.
8. What is internet? How does internet help promoting education?
9. Write short notes on:
    a. Email,
    b. Search engines,
    c. Info-savvy skills,

d. Digital age skills,
   e. Safe surfing mode,
   f. E-learning,
   g. M-learning,
   h. Distance learning,
   i. Online learning content,
   j. Virtual university,
   k. Wikipedia,
   l. MOOCs,
   m. Social networking.
10. What do you understand by technopedagogic skills? How this skill is related to media message compatibility, contiguity of various message forms, message credibility and media fidelity, message currency, communication speed and control, and sender-message-medium-receiver correspondence?
11. Discuss briefly the following ICT tools.
    a. LCD/LED projector,
    b. Digital camera,
    c. Camcorder,
    d. Scanner,
    e. Printers,
    f. Interactive whiteboard,
    g. Word processors,
    h. Slide presentations,
    i. Blogs,
    j. Google groups,
    k. Google docs.
12. Write down the approaches of using ICT tools. Write the processes of navigating, searching, selecting, saving and evaluating the authenticity of the material.
13. What is digital learning design? How does it different from traditional learning design?
14. Briefly describe the salient aspects of learning design with digital pedagogy.

Chapter 6

Open Educational Resources

Objectives of this chapter

- To introduce the concept of open learning.
- To explain the blending of technology with existing educational paradigms.
- To introduce the concepts of OERs, MOOCs, flipped classroom strategies, spoken tutorial, SWAYAM, and YouTube Channels into the education system.
- Explain the requirement of online professional development for teachers to cope up with the huge drift in education system.

Expected outcomes of this chapter

After going through this chapter learners will be able to:
- Understand the concept of open learning and how it can revolutionize the existing education system.
- Analyze the importance of technology and its role that it plays in the system of open learning.
- Understand the concepts of MOOCs, flipped classroom, spoken tutorial, SWAYAM, and YouTube Channels.
- Understand the importance of professional development required for the upliftment of teachers.
- Apply the appropriate OER in classroom practices and appreciate its use in the modern education system.

6.1 OPEN LEARNING

Open learning can be hailed as the learning "for the learner and by the learner". It refers to the tasks that open the boundaries for the learner beyond the conventional teaching methods. Open learning aims at helping education to reach out the masses through multiple methods. Access permission, content responsibility and fund management ability are the three concerns lurking behind the system of open learning. Open learning can be treated as a three-dimensional educational approach comprising the following.

Open Courses

The onset of open courses or more colloquially used massive open online courses (MOOCs) into the arena of open education has completely transformed the scenario of existing traditional learning paradigms. The contents were now the only priority of these courses. Appropriate content delivery and their proper assessment along with the facility of interaction with peers made these courses complete. It is predicted that the adoption of these varied techniques in educational institutions can lead to engagement of larger sections of students, as those tools are reasonable and achievable by nature.

Open Educational Resources (OERs)

This is the system by which premium standard contents are made freely available in the public domain. This open process enables teachers to customize their teaching content along with the stipulated textbook so that the learner can indulge deep into the subject and help understand the concept better. To create a benchmark of OERs, guides like CARE Framework and TEMOA Rubric are also used to judge the quality of resources.

Open Pedagogies

This method proposes to entangle students in real work within the classroom tenure so that they can earn beyond the syllabus. The main aim of incorporating this method was to convert the concept of assignments from 'use and throw' ones to 'sustainable' ones. Students generally complete the assignments and dispose them once they acquire the final marks, but the idea should be doing their assignments in such an order that it can be updated, preserved for future use and at the same time these can be shared with all.

Open learning ensures a lifelong learning possibility for professionals. It provides students to enjoy hassle-free education related to complex admission procedures in universities following their schedule as per their convenience, needs to travel less and finally have the option of choosing our own course as per requirements.

6.2 TECHNOLOGY AND OPEN LEARNING

Though there is a recent drift in education where technology is being imbibed to the teaching and learning process, the considerate appliance of the same is anticipated to bring in varied methods which ultimately results in the upliftment of the learning standards. Ideas for learning and basic ethics should be maintained while blending education with technology towards imparting intended education. The role of a teacher should be that of a facilitator and it would be apt if there was a one-to-one association maintained by each student so that the teachers can cater their needs.

Different forms of communication can be utilized while using technology in open learning. Asynchronous communication includes technologies that utilize previously stored learning resources. Video tutorials are a perfect example of asynchronous communication. On the other hand, synchronous communications are instantaneous. These technologies prefer to live interactive sessions like audio or video conferencing. The use of technologies can further be required to evaluate or assess a student, to be able to differentiate between separate requirements of learners, to involve students in more interactive and innovative methods of teaching and to be able to analyze the concerns associated with technology. Few of the common type of technologies available for spreading education digitally among one and all are:

- Emails
- Interactive tutorials
- Free downloadable content
- Real-time interactive approaches, etc.

6.3 OPEN EDUCATIONAL RESOURCES AND THEIR USEFULNESS

OER is the freely available resources that are mixed with the conventional education practices to assist training, knowledge gaining, evaluating and research functions. The usage of the word was first found in UNESCO's 2002 Forum on Open Courseware. OER comprises entire courses, course materials, modules, manuals, workbooks, video contents, and examination-related resources along with answers, software or any other available methods which aid knowledge sharing. There are many existing definitions of OER which mainly concentrates around the following important aspects.

- The usability, reusability, recycling, remodeling, reprocessing, recovering and regeneration of the resources as per requirements.
- All the resources have to be made free and readily available for teaching and learning purposes.
- It should embrace all categories of digital media.

Along with all availabilities, there are certain sides to the definitions of OER, which need much concern. Clarifications regarding the nature, source and the rank of availability of the materials should be meted out while using these resources. The essential criteria for an educational resource to be claimed as an OER requires the presence of an open license. It is advisable to use the Creative Commons license which is both nationally and internationally the most frequently used authorization structure for OERs.

OERs can be defined as the varied types of learning resources available in either digital or non-digital form that finds its existence in the unrestricted domain or may have been incorporated with a free-to-use license which allows modification and reorganization of the document with minimum or without restrictions. To think of a wider aspect, this method of making resources available helps enhance the standard of education at the international level. It comes across the developing countries as a great boon, where due to financial reasons students are not able to procure books which are of a high price or where there is inadequate admittance to classrooms for students of all categories. Other than economic constraints, inefficient teaching–learning processes can take the help of OERs as an instrumental medium in imparting a plethora of knowledge in any field of study. In affluent countries, there may have cost cutting including OERs in the course of study. From the student aspect, OERs provide open yet authorized access to the best resources and degree programs from around the globe. The resources obtained through these processes can hence be converted into multiple languages to help initiate innovation. The best part of accessing OERs is that people of any age group can benefit from this system.

There are many sites offering materials categorized by different criteria which can be proved to be beneficial to all learners. Following are some of the sites which can be accessed as OER.

A. https://coteducation.com/continuing-our-support-for-open-textbooks/
   This site provides free access to textbooks categorized by different subject regions.
B. http://www.learningpod.com/
   This site is hailed as the biggest library of freely available questionnaires to help students practicing.
C. https://lumenlearning.com/
   This site offers exceptional learning capabilities to students. Other than course materials, affordable materials are provided so that the students can enhance

subject knowledge, complete the course successfully and retain the knowledge and skill.

D. http://www.merlot.org/merlot/index.htm
Though this California State University System's site contains more than 50,000 resources, more than 3000 open textbooks are available containing accessibility information for physically-challenged candidates.

E. https://ocw.mit.edu/courses/online-textbooks/
Managed by the Massachusetts Institute of Technology, this site contains freely available textbooks for varied disciplines.

F. https://www.oercommons.org/
Managed by the Institute for the Study of Knowledge Management in Education, this site provides 23000 types of OER. Additional information including the process to create OERs, necessary training to use them and the capability to generate 'OER Commons', which is a general platform where common shared resources are provided in this site.

G. http://opencourselibrary.org/
This course oriented resource site is managed by the Washington State Board for community and technical colleges.

H. https://www.oeconsortium.org/
This site prioritizes the concept of 'open education', and is a community of 240 schools consisting of OER resources, webinars, links to textbooks among others.

I. http://oli.cmu.edu/
This site provides different courses to the students mainly based on computing.

J. https://cnx.org/
This site is managed by Rice University and thousand of learning resources are present in this site, which can easily be prepared to transform into books.

K. https://www.coursera.org/
This site is an American online learning website which associates with high level universities and organisations to allow access to the world's best knowledge providers. Stanford professors Andrew Ng and Daphne Koller were the founder members of this website that provides numerous MOOCs, special certification courses and degrees. Reports suggest that until June 2018, there have been 33 million registrations for around 2400 courses. These courses are of 8 weeks-12 weeks duration and the student performances are assessed by various methods like weekly assignments, quizzes, projects and a final examination. All courses include video lectures by distinguished instructors from premier institutions and the provisions of forums are offered to allow peer discussion regarding specific topics of the course.

L. https://www.edx.org/
This site was created in May 2012 by Massachusetts Institute of Technology and Harvard University and is one of the gigantic MOOC contributors of the world. It is the only non-profit association hosted in the open source Open edX software. edX is used widely for both its free and chargeable online university level courses it provides. It also conducts study on the methodology of learning on the basis of which learners use their courses.

For further resources, interested learners may check on the link https://educationaltechnology.net/open-free-educational-resources-oer-teaching-learning/.

There are several motivations behind prioritizing the OERs in mainstream education. The constant rise in the price of textbooks, the ability to distribute and recycle resources, the right to use high quality materials, the facility of returning back to the course once it has been completed and the main aim to be able to provide free education to all are the important few. OERs are learning resources that can be refurbished because their creators have given the facility to do so. OERs may include presentation slides, podcasts, syllabi, images, lesson plans, lecture videos, maps, worksheets, and even entire textbooks under authentic tools like Creative Commons licenses. It is most beneficial to be able to combine different educational materials on a common platform. But it is to be kept in mind that OERs are freely available resources but the converse is not true. Free resources have a temporary lifespan and have various access restrictions imposed on them, whereas, OERs are free resources that are publicized under proper copyright formats.

6.4 WIDELY USED OERS

There are a huge number of good OERs available worldwide. Here we have presented some of those which are relevant to Indian educational situations.

NPTEL

NPTEL is another name for National Programme on Technology Enhanced Learning which is a project lead by seven Indian Institutes of Technology (IIT Bombay, Delhi, Guwahati, Kanpur, Kharagpur, Madras, and Roorkee) and Indian Institute of Science (IISc) for creating affordable course contents both in the domains of engineering and science (Fig. 6.1).

OERs in the forms of web and video resources are available in a variety of 23 disciplines in the portal www.nptel.ac.in. Students have to learn the concepts first in a week through provided videos and then weekly assignments are to be solved based on the knowledge acquired through those videos. These assignments are to be submitted in the online mode within the stipulated time. There is a presence of a forum where the students are open to discuss any doubts, which are promptly answered by the teacher teaching the course or any member of his/her team. To achieve certification for these courses from the most premier institutes of the nation like IITs, a student have to appear a written exam in person with a negligible amount of fees. The final evaluation is based on a calculation of 75% from the final written exam and rests 25% from the previous assignments submitted during the tenure of the course.

Students are benefitted through these courses as these can help in their credit transfer in their curriculum which further helps to yield them a better credential. For the faculties, these courses can be considered as AICTE recognized FDPs and can also help as refresher courses. Besides these, professionals in varied fields can opt for these courses to uplift and enhance their knowledge and skills.

Fig. 6.1

GitHub

GitHub is the most popular code hosting website which boasts a repository of more than 1 million codes from all over the world. As in OERs, these codes can be stored in GitHub, create projects as per your choice, changes made to other codes, track changes others make in your code and release suitable versions of the code as and when required. GitHub has acquired the trust of business companies like Airbnb, IBM, PayPal, etc. The team at GitHub reviews the codes hosted on their platforms, manages the projects hosted by users, integrates different parts of the codes in a project, manages the team at work, helps each other in codes and finally helps in the process of code hosting. All actions are added by feedback, in the end, to help users review their work.

MOOCs

Massive open online courses (MOOCs) are online courses available to any person with a computer and access to the World Wide Web. Anyone has the privilege to enroll in these courses and they help achieve a cheaper yet lithe way to become skilled at learning a new level of competencies. This further leads to the enhancement in the respective profession and to be able to convey value worthy educational experiences. MOOCs facilitate the use of interactive courses along with the conventional resource sharing methods allowing feedback collection, taking quizzes and allotting assignments. MOOCs were introduced in 2006 but gained momentum from 2012 onwards.

Different innovative courses through sites like Coursera, Udacity, Khan Academy or edX have enrolled millions of students worldwide for MOOC courses. It was found in a survey that most of the students who opted for MOOCs had already earned their college degrees. The importance of MOOCs has now compelled many universities to include these courses in the curricula to help fulfill the gap of prerequisite knowledge required for varied courses. Though a huge effort is required to create a course through MOOCs, one concern that constantly bugs is the rate at which students opt out from these courses. Though there are multiple reasons why students enroll into such courses, it has been studied that the active participation of the students in the initial weeks of the course leads to less number of dropouts from a course. And as we know, that we like to follow what people do, rather than applying our knowledge for our own purpose, the dropout of a single student might many-a-times lead to the exit of his/her group or circle of friends from the course. Too much of the time consumption and absence of self-motivation are the other factors that lead to the reason for exit from these MOOCs.

Though there are many advantages, it has to be kept in mind that students need to be digitally literate to handle these courses. There should be constraints on the resources as the entire course stands on materials provided by users. Students shall be able to devote the time and effort that are required to complete these courses. Language constraints should be customized as per the requirement of the enrolled learners and participants must self motivate themselves by setting their individual goals to pass through MOOCs. Successful MOOCs contain the learning of the courses, applying the acquired knowledge and assessing them. Developing MOOCs is a humongous task as many restrictions are to be kept in mind. It should start from the very basic, interactions must be prioritized, there should have an efficient team to build-up the course together, it should be ready before releasing where the success of the learners is the ultimate fruit.

Flipped Classroom

A flipped class is one that inverts the typical series of content attainment and application so that:
- Students achieve the required information before class, and
- Instructors direct students to energetically and interactively clarify and apply that knowledge during class.

This approach supports instructors playing their most important role in guiding their students to deeper thinking and higher levels of application. A flipped class keeps student learning at the center of teaching.

A flipped classroom is one where learners are provided content to study at home and discuss it during the class hours. This is a blended learning approach where the face-to-face interactive study is mixed with a self-governing study with the assistance of technology. This helps in the fact that students come prepared on a particular topic from home and hence will be able to participate in discussions on the important points related to that particular topic. This can be termed as a double fold approach where students are having access to the same topic twice, one at home and one during problem-solving within the class hours. Though these methods go apart from the traditional styles of teaching, yet to imbibe these in our curriculum, the video quality of the content, the precise information in the video, the amount of sound in the video, the method of instruction, the tasks asked to do, the presentation or way of communication and the process of assessment should be of concern (Fig. 6.2).

Educators are mainly flipping their classes as students obtain a deeper perceptive of the content and how to employ it. Students are converted from being passive listeners to active learners. It increases the rate of interaction between students and teachers. The knowledge base of the students builds inside and outside the classroom in this way. Students interact with themselves and this helps in learning from one another. Thus, the received feedbacks help to understand the vibe of both the sides appropriately. There are five tasks to flip a class given below.

Step 1: The instructor needs to find out where the flipped class shall be appropriate in the course.

Step 2: Students should be engaged in the application of the knowledge during the class hours and proper feedback should be collected.

Step 3: The relationship between 'homeworks' and 'classworks' should be addressed.

Step 4: The resources should be designed in such a way that will cater to the requirements of the course.

Step 5: The students should uncover the learning beyond the scope of the class hours through combined practice along with their peers.

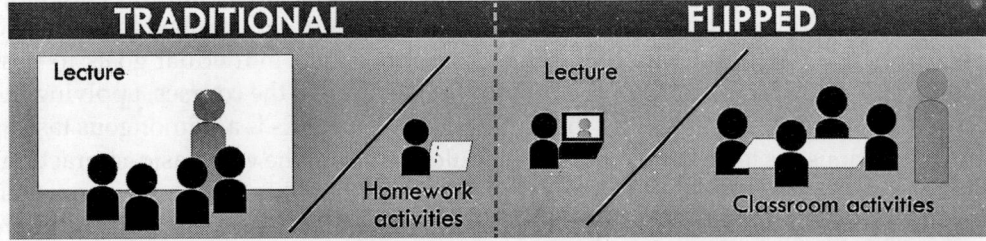

Fig. 6.2: Concept of a flipped classroom (source: University of Washington)

Spoken Tutorial

Spoken Tutorial is a multi-award winning educational content portal initiated by IIT Bombay for MHRD, Government of India. Free and open source software may be learned through these platforms all by oneself. A computer and an internet facility is all that is required to register for these courses and these can be learned in a place, time and language comfortable to the learners. All the contents published in these sites are shared under the CC-BY-SA (Creative Commons Attribution-ShareAlike License) license. These courses are easy yet effective and are suitable to cater to the needs of naive learners. There are three levels of content delivery methods in these courses—basic, intermediate and advanced. All facilities like assignments, the presence of online forums, active participation from learners are incorporated into these courses. The presence of fundamental courses like mathematics and science can also prove to be beneficial for school students. If the time permits, then one student can complete up to a maximum of three courses in a semester. This project aims to make a famous software learning initiative of the 'Talk to a Teacher' activity of the National Mission on Education through Information and Communication Technology (NMEICT), launched by the Ministry of Human Resources and Development (MHRD), Government of India.

SWAYAM

SWAYAM is a programme initiated by the Government of India and intended to attain the three fundamental principles of education policy, viz. access, equity, and quality. The object of this endeavor is to take the finest teaching–learning resources to everyone counting the most deprived. SWAYAM seeks to bridge the digital divide for students who have previously remained untouched by the digital revolution and have not been able to adhere to the mainstream of the knowledge economy.

Original IT platforms are utilized to help the hosting of all the courses which are present in the syllabus from class IX till postgraduation and available any time to all. Interactive sessions are a must in these courses which have been prepared by the best-selected teachers available nationwide at zero cost.

The courses hosted on SWAYAM are in four quadrants—(1) video lecture, (2) specially prepared reading material that can be downloaded/printed, (3) self-assessment tests through assessments and quizzes and (4) an online discussion forum for clearing the doubts.

Techniques have been devised to augment the learning familiarity by using audio–video, interactivity and state of the art digital pedagogy. In order to ensure the best quality content are produced and delivered, nine national coordinators have been appointed—AICTE for self-paced and international courses, NPTEL for engineering, UGC for non-technical postgraduation education, CEC for undergraduate education, NCERT and NIOS for school education, IGNOU for out of the school students, IIMB for management studies and NITTTR for teacher training programme.

SWAYAM platform has been developed by MHRD, Government of India and All India Council for Technical Education (AICTE) with the help of Microsoft and would be ultimately capable of hosting 2000 courses and 80000 hours of learning covering school, undergraduate, post-graduate, engineering, law, and other professional courses.

YouTube Channels

Educational YouTube channels are constructed to put forward contemporary educators plenty of resources and information for adding up a zing in teaching. Daily, there are over a billion users uploading informative videos on YouTube. Videos that inspire and educate, can help people brainstorm, being original, being true to the idea of sharing information to the known and unknown and being easily understandable and reliable are the key factors to create a video in YouTube Channels.

Few of the top-rated educational video related websites/channels are mentioned below.

- TEDED—with 6 million subscribers, TEDED rules the list of being the best educational website.
- COMMON SENSE EDUCATION—this channel is dedicated entirely to offer the most excellent digital tips and tools for contemporary educators.
- EDUTOPIA—this is hailed to be a gold mine for teachers of this generation.
- BIG THINK—this channel dedicates itself to help us think out of the box about the big shot ideas and skills that define knowledge in the current scenario.
- TEACHING CHANNEL—videos from this channel can be watched, shared and taught to help students develop their knowledge.
- Other channels include KHAN ACADEMY, NATIONAL GEOGRAPHIC and EXPERT VILLAGE which are responsible for revolutionizing how we acquire information nowadays. For a list of numerous channels, please follow the link https://blog.feedspot.com/educational_youtube_channels/.

6.5 ADVANTAGES AND DISADVANTAGES OF OERS

Advantages

- Learners can learn from OERs wherever, whenever and however they want.
- These resources are free of distribution costs and hence can reach all.
- OER resources help as additional assistance to the teachers teaching courses as part of the curriculum.
- The biggest help that OERs gift students is to reduce the cost of procuring these materials from markets.
- The ability to continuously improve the OER resources helps in enhancing its standards. It also can be customized as per requirements.

Disadvantages

- As these OER resources are widely available for use, the quality is to be maintained throughout. Releasing of poor quality material leads to defy the goal of properly educating one and all.
- Though education is planned to be digitized, the direct interaction between students and teachers should not be made obsolete. Students should self-learn but under the proper guidance of the teachers.
- Multilingualism is an issue that needs to be addressed in OERs.
- Users should be made digitally aware before they intend to use OERs in their daily lives.
- The materials released as OERs should be maintained through self-motivation even though there is no reimbursement for the same, and it should be assured that proper use of copyrights is made in all the resources.

6.6 OERS IN ACTION—A PRACTICAL EXAMPLE FROM THE K-12 SECTOR

OER converges from associations belonging to multiple sections of the educational society. OERs have proven to perform better in cases of student performance and satisfaction. The allowance of users to reuse the OER resources at the school levels create a possibility of varied usage through numerous adaptation techniques than other available online materials. It proves to be crucial in improving the status of the backward students in a class and they can enhance their knowledge on the related subject or course through the retentive facility provided by OERs. On the side of the educator, an application of OERs in the K-12 (KG to class XII) sector shall help develop the essential reflection of the teachers towards a particular student. Vast exposure of educators to OERs tends to involve a wide range of content while teaching students. Finally, the inclusion of OERs in institutions may come as financial relief in third world countries like India. OER claims to have a positive impact on children before going to college and which will further help them imbibe them in the next learning phase of their lives.

6.7 ONLINE PROFESSIONAL DEVELOPMENT FOR TEACHERS

Professional development means making ready a person to be competent for their professional role, so that, they can deliver their duties effectively. As they say that the future of the nation is in the hands of teachers, professional development should be made a mandate for all the teachers as they need to cope up with the constant change occurring around them and the need to imply changes in the methods of education based on the needs of the students. It provides flexibility and adaptability to the teachers, and helps in the creation of communities amongst the teachers and enhances the retention of the teachers by directly involving them with the process of learning. After the vast improvement in technology, many online resources provide ample scope for the professional development of the teachers. Some of them are:

- ASCD-ASCD (association for supervision and curriculum development)—offers an enormous range of subject matter as well as resources on teaching, STEM subjects, Common Core as well as efficient teaching through technology.
- Intel Teach Elements—the courses designed help teachers in learning about various social topics such as learning about social media, technology and 21st-century assessments.
- Library of Congress Teacher Modules—this site provides online 'Teacher Modules' without any fee. Courses designed here assist teachers to utilize the enormous resources available in both online and offline mode.
- ISTE (international society for technology in education) professional learning—offers a lot of professional learning services along with commodities for the teachers that are helpful and easily available having great worth.
- TEQ Online PD (an acronym for TV channel, Télévision Ethnique du Québec, online professional development)—this site offers almost 50 courses on the most necessary tech integration hurdles faced by the teachers as well as professional development programs.

6.8 OER AND DIGITAL PEDAGOGY

Digital pedagogy is not only about using digital technologies for teaching and learning but rather resembling digital tools from a significant pedagogical viewpoint. It is about settling on when not to use digital tools, and about paying notice to the impact of digital equipment on education. Digital pedagogy pays importance to OERs, sharing of the common syllabus, sharing teaching resources through GitHub and Creative Commons, projects designed by students and publishing content through open access. The experimental nature of this method of teaching makes it an important criterion for education in today's generation. It emphasizes on blended learning in classrooms and incorporates the same using LMS and mobile learning. LMSs like Canvas is very much into practice in today's teaching arena. The Canvas LMS offers data, deep analytics, and views into gains on student achievement. It acts as a central management hub for all your teaching apps. It brings all your teachers together in one place to share content and ideas. And that's how it helps districts provide equitable access. The implementation of digital pedagogy calls for the usage of mobile learning apps like Sololearn, Polleverywhere, Decoder, Photomath.

EXECUTIVE SUMMARY

- Open learning is a method of education that allows people to learn at their convenience even at geographically dispersed locations.
- It's high time that the potential of technology to act as a catalyst to cause a huge change in the existing education system should be recognized and absorbed for keeping at pace with the paradigm shift in education.
- OER helps in fulfilling the learning needs of all ages. It helps learners to get access to affordable resources, helps teachers to modify their syllabus as per the requirement of the students which benefits the content delivery in class.
- Students of the school level should be made familiar with the concept of OER.
- Teaching–learning processes must include emerging approaches like MOOCs, flipped classrooms, spoken tutorial courses, SWAYAM courses, videos from YouTube Channels to help students offer a variety of resources to dig deep into a particular topic being taught in class.
- Digital instructions with technology blended with normal classes lead to increased use of formative assessments, peer assessment, self-assessment, revision of the work done by the students and high student engagements.

Review Questions

1. What is the aim of open learning?
2. What are the technological means which can be imbibed in regular classroom teaching?
3. What are open educational resources? How can they help learners in today's educational scenario?
4. How can MOOCs assist students in their curriculum?
5. Explain in your own words how you as a teacher would implement a flipped classroom in a class. How would you engage students in the entire classroom?
6. How do you plan to include spoken tutorial/SWAYAM courses besides the regular courses of study and how do you feel it will improve the education system as a whole?
7. Do you feel that the prime motives of developing spoken tutorial/SWAYAM/MOOCs courses help the learners at all?
8. What is the necessity of professional development for teachers to survive in today's changing educational scenarios?

Chapter 7

Learning Management Systems

Objectives of this chapter

- To explain the concept and importance of CBT, CMS and LMS in education.
- To present the concept of SCORM and its importance in learning management.
- To explain how to work with popular freely available LMS like Moodle, Google Classroom, Canvas and social networks (Facebook).
- Discuss the significance of consortia in higher education.
- To introduce the technology of NGDLE preceded by LMS.

Expected outcomes of this chapter

After going through this chapter learners will be able to:
- Understand the definition, elements and working procedures of major LMS.
- Analyse the technological innovations followed and preceded by LMS.
- Use open source LMS like Moodle, Google Classroom, Canvas, etc. for their practice.
- Judge the requirement of learning technological implementation in their practicing or relevant education system.
- Develop courseware using popular freely available LMS.

7.1 LMS INTRODUCTION

It has been proved that technology has the potential to improve teaching and learning process. Technology is rapidly changing the dynamics of education. With the use of computer and internet, the teaching–learning process has changed. Teachers are using modern technology to replace old models of rote learning and creating more personalized, self-directed experiences for their students. There are plenty of mobile applications that instigate learners with special needs into the learning environment by enabling and facilitating them with digital education. Through the use of LMS, students can access online resources to get assistance on demand beyond the physical reach of their teacher. Fast advancements of computing techniques and ICT are contributing massively towards design and development of new learning technologies.

7.2 COMPUTER- AND WEB-BASED TRAINING (CBT/WBT)

CBT is the acronym for computer-based training, which depicts a type of education in which the learner learns by executing special training programs on a computer through online or offline mode. CBT is especially effective for training people to use computer applications because the CBT program can be integrated with the applications so that the learners can practice using the application as they learn. CBT is the more developed version of CAI, which involves proper use of multimedia to ease the teaching–learning process. The most important feature that makes a CBT popular and successful is its interactivity. Anything that can be communicated using text, multimedia (graphics, color, sound, animation and video) and interactive response techniques can be subject to CBT. CBT can integrate text, graphics, video and audio. If the training is particularly content-dense that means many new concepts are presented together or uses a hierarchy of skill acquisition, a proper CBT can be very effective on those cases. On an average, it is said that the people remember 20% of what they see, 40% of what they see and hear, and 70% of what they hear, see and do. So CBT's rich, multisensory delivery system can facilitate greater retention of new knowledge. The immediate feedback in most computer based training allows both instructors and trainees to monitor progress and adjust instruction accordingly.

Components of an Effective CBT

Following are the components of effective computer-based training.

Learning Objectives

Without knowledge of learning objectives and desired outcomes of the instruction, the program will likely be unfocused, confusing to the end-users, and quite possibly, useless. It is difficult for an end-user to navigate through the different modules of a CBT application without understanding the learning objectives and therefore the chances of learning anything from the program are slight. To focus on the learning objectives, other technical design should be kept simple and standard like screen should be simple, yet informative, toolbars and text size should be standardized, and color schemes should be aesthetically pleasing, sound file should be used only where necessary for impact, actions should require from the trainee to use a mouse in order to move from screen to screen.

Learning Effectiveness

Learning effectiveness is an important aspect of any learning program. To accomplish this, trainees are evaluated through preliminary and postlearning tests. In other words, effective CBT programs should include tests to measure a learner's mastery of the material. The incorporation of multimedia, including graphics, sound, video and animation should also be a factor when designing CBT. Including video clips can have a positive influence on CBT participants. The positive influence likely comes from the fact that the end-users see the relevance to themselves when the instructional situations are specific to their domains. Incorporation of interactivity helps to make the training experiences more engaging and hands on interactive experience increase the retention.

Feedback

When a participant receives feedback on how he/she is performing during learning, it adds to the likelihood of knowledge retention.

These components comprise merely a partial list of what to consider when developing instruction, but among these, we have to focus on how to organize several multimedia components and how to incorporate interactivity because, without these factors, a CBT program could be boring, ineffective, or even worthless.

Organizing an Interactive CBT

Apart from interactivity, the other main feature of a CBT is its multimedia components. The success of multimedia presentation depends heavily on its design. The most fundamental type of presentation communicates a single message to a small, receptive audience. The development of multimedia components of a CBT follows a typical path.

Story

A story is a message that tells the particulars of an act or occurrence or course of events. It is presented in writing or drama or cinema or as a radio or television program. The art of writing a story is identifying the main ideas behind it and the order in which they will be presented. It is a big challenge to figure out the sequence in which we will tell the story.

Script

It is the blueprint or roadmap that outlines a movie story through visual descriptions, actions of characters and their dialogue. Scripts are normally used by the production team. Scripts are also used by the programmer and graphic artist to understand more about the tone and flow of the program. When one writes about the scripts it must have a layout that has provisions for five basic areas—(i) title, (ii) action, (iii) narration, (iv) dialogue and (v) interactive control.

Flowchart

The flowchart is a schematic representation of the interactive flow of a program, usually produced by the interactive designer. All possible user interaction pathways, expressed through labeled boxes and directional arrow, are traced through any hierarchical menu tree structures and along various screen branches. A flowchart represents the entire process from start to finish, showing inputs, pathways and circuits, action or decision points, and ultimately completion. It can serve as an instructional manual or a tool for facilitating detailed analysis, optimization of workflow and service delivery.

Storyboard

A storyboard is an expression of everything in the form of layout which is to be presented. It will be contained in the program—what menu screens will look like, what pictures (still and movie) will be seen when and for how long, what audio and text will accompany the images, either synchronously or hyperlinked.

7.3 SHARABLE CONTENT OBJECT REFERENCE MODEL (SCORM)

In the mid-90s, several government agencies latched onto e-learning as a way to train workers in different departments. In 1999, the Department of Defense, under an executive order from President Clinton of USA established the Advanced Distributed Learning (ADL) research group to develop a set of standards so that content creation tools and an LMS could communicate one another and operate in unison. ADL devised those guidelines, which eventually formed the basis for SCORM. Still operating today, ADL oversaw subsequent iterations of SCORM. Current content creation tools and LMS are typically categorized as SCORM 1.2 and SCORM 2004 compliant or SCORM 1.2/2004 for short.

The SCORM is a web-based e-learning standards and set of technical specifications that were developed to provide a common approach to how e-learning content is developed and used. It standardizes the way in which e-learning courses are created, and how they're launched. When creating an e-learning course with a SCORM compliant authoring tool, the output is a zip folder. It defines the communication between client side content and run-time environment. LMS and authoring tools are built with this specification and as a result, these tools interact with each other. There is a variety of SCORM versions and each version specifies the methods that support run-time environment and how those methods should behave. The two main components of SCORM are sharable content object and reference model given below.

Sharable Content Object or SCO

SCOs are the assets used in online courses. This describes the elements of the SCORM package that can be reused across multiple tools and platforms. Once the various elements of the package are SCORM compliant, the content should be understood by all compatible learning platforms and tools.

Reference Model

This part of the term tells that SCORM is a standard, the specification for which can be understood and applied in a consistent way by all who work in the e-learning industry. These are the 'rules' everyone follows.

Literature shows that there are three different published versions of SCORM, these are:
- *SCORM 1.1*: It is the first published version of SCORM released in January 2001. This version is not widely accepted by the industry.
- *SCORM 1.2*: It is the second and improved version of SCORM 1.1. It has resolved lots of issues of SCORM 1.1 and it is widely accepted by the industry. It was released on October 2001.
- *SCORM 2004*: It is a more complex version of SCORM and was developed to support the sequencing of content in paths the user could take. It is released on January 2004.

The figure 7.1 depicts the components and architecture of SCORM.

7.4 CONTENT MANAGEMENT SYSTEMS (CMS)

CMSs, in general, have two parts—one, which is termed as the content management application (CMA) and the second, content delivery application (CDA). The CMA is the graphical interface where the user has access on any content related to adding, deleting or editing content without knowing much about HyperText Markup Language (HTML). On the other hand, the CDA is responsible for managing and delivering the stored content of the CMS to the front-end CMA. To deploy a website using CMS, the website hosting services is to be hired and domain name to be registered. The domain name refers to the URL of the website that is being deployed. According to the

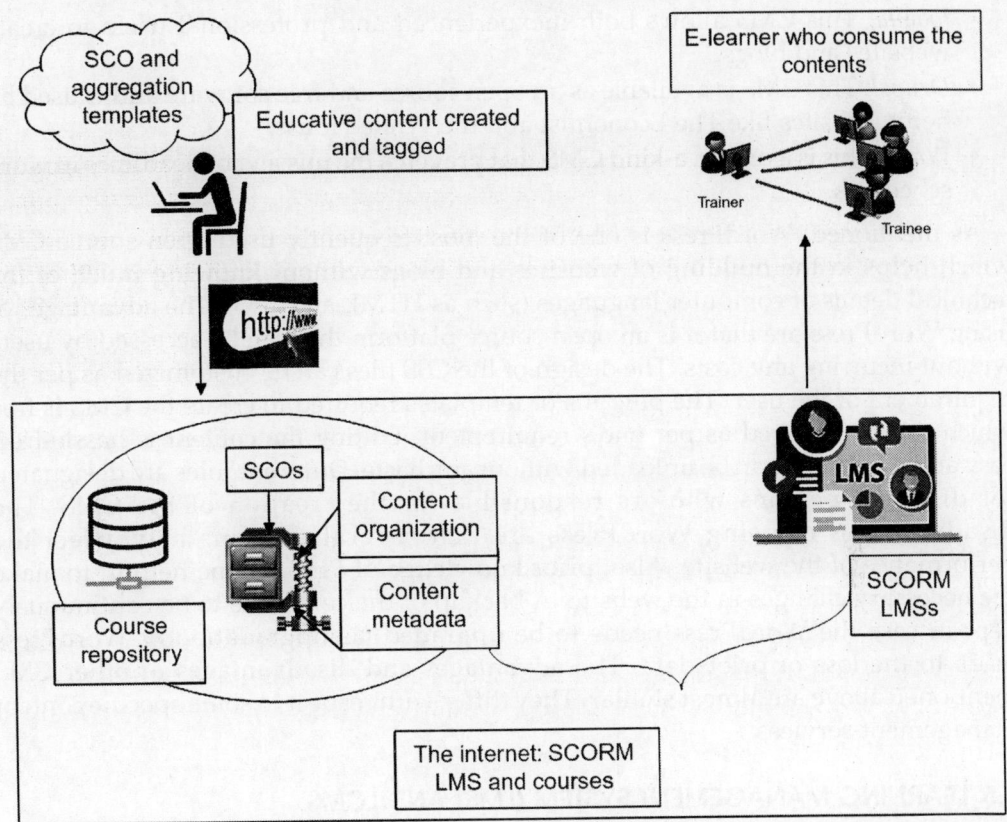

Fig. 7.1: A diagram on SCORM architecture

requirement, the CMS interface is then to be modified following which the content creation is to be initiated.

The basic functionalities of CMS include preparing content, accumulating them, allocating the roles and responsibilities to the persons involved in the publishing of the content and finally issuing the content on the web. Other features include helping to search and extract data, formatting selected documents to HTML or PDF, reconsidering the content that is already available on the website, trail the users who have made changes to the content in the CMS and publishing facility with a wide variety of templates.

CMS are mainly used in enterprise content management (ECM) and web content management (WCM) purposes. While ECM helps to enhance the collaborative working environment in an organization by assimilating all documents and handling them digitally, it also provides access to the digital assets of the company by imposing certain restrictions on the role of the user. Similarly, a WCM prioritizes on the cooperative working along with several websites. Other than this, CMSs like WordPress, Joomla, etc. are applied in universities, big and small business organizations, web directories, blogs, etc. Following are the four most used CMS freely available.

- *WordPress*: WordPress is the most widely used open-source CMS to prepare blogs and websites.

- *Joomla*: This CMS allows both inexperienced and professional users to create websites and blogs.
- *Drupal*: This CMS is available as an open source and free software and is used by hefty websites like The Economist and the White House.
- *Wrike*: This is a one-of-a-kind CMS that prevents the missing of deadlines in work schedules.

As mentioned, WordPress is one of the most frequently used open source CMS which helps in the building of websites and blogs without knowing much of the technical details of computer languages (such as HTML and CSS). The advantages of using WordPress are that it is an open source platform that can be accessed by users without incurring any costs. The design of the CSS files can be customized as per the requirement of the user. The plug-ins or templates required to create the CMS is free which can be changed as per one's requirement. Editing the content is hassle-free, easy and media files can be uploaded without any haste. Different roles are designated for different persons who are responsible for the creation of the CMS. The disadvantages of using WordPress are that several plug-ins may affect the performance of the website. Also, prior knowledge of PHP will be helpful to make the necessary changes in the website. A backup of the content is to be continuously kept in case the WordPress needs to be upgraded, as upgradation of WordPress leads to the loss of prior data. The advantages and disadvantages of other CMS mentioned above are almost similar. They differ with respect to some specific content management services.

7.5 LEARNING MANAGEMENT SYSTEM (LMS) AND LCMS

Learning management system, also known as LMS or learning content management system (LCMS), is a software system that assists in innovating, managing and distributing e-learning courses. Learning signifies the education that is imparted through these courses. Management signifies the organization of the entire process of course content designing, editing, allotment to learners and their gradation. The system refers to the fact that all these are automated with the help of computer software.

Architecture of LMS

An LMS is the main driving force behind e-learning. In the backend, there is an existence of a server that is responsible for maintaining the course contents, validation and verification of the users, scheduling periodic notifications, etc. The frontend comprises an interface that is executed within the web browser and is handled by the admin, teachers and learners. LMS mainly works in five stages while organizing and deliverance e-learning courses.

- *It composes e-learning resources*: Resources appropriate for the LMSs may be created from the beginning or by editing already existing content. The inclusion of ICT tools like YouTube videos and Wikipedia links is mandated in these contents.
- *Categorizes the available resources into required courses*: Course creation requires the idea of the fact for which the course is being designed.
- *Presents the courses*: What amount of the content shall be revealed to what group of people always remains a doubt while designing the course. LMS should be able to

impose these types of restrictions on the software to be allowed to specific content to the unrestricted group of people. LMS should also be flexible in allowing learners to view the contents through all variants of handheld devices.

- *Register learners to the courses*: Generally, there are three groups of people (admin, instructor, and student) who use a LMS. Administrators are the people who maintain the LMS, instructors are the persons who arrange the class curriculum and evaluate the improvement of the learners, and students are the set of people who acquire knowledge through the LMS. Managing the registered users to the course, talking to them as teachers, specify the course as per the learner requirement, preparing seminars, schedule tests and finally grading them are the important tasks of LMS to be performed.
- *Evaluates the performance of the learners*: The major advantage of incorporating LMS into everyday learning is that it automatically tracks the progress of an individual student based on numerous characteristic features. LMS should also notify the users regarding any upcoming or pending event and also understand the drift of issues within its domain.

LMS should incorporate some special characteristics for its better use. It should automate administration-related functionalities. It should also keep track of certification processes and allow the collaboration of content from third parties. Content should be accessed at any time, from any place and especially in mobiles. Course catalogs should be provided for easy navigation of the users and accessibility to the courses is to be provided in other compatible LMS. Automated notifications must be provided periodically and it should offer some unique services within itself to get some branding. To make learning more interesting, techniques such as badges, points, etc. may be awarded. Customized reports should be generated in view of the personalization of the users.

Organizations, business houses and agencies belonging to the government or private educational institutes mostly use LMS. The LMS other than performing remarkably as effective business tools are used for a variety of other purposes. Training employees through LMS and providing scope to learn at their convenience under supervised trainers who will scrutinize their improvement and report it accordingly. An employee after joining a company may go through all the information provided in the LMS as a reference, instead of touring around to gather all the detailing required performing his/her assigned tasks. LMS's can also be effectively used to help in the preservation of information which can be further reused for knowledge gain of new employees. It is aptly designed for educational purposes irrespective of the institution, but e-learning promises are to be a rage in the upcoming future.

Following are the five most used LMS available in the market.

- *Canvas*: One of the most dependable LMS used in higher schools and colleges.
- *Moodle*: Open source platform used widely for e-learning purposes.
- *Google Classroom*: Open source platform used widely for e-learning purposes.
- *WizIQ*: E-learning LMS with the added feature of proving virtual classroom learning.
- *OpenedX*: Open source course management system for e-learning purposes.

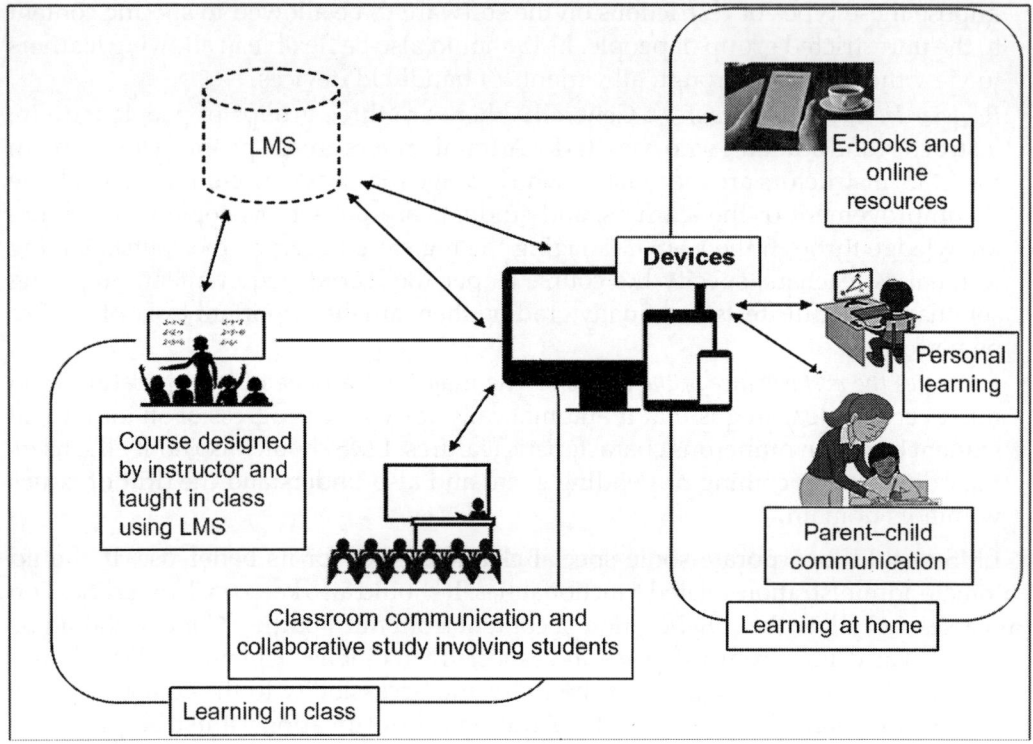

Fig. 7.2: Example of how open source LMS can be utilized in education technology

7.6 MOODLE

Moodle is a knowledge sharing platform that allows teachers and students a distinctly strong, protected and integrated structure to produce a custom-made learning atmosphere. The software is freely downloadable by commoners and has been created by the Moodle project synchronized by Moodle HQ. Some features of Moodle are:
- It is designed in such a manner so that it can be used worldwide.
- It is dependable and is the most widely used knowledge sharing platform worldwide.
- Both teaching and learning are supported by Moodle. Methods incorporated are learner-focused with provisions for encouraging shared learning.
- The documents provided in support of learning Moodle precisely describe the detailed methodology to implement them in our machines.
- Continuous improvement is involved in the development of Moodle and hence it is always up-to-date.
- Moodle is available in multiple languages making it more available to the education fraternity.
- External tools can also be accessed through Moodle, making it a one-step solution of all knowledge sharing-related purposes.
- Moodle can be easily customized as per the need of the individual or the institution. Hence, plug-ins can be installed to achieve particular functionalities and get the Moodle connected to external apps.

Learning Management Systems

- Moodle can be customized to be used by any number of students, from minimum to maximum.
- Data within the Moodle is constantly guarded and hence there is no possible chance of the data getting lost and distorted.
- It can be accessed at a time, at any place and from any device within the world.
- There is always control on the data and the way it shall be represented.
- There is a huge collection of materials that backs up the Moodle.

There is a huge team that is constantly working towards the removal of bugs within the software and incorporates enhancements.

Process to use Moodle as an LMS

1. An account has to be created initially, the verification of which is done through mail (Fig. 7.3).

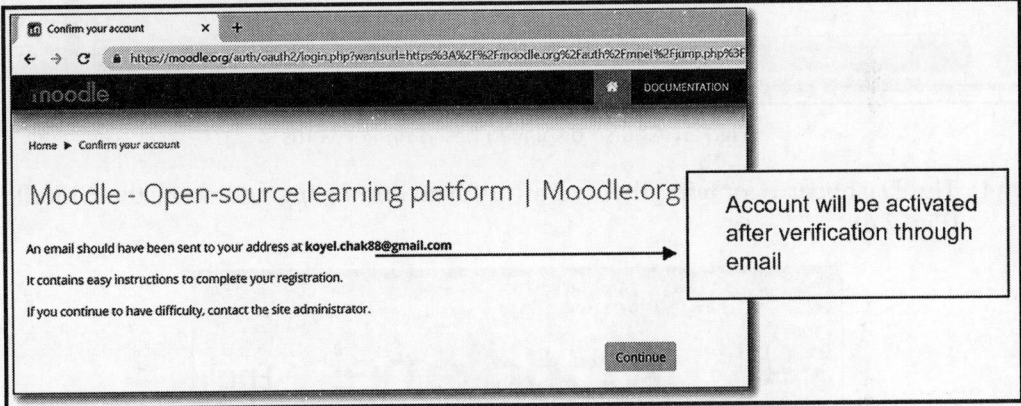

Fig. 7.3: Process of activating account after verification via email

2. Once the account is created, the option for Enrolling or Downloading a course is provided (Fig. 7.4).

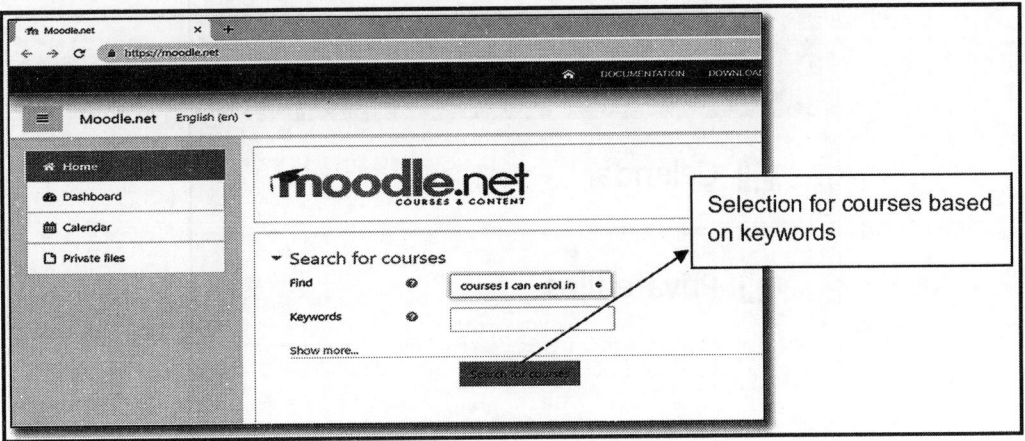

Fig. 7.4: Course enrolling options provided and search available based on keywords

3. Based on the keywords, available courses are shown to users (Fig. 7.5).

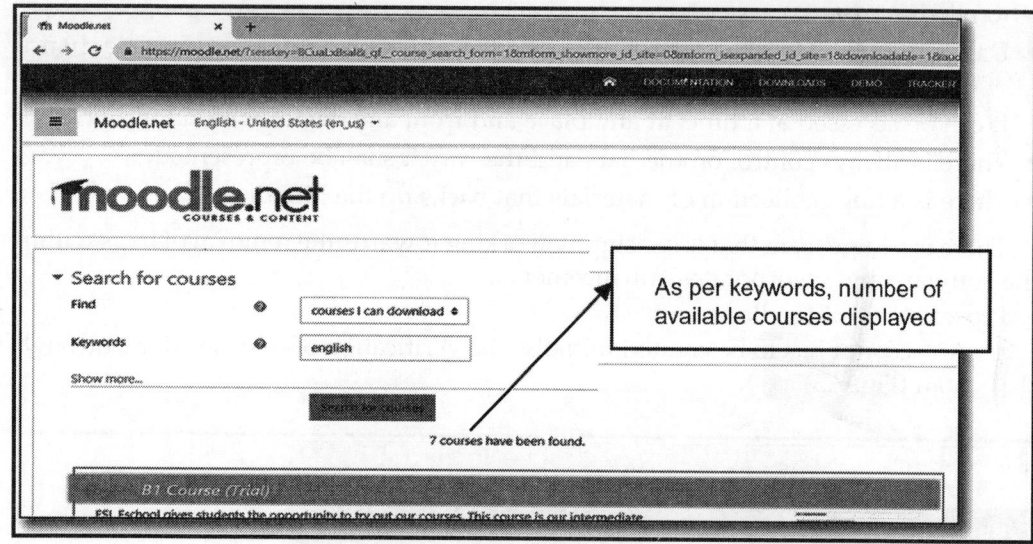

Fig.7.5: Course displayed based on keywords

4. The Dashboard contains the overall information of the course in the Moodle (Fig. 7.6).

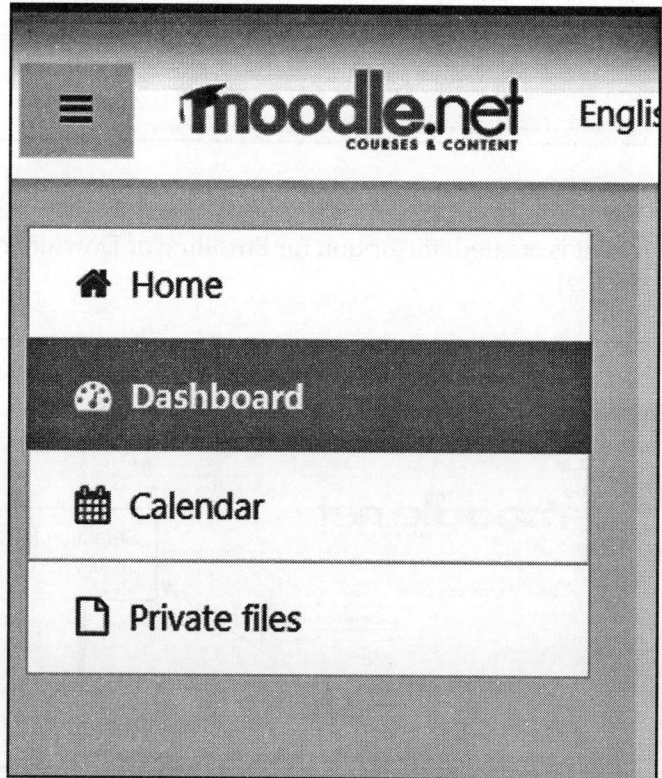

Fig. 7.6: Dashboard is basically the information bearer of Moodle

5. Provisions are available so that teachers can take online tests/quizzes through the Moodle (Fig. 7.7).

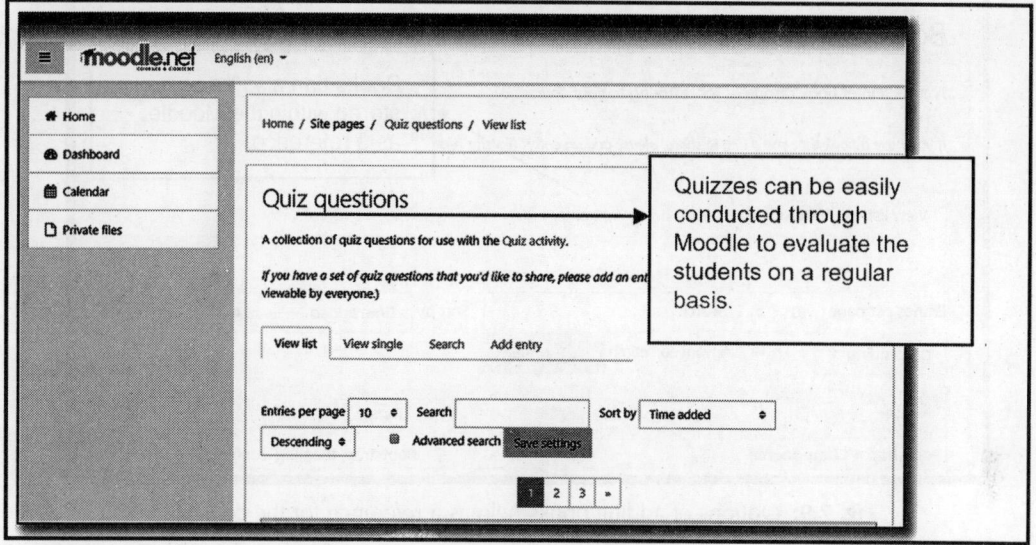

Fig. 7.7: Page displaying the quiz taking options

6. A timeline helps keep track of events and also helps to schedule tasks (Fig. 7.8).

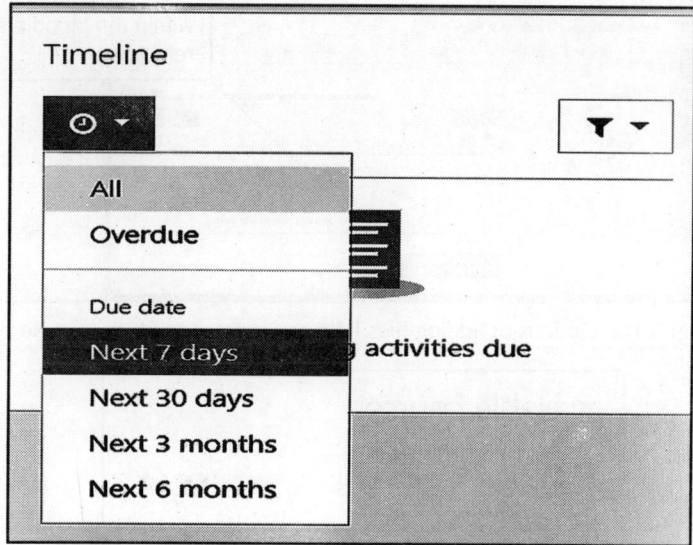

Fig. 7.8: Timeline representing schedule of activities

7. To help in the course, books can also be added to the Moodle so that the learners go through them in case of any emergency (Fig. 7.9).
8. Other than books, files can be also uploaded and kept ready for reference to the course (Figs 7.10 and 7.11).
9. The entire dashboard of a self-created course looks like this (Fig. 7.12).

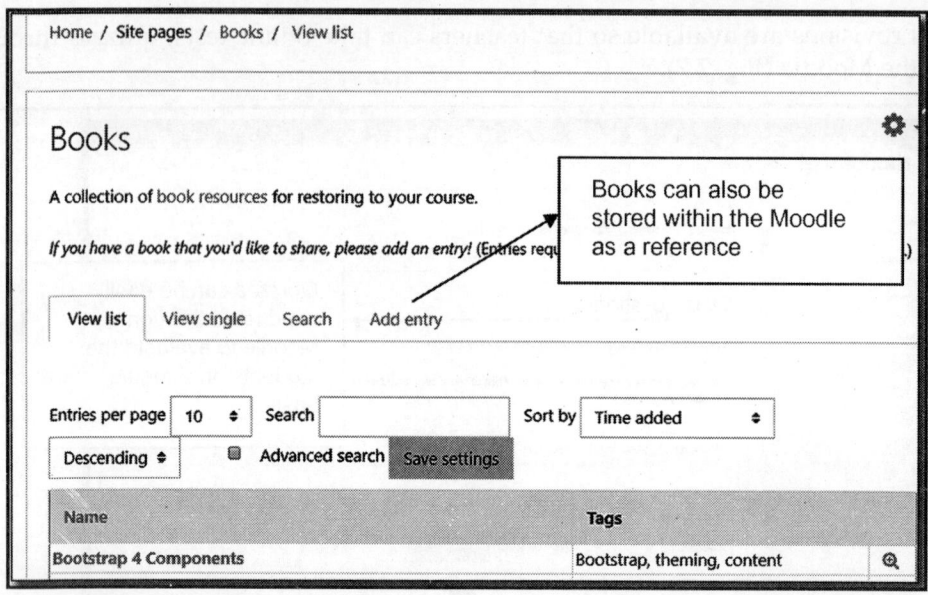

Fig. 7.9: Options of adding books help as a reference for the course

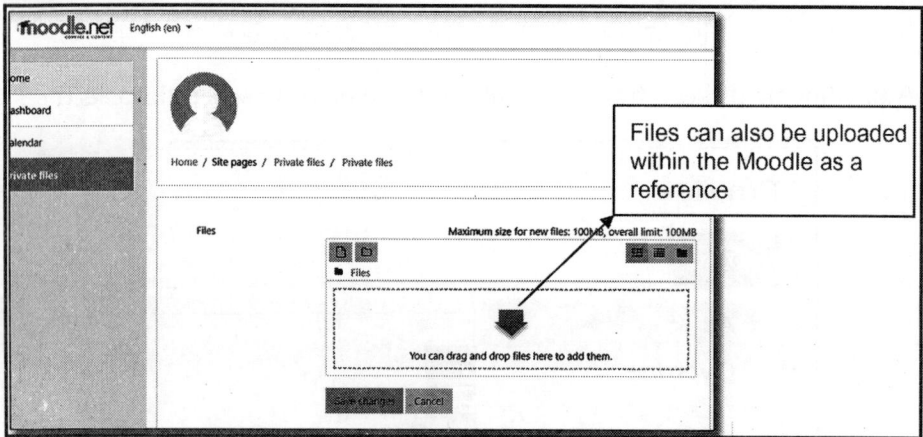

Fig. 7.10: Options of adding files help as a reference for the course

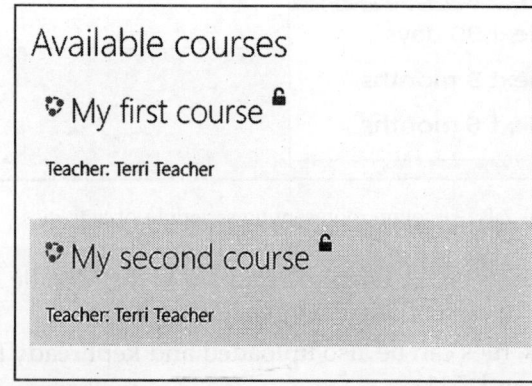

Fig. 7.11: Figure showing the list of all customized courses prepared by the educator

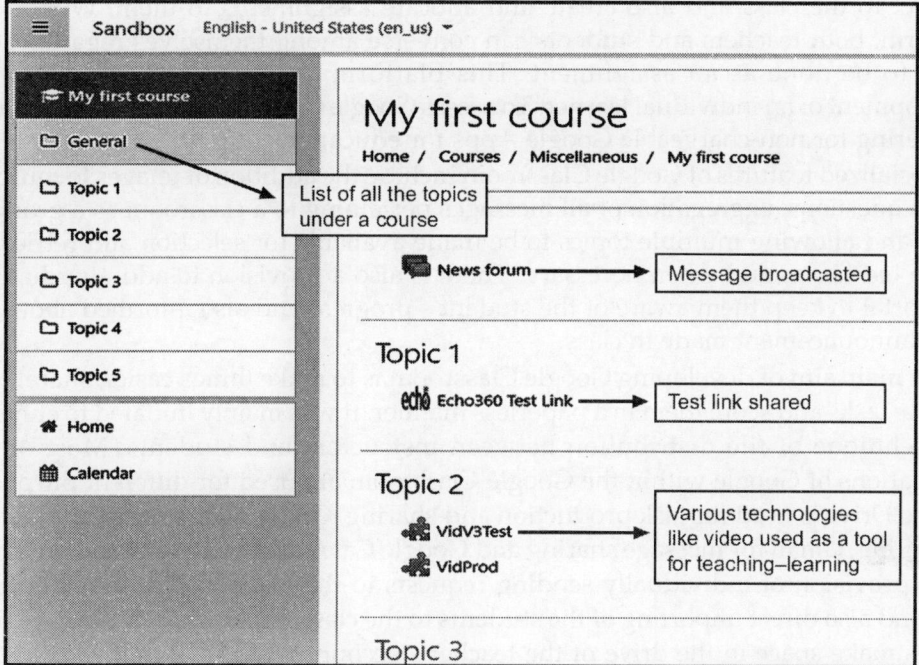

Fig. 7.12: Course details containing all the topics and various methods of ICT enabled resources imbibed to impart the course

Products Available within the Moodle

- *Moodle LMS*: This works as the world's largest open source learning platform. It is free, integrated, tailored, easily accessed, handy and data within this can also be tracked and scrutinized.
- *Moodle App*: This feature helps to access Moodle at any place, any convenient time and from any device present nearby. Users can be offline and learn, keep track of deadlines, be updated and learn at their convenience through this app.
- *Moodle Workplace*: This deals with the creation of the LMS by the team with an idea to maximize learning and expansion policy. Various employee programs can be designed, reports can be tailored and centrally handled using this workplace.
- *Moodle Cloud*: This provides the infrastructure required to facilitate the learning of the students. It is handy, elastic, can be increased without space limitations, simple in nature and free of preservation.
- *Moodle Net*: This is a discussion forum that aims to collaborate and share knowledge within the community to learn yourself and also let others learn. It is open, visible, secured, always linked, confidential and ethical in nature.
- *Moodle Education*: This is responsible for maintaining the quality of education and quantifies the digital proficiency of the instructors.

7.7 GOOGLE CLASSROOM

Google Classroom is free of cost collaborative resource for instructors and learners. It was released on August 12, 2014. Here there is the facility where teachers can conduct classroom teaching by generating an online classroom, send requests to students to connect to the class and also create and allocate assignments to them. Within this platform, both teachers and students can converse among themselves regarding the work to be done as an assignment. This platform also enables tracking of the development of an individual learner. To access Google Classroom, institutions require registering for non-chargeable Google Apps for education account.

Specialized features of Google Classroom include the addition of images to multiple choice questions, aggregation of all messages pertaining to a classroom as a group in inbox and allowing multiple topics to be made available for selection and retrieving by the teacher as and when necessary. There is also a provision to add guardians in this portal to keep them aware of the student's progress and also informed about the latest announcement made in class.

The main aim of developing Google Classroom is to make things easier, share, help allocate tasks and score them in a paperless manner. It was mainly initiated to enhance the technique of file distribution between instructors and students. Most of the applications of Google within the Google Classroom are used for different purposes. Google Drive is used for task production and sharing, Google Docs, Sheets and Slides for writing, Gmail for message sharing and Google Calendar for time schedules. There is the provision of individually sending requests to the students to join the current class and also direct importing of the students to the class. Separate folders for distinct classes make space in the drive of the teacher's account which makes it easy for the teacher to grade the student against his/her performance.

Hence, Google Classroom helps make an association between the teacher and the learner, facilitates adding more students into the digital class, enhances distribution of assignments to students, increases the interaction between the instructor and the learner, allows teachers to create, distribute and review assignments and provides a one-step solution for students to access these at one place. The main ingredients that make up Google for Education suite comprises Classroom, Gmail, Drive, Calendar, Vault, Docs, Sheets, Forms, Slides, Sites and Hangouts. Classroom app can be accessible for educators and while registering for the account the school's email domain is used and the apps are devoid of promotion while the support is non-chargeable.

Some snapshots of help login to Google Classroom and use its features are provided below (Figs 7.13 to 7.18).

7.8 CANVAS

Canvas is another widely used LMS to integrate modernization in education. It has been designed to strengthen instructors and employ students to acquire the required skills. Canvas makes simpler the methods of teaching, promotes learning and abolishes the pain of sustaining and increasing conventional learning equipment. Canvas comprises a collection of extreme integrated knowledge sharing products to provide a one-stop solution for institutions which imbibe this. A survey conducted by the Canvas team showed that using LMSs saved around 1 hour on an average in a day, more than 33% of students have adapted to these methods of learning, the maximum amount of pedagogical litheness is faced and 98% of learners cover a maximum of the expected syllabus. Canvas consists of 5 lakh skilled members who can provide help when required, provides security, robustness and reliability for which it is widely accepted.

Learning Management Systems

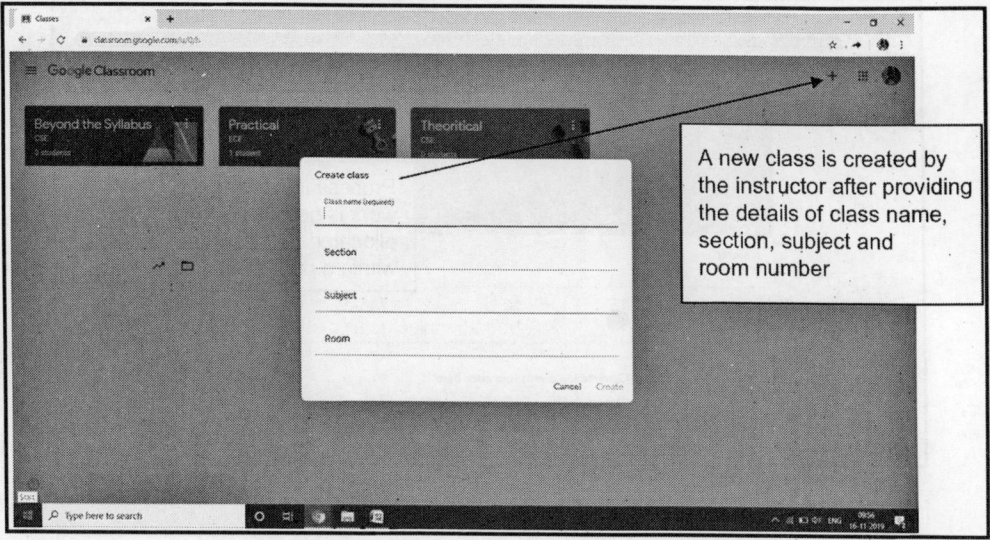

Fig. 7.13: Process in which a class is created by a teacher

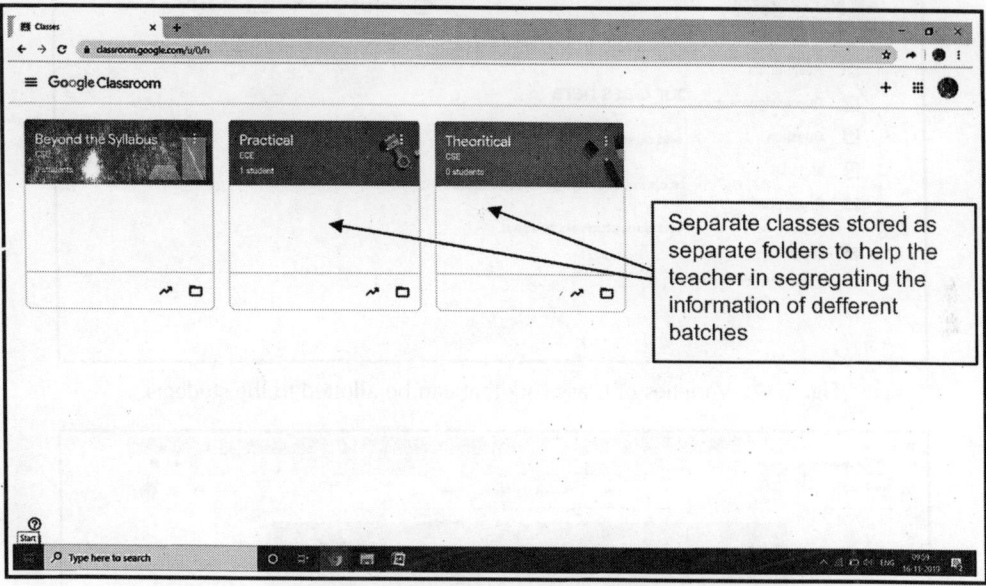

Fig. 7.14: Page displaying multiple yet distinct folders for separate classes

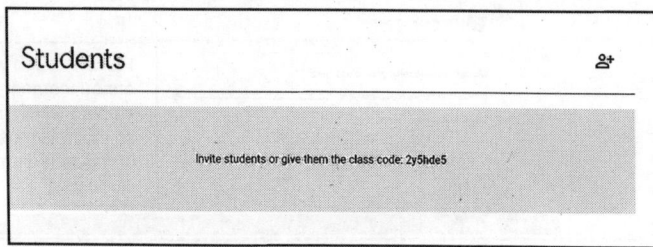

Fig. 7.15: Students can be added to the class via the given code or manually by adding the mail-id

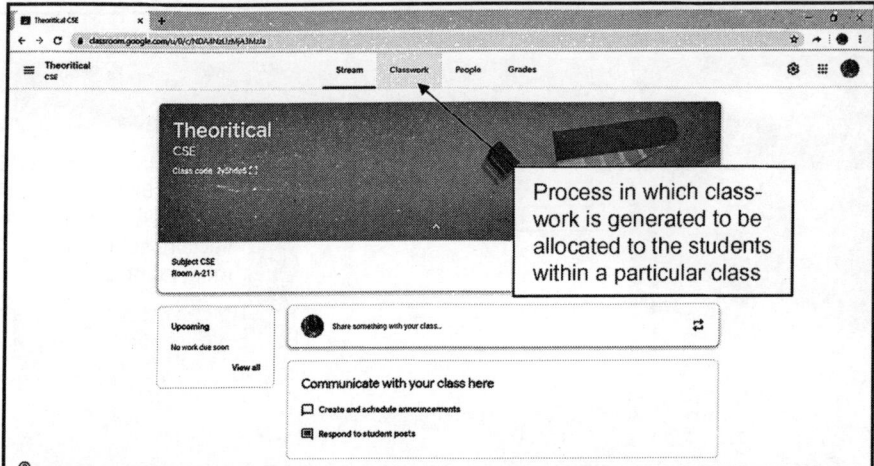

Fig. 7.16: Process to create Classwork for the students

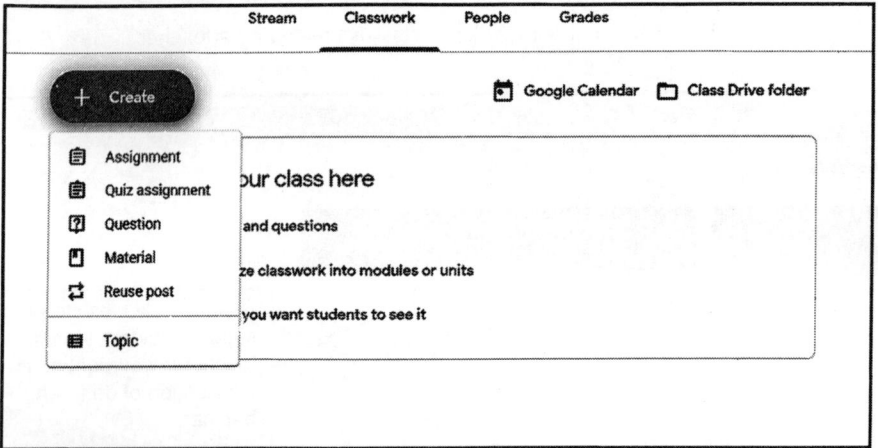

Fig. 7.17: Varieties of Classwork that can be allotted to the students

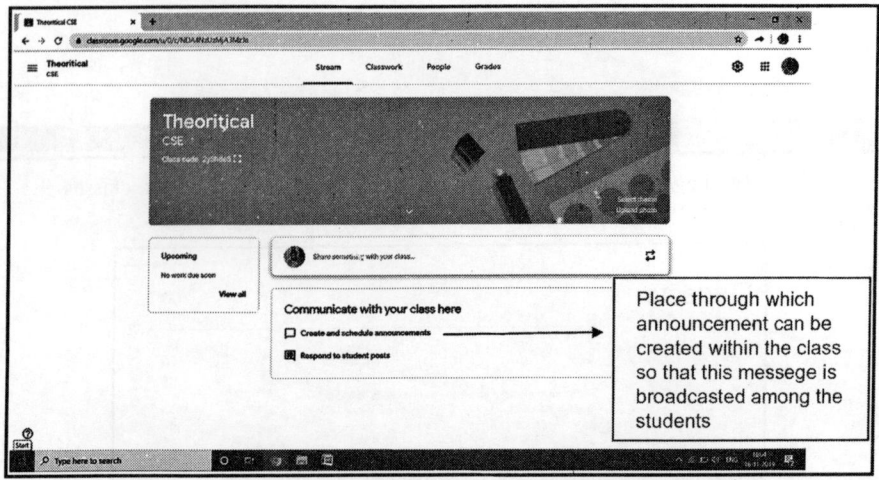

Fig. 7.18: Messages can be broadcasted to the students in the classroom

Canvas allows teachers the scope to teach in the way that they prefer. Presence of interactive videos, engagement of the students in their convenience and personalized learning experience provides reasons to prefer canvas by the students as well as teachers. Canvas incorporated in K-12 schools helps increase the level of teaching, helps progress student accomplishment, and allows integrating with various technologies.

The main features of Canvas are:
- Open entrance and access for learners worldwide.
- The presence of Canvas Commons allows recycling, modifying, preserving and reallocating of resources present within the Canvas.
- The open platform allows incorporating third party applications in the Canvas.
- Data available in Canvas can be further analysed by researchers.
- The platform provides neutrality for modernism and experimentation.

7.9 FACEBOOK (SOCIAL NETWORK) AS LMS

Facebook is a social networking website where users can place remarks, share snaps and post links to a news broadcast or other remarkable content on the internet, chat live, and watch short-form video. Facebook was started in 2004 by Mark Zuckerberg and Edward Saverin. Its availability to both common people and organizations along with its interaction facility with third parties all through the same account results in its worldwide popularity among all age groups. It comes across as very user compatible, provides access to everyone, requires less or no technical knowledge to use it, acts as a great medium to connect with friends and helps track down several lost people in the hustle of daily life. In the business front, Facebook allows business organizations to identify their target audience and hence promote their products and services to the clients who prefer them. It is very easy to upload photos, share messages and acts as a great entertainment platform for users. Customized set of privacy controls provides a great advantage to the users to confine their information to their choice only, in a way, restricting access to user content.

There are some potential differences between Facebook and an LMS. It is said that if these differences are resolved then Facebook can be effectively used as a good substitute for learning management systems. While an LMS is controlled and owned by an institution, Facebook is neither to the students nor to the teacher. Though there are no charges levied if Facebook is used as an LMS, still, it has its content quality and security risks that need to be seriously looked after. To join an LMS, a user has to enter through the password credentials provided by the institution, but on Facebook, though having a profile can allow the user to join various groups, it becomes a question for learners who are not interested in creating a social media profile. A variety of resources types which are allowed to be uploaded in an LMS is more compared to that on Facebook. Control of the content in an LMS is mainly given to the instructor who is responsible for uploading the managing and deleting the contents, while on the contrary almost similar rights are provided to the instructor and the learner where both can produce as well as remove contents. The main mode of interaction in Facebook is synchronous but Facebook lacks behind by being unable to assess an assignment as that of an LMS.

The main part of Facebook where the contents can be uploaded or shared is the wall. Contents can be 'liked' by users or be commented on directly. The orientation of the wall is such that the latest content is always on the top with the initially uploaded ones going down to the bottom. Events can also be added for the group members to join at their convenience. To get knowledge of all the members within the group, the profile pictures are displayed on the page of the group. Participants who are online are depicted by an active 'green' sign beside their profile pictures.

To use Facebook as an LMS, initially, a page needs to be opened. Students are to be made to join the group so that they can access all resources from the page. For the instructor, presentations may be uploaded in the group, or links can be shared. Google Docs can be utilized to allocate assignments to the students through this group. Students are also allowed to post their queries in the group for the educators to respond.

Properly implemented, student learning through Facebook may result in rigorous and mutual in nature. There shall exist a dynamic learning environment for the students if taught in this manner. Participation can be expected from both active and passive students by simply indicating their presence in content by pressing the like button. With appropriate methodology, Facebook stands out to provide a unique learning ambiance to enhance collaborative and active learning within the students.

Other than making the students learn through Facebook as an alternative to LMS, there lies a great responsibility of the instructors to maintain the quality of teaching–learning process. The speed at which responses are made, the nature in which the interactions are faced, the style in which the questions are answered heavily affects the manner in which the students will perceive this medium as a serious mode of teaching. There lies great potential in creating an influence of Facebook groups as a learning environment.

7.10 CONSORTIA (UNIVERSITY) IN HIGHER EDUCATION

A consortium is an association or collaboration (educational mainly) of institutions to achieve mutually beneficial goals. Higher educational institutions foster inter-institutional cooperation among a group of colleges and universities for the purpose of enhancing services. With the advancement of ICT, universities have joined for resource sharing along with research and development activities. The universities and institutions have joined with cooperation from government agencies to form national and international consortia. The norms of academic cooperation may vary in the scope by the level of:
- Control (public–private).
- Discipline (computer science, engineering, medicine).
- Service provider (libraries, universities, science laboratories).
- Institutional level (research institute, government agency, corporation).

The initial consortium structure consisted of three or more colleges and universities signing an agreement to cooperate in providing joint ventures. Some of the joint ventures were tuition waiver for cross-registration, faculty exchanges and professional development, interuniversity library privilege, joint purchasing of goods and services, and outreach projects. Consortia design got momentum after 1990 with the rapid growth of ICT and investment from industry and government. At the present time we have noticed the following types of consortia.
- Multipurpose academic consortia
- Technology-planning consortia

- Local business and industry-linked consortia
- Research and academic library consortia
- Scientific research and development consortia

Numerous instances of informal coalitions and partnerships can be formed. But in practice, the formalized agreements of consortia offer structural opportunities of another dimension. The consortium can be likened to an interorganizational network in which environmental conditions affect its functioning. The ideal consortium will be based on an understanding that organizational change in response to market shifts necessitates flexibility, long-range planning, and adequate resources among equal partners.

7.11 NEXT GENERATION DIGITAL LEARNING ENVIRONMENT

Researchers and practitioners are trying to go ahead with the technology innovations preceded by LMS technologies. In this way, the term 'next generation digital learning environment' (NGDLE) has evolved. It is a digital technology for teaching–learning practices providing an ecosystem or environment for an interconnected, dynamic, ever-evolving community of learners, instructors, tools, and content. Classrooms and LMS are an instance of the built pedagogical models. In the process of transitioning higher education, new issues to be addressed with the 'line of codes' of ICT practices to transmit the model of education to one built on a concept like active learning, hybrid course designs, personalization, and new directions for measuring degree progress. NGDLE is the next generation in this sense. Five functional domains of NGDLE are:

- Interoperability and integration
- Personalization
- Analytics, advising, and learning assessment
- Collaboration
- Accessibility and universal design

NGDLE includes traditional LMS as a component. It is not a single application like enterprise applications. It is rather an ecosystem characterized by the following.

- NGDLE is a union of IT systems including content repositories, analytics engines, and a wide variety of applications and digital services.
- One key to building such a union work will be full adherence to standards for interoperability, as well as for data and content exchange.
- Full adherence to the standards for interoperability along with data and content exchange is the key to constructing this union.
- NGDLE will not be exactly the same for any two learners, instructors, or institutions. Rather it will support personalization.
- It appears to be a cloud-like space to connect content and functionality like a smartphone environment with self-selected apps.
- The union-based NGDLE will be mashed-up at both the individual and the institutional levels, as opposed to consortia forming to create open enterprise applications.

EXECUTIVE SUMMARY

- Technology has the potential to improve teaching and learning process and through the use of LMS, students can access online resources to get assistance on demand beyond the physical reach of their teacher.

- An effective CBT (improved CAI) with components like learning objectives, learning effectiveness, and feedback system, executes special training programs on a computer through online or offline mode. Its development consists of the steps such as story collection, script writing, flowchart or flow diagram design, storyboard designs.
- SCORM is a web-based e-learning standards and set of technical specifications that were developed to provide a common approach to how e-learning content is developed and used.
- CMS are mainly used in enterprise content management and web content management purposes. It consists of CMA and the CDA. WordPress, Joomla, Drupal, etc. are freely available CMS.
- LMS is a software system that assists in innovating, managing and distributing e-learning courses. It composes e-learning resources, categorizes the available resources into required courses, presents the courses, registers learners to the courses and evaluates the performance of the learners. Moodle, Canvas, Google Classroom, etc. are freely available LMS.
- Modular object-oriented dynamic learning environment (Moodle) is an online knowledge sharing platform that gives customized learning atmosphere to learners. Instructors can use Moodle to generate lessons, supervise courses, and cooperate with teachers and students.
- Google Classroom is emerging as one of the most prominent tools in education technology. It acts as a clever virtual classroom that focuses less on technology and more on training. It utilizes the celebrated Google's templates to help teachers and students collaborate and all in a paperless manner.
- Canvas is one the 21st century LMS which is flexible, dependable, customizable, easy to utilize, movable and time-saving. It has all the ingredients that help make the process of teaching and learning much easier.
- To engage students as lifelong learners, the utilization of social networking tools (Facebook) as an LMS can prove to be much effective. The quantity of dealings of the students and the evaluation process is enhanced due to the integration of social networks in education.
- A consortium is an association or collaboration (educational mainly) of institutions to achieve mutually beneficial goals. Consortia design got momentum after 1990 with rapid growth of ICT and investment from industry and government.
- Researchers and practitioners are trying to go ahead with the technology innovations preceded by an LMS technology. Next generation digital learning environment (NGDLE) is an evolving digital technology for teaching–learning practices providing an ecosystem or environment for interconnected, dynamic, ever-evolving community of learners, instructors, tools, and content.

Review Questions

1. How is CBT different from WBT? Write the components of a CBT. How to organize a CBT?
2. What is SCORM? Illustrate the architecture of SCORM with block diagram.
3. Describe with a block diagram how a CMS works and what type of rights are imposed for different roles. Give four examples of CMS.
4. What is a LMS? Describe how LMS works. Discuss with a block diagram how open source LMS can be utilized in education technology.

5. Write the concept and importance of the following (or write short notes on).
   a. SCORM
   b. CBT
   c. WBT
   d. CMS
   e. LMS/LCMS
   f. NGDLE
   g. Moodle
   h. Canvas
   i. Google Classroom
6. What are the features of Moodle? Explain how to work with Moodle. Write the different products available from Moodle.
7. Explain how will you plan your teaching through Google Classroom.
8. What are the functionalities of Canvas LMS?
9. How can social networks/Facebook be used as an LMS in today's education scenario?
10. Write down the necessity and usefulness of consortia in the higher education.
11. What is next generation digital learning environment (NGDLE)? Write the function domains and characteristics of NGDLE.

Chapter 8

Personalization and Adaptive Learning

Objectives of this chapter

- To introduce the concept of personalization and service oriented architecture in educational web environment with ICT supports.
- To introduce personalization of learning in prevalent education system in schools.
- To explain the key concepts of self-regulated personalized learning pedagogical model and its implementation methods.
- To introduce the concept of adaptive learning and discuss different models supporting adaptive learning along with its benefits, limitations and future prospects.
- To explain adaptivity and personalization in mobile learning towards student modeling.

Expected outcomes of this chapter

After going through this chapter learners will be able to:
- Understand the change of learning style according to learner requirement through personalization using ICT and service oriented architectures.
- Understand SRPL pedagogical Model and the relation between its key components which increase learners' development and participation.
- Analyze SRPL and other different approaches in the field of personalization.
- Understand the concepts of adaptive learning and explain the different models supporting it.
- Explain the benefits, limitations, and future prospects of adaptive learning.
- Analysis adaptivity and personalization in mobile learning towards student modeling.

8.1 PERSONALIZATION OF LEARNING

The term personalization focuses on things that are personal, i.e. it gives attention to each individual person. The act of fabricating something which meets individual requirements is known as personalization. The following Table 8.1 provides a comparison between traditional learning and personalized learning.

Adaptive learning or adaptive teaching provides customized learning experiences that address the unique needs of an individual (personalized) through just-in-time feedback, pathways, and resources. Following are the issues which govern personalization.

- Based on learners content.
- Based on learners preferences.
- Learner's educational background and experience.

Table 8.1: Comparison between traditional learning and personalized learning

Traditional learning	Personalized learning
Mass production	Mass customization
Fixed place, school-based	Anywhere and everywhere, mobile
Teach the content	Teach the student, collaborative learning communities
One-size fits all instruction/resources	Differentiated instruction
Institution/teacher-cantered	Student-cantered
Physical/face-to-face learning	Online learning platform to enable blended learning

8.2 BENEFITS OF PERSONALIZED LEARNING

Every single student's learning requirements and preferences are different. So there is no one-size-fits solution for each individual. Personalization is a unique approach in education technology which helps the teacher to deeply understand the learner's needs.

i. Personalized learning distinguishes all students who learn in a different way and have their own unique paths to mastery.
ii. It ensures that each student is suitably placed to exploit his or her prospects for accomplishment.
iii. It makes stratagem that evolves to each individual learner's progress and understanding.
iv. It maximizes student engagement throughout the learning journey.
v. It exploits understanding about each student's strengths and weaknesses to authorize teachers in the classroom.
vi. It improves the learning outcomes and allows instructors to focus on what actually is the difficulty.

8.3 PERSONALIZED LEARNING ENVIRONMENT AND ICT

Personalized learning provides instructions that offer pedagogy, curriculum, and learning environments to meet the individual student's needs. In this environment, a student is not bound in their classroom study. Focused on learner's priority, the learning objectives, content, and pace all vary as per the needs of the learner. The personalized environment offers a digitally-rich environment as most of the learners prefer to use laptops and mobiles because they are technologically fluent.

Personalized learning should have an environment that supports appropriate technology, learners flexibility based on physical space around them, learning time structures and also instructional modalities. As each learner has a completely unique set of mind, therefore, personal learning environment (PLE) is the combination of tools, people, and services that make-up individualized resources and is a unique approach to learning.

In an education system, ICT is used to support, enrich, enhance and optimize the delivery of information. It is already established that ICT improves student learning and also enhances learning methods. To make justice to the different learner's needs, ICT supports personalized learning. Use of different ICT-based applications for this purpose here include accessing course materials through remote devices, developing online digital repositories for lectures, course materials, and digital library along with cloud-based academic management systems, implementing flipped classroom concepts, accessing different electronic devices like computers, tablet computers, audio players, projector devices, etc.

The encroachment of ICT and the development of various tools as digital resources made personalized learning available in wider audiences. Following are the advantages of ICT in personalized learning.

i. The content is more engaging and attractive.
ii. It helps the teacher to monitor the learners constantly providing the scope of improvement of each individual learner.
iii. The study material is relevant and customized for each individual learner.
iv. It supports virtual social communication among different organization which helps the teachers as well as learners to develop their knowledge.
v. It simplifies learning-to-learn abilities.

A service-oriented architecture is an effective component in the web-based learning environments. It is the collection of different types of services. The term services are the most significant component, which provides communication with each other and satisfy their needs. Web services are the set of protocols by which services can be published, discovered and used in a technology-neutral, standard form. This architecture helps the learners to organize, realize, participate, apply, supervise, and invoke the e-education service system and also enhances the personalization aspect by providing the individual learner's needs. As the content in the form of web documents are increasing drastically, there is an immense difficulty for the learners to recognize the appropriate track. To overcome this difficulty, customization of documentation is needed according to the user's preference. Service-oriented reference architecture describes the essence of software and most relevantly it supports personalized e-learning systems. This architecture provides a business-level software service that can be executed in heterogeneous platforms. Those services are location independent. This means it is applicable to any system and in any network. This service-oriented architecture also enhances reliability and reduces hardware acquisition costs. It also provides loose-coupling across application services and granular authentication supports.

8.4 PERSONALIZATION OF LEARNING AND PREVAILING SCHOOLS

Personalized learning is a learning approach. Personalization is a complex concept which fulfills distinct needs. The goal is to customize learning for each student's strengths, requirements, skills, and interests. An individual student gets a learning plan that's established on what he or she identifies and how the learners acquire the best knowledge. Organization achievement depends on the sum of personalization accomplishment. Nowadays, personalized learning offers fundamental challenges in school education. In school and higher-level education system particularly, personalization is perceived as an extension of a long-standing agenda for differentiation of learning to ensure the different requirements of individual learners.

Children learn from diverse ways and in different places. Personalized learning is a teaching model based on that principle. Individual learners get a learning plan based on the learners learning the way, skill and interest. This is just the reverse approach that most of the school follows. Teaching–learning is not a short term approach. It has several long-term goals. This process supports students taking ownership of their own learning. Project-based learning can be considered to suffice this type of education standard. It is an approach that supports individualized education programs.

Every single school using personalized learning will differ from each other. But there are certain models that schools generally follow.

Usage of Learner Profile

In this model, schools update learner's information on a regular basis and try to deeply understand each individual learner strengths, requirements, impulses, progress and objectives. These profiles are updated and they generate a standard report card. This detailed report card helps the teacher to understand the learner and also supports them to take positive decisions in terms of improving the educational impact. On the other hand, learners also recognize their own progress. There is a scope to modify own learning style or make changes in their objectives to avoid acquiring poor or unsuccessful grades in exams.

Usage of Personalized Learning Path

In this model, schools help each learner to customize a learning path based on their progress, motivations, and objectives. Schools can create a learner's schedule based on weekly updates focusing on academic development and benefits. Each learner's schedule may differ from each other. There are several learning approaches commonly known as modalities. Here teachers carefully monitor each learner and deliver additional support as required. Project-based learning, independent work, one-to-one tutoring supports this type of personalization path.

Usage of Competency-based Progression

This model mainly focuses on learner's progress. This system makes clear of learners prerequisites to help achieve mastery in a particular skill. These capabilities prioritize specific skills, knowledge, and mentality of the learners. The learner works on numerous competencies simultaneously. When a learner becomes a master in a particular topic, s/he moves on to the next. The learners get the support and services to become masters on the skills. It does not focus on examination system. Continuous learning and incessant improvement is the most significant part of this model.

Providing Flexible Learning Environments

This model mainly focuses on the environment where the learner learns the best. It includes space, time and resources in the classroom.

These models of personalization are not yet fully operational in different schools as they are still developing and appearing as modern tools. But these have great potential to change the teaching–learning system. There are many more aspects which are still required to enhance these personalized learning approaches at the school level.

8.5 THE SELF-REGULATED PERSONALIZED LEARNING PEDAGOGICAL MODEL

In 21st century teaching–learning, the pedagogical model describes the functions of an effective teacher so that the students are involved in the classroom and do intelligent yet challenging works. It provides a cycle of five (5E) phases such as engage, explore, explain, elaborate, and evaluate. The main focus is on improving teaching practices to increase student learning outcomes. Since the outcome is the ultimate goal, learning is also the most prime factor in this pedagogical model and we must contemplate each individual learner's need.

The objective of the self-regulated personalized learning (SRPL) project is to develop an innovative system to adopt the requirements of individual learners. It has some unique features to structure learning that develop coherent pedagogical results. These are given below.

 i. Guarantees that learners are capable of making informed educational results.
 ii. Differentiate and distinguish diverse forms of skill and knowledge.
 iii. Create such a learning environment which differs according to the learners need.
 iv. It prioritizes learner's opinion such as their response and assessment so that continuous involvements and developments take place.

The rapid growth of ICT can materialize the dream of several generations of educators and intellectuals. Pedagogical models today support personalized learning to a large extent in European schools to satisfy the SRPL goals. They are more focused on develop additional methodologies based on SRPL which gives a better result of experiments with teachers in schools.

The objective of the model is to sustain personalization entrenched in self-regulation along with the improvement depending on essential motivation. Personalization is an adaptation of the learning process here. Its content varies from personal individualities and preferences to the learner's choice. Adaptation should be based on the development of learner's choice and exploration. While developing a learner's choice, multiple options are provided to learners and they have the freedom to select according to their individual parameters and personal preferences. But whenever the learners choose two considerations, one has to be met for support towards mindfulness and other for meaningfulness. On the other hand, exploration is a behavior in which an individual translates distinctive inquisitiveness to a thoughtful active non-linear search for information, its examination, and assessment in a self-reflective way.

Self-regulated Learning

It mainly focuses on three major components like consideration, performance, and self-reflection. There is a scope of comparison of self-observed performance against some standard performance so that learners can judge his/her ability by oneself.

Intrinsic Motivation

To improve learner's motivation some psychological needs are required like perceived competence, sense of autonomy, and sense of acceptance. Perceived competence provides a slow introduction of new concepts by breaking the entire task into sub-tasks according to the learner's development. This step helps to understand the learner's ability. A sense of autonomy supports self-determined behavior and tries to understand what one actually wants to do. Sense of acceptance is supported by the language of acceptance, assessment of actions rather than by the individual, and group reflections like forums, chats, and another communication tool.

Relationship Among the SRPL Model Entities

SRPL has three basic goals in the education system—personalization, self-regulation and essential motivation. Each of these is dependent on each other and partially overlaps each other. These three entities support accompaniment and enhance each other. Each of them performs in tandem to achieve the goal. The figure 8.1 demonstrates the relationship among the SRPL model entities.

SRPL is not a specific teaching–learning approach. So, this is not restricted in a particular teacher or learner. This self-regulated model acknowledges personal differences between individual learners and teachers depending on various learning circumstances, different pedagogical goals based on school-specific activities and also the social and cultural values of the learners. It analyses the approaches and modifies according to the prerequisite. The objectives of the pedagogical model are to accommodate all teaching–learning approaches in a minimum number of choices.

Self-regulation and reflection increase the SRPL level which is more meaningful and specific for the individual learners. School administration changes their methodology supported by both teachers as well as learners and gradually moving towards the two varieties of the learning process, namely open-endedness and openness. This tool permits teachers to illustrate their approach in a tangible way through classroom pedagogies, content development methodologies, and changing school management methodology.

Practicing SRPL

SRPL provides the option to allow various degrees of openness and choice in different leaning ambiances. The user will be able to decide which level and the scope of directness shall suffice his/her preparation procedure. As there are multiple options from which the students can choose their preferences, users are liable to decide on all aspects of the planning process initiating from setting the goal of the plan to the execution. However, with the gradual use of the planning tool, more and more aspects of the planning process can be open to the choice of each individual student and thus promoting the personalization of learning.

Practicing SRPL is overall an echo-system that encompasses all facets of the learning procedures. It is advised that students should be systematically motivated to query themselves regarding their choice of option, activity, interests, preferences, and identity as a whole. The main advantage is students not only learn about themselves, but also understand how they learn. Students will understand the status of their progress, explore their learning style and hence readily adapts their interests through explorative accomplishments.

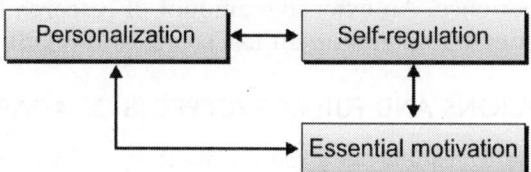

Fig. 8.1: Relationship among the SRPL model entities

8.6 ADAPTIVE LEARNING MODELS

Adaptive learning is an online educational system supported by different artificial intelligence techniques. Adaptive learning is also recognized as adaptive teaching. The foremost constituent of this adaptive system is student performance so that the system can modify the presentation according to the learner's need. Learning management systems (LMS) delivery, often taking part, includes management, documentation, tracking, progress reporting, and user supervision. Different algorithms are used to organize communication with the learner and deliver of personalized resources to accomplish the distinctive requirements of each learner. Adaptive learning has appeared as the cornerstone of education to support real-time learning with the provision of personalized educational experiences.

Each student has distinct features such as information, objectives, involvements, interests, experiences, personality traits, learning styles, learning activities, and study outcomes. Adaptive learning systems have conventionally been distributed into separate 'models'. It is from these features, that the learner model is constructed. The procedure to build-up the learner model is called the user modeling process or learner modeling process (also called student's modeling). The adaptive learning system uses learner's model to make an adaptation. In other words, an adaptive learning system takes advantage of individual information available in the learner's model given below in order to tailor learning constituents and teaching methods to each student.

Expert Model

An expert system is constructed on fundamental information about the design and function of an object. Such systems are used to diagnose equipment difficulties, for instance, as done in contrast with the rule-based expert systems.

Student Model

A student model is a demonstration within the architecture of an intelligent tutoring system (ITS) or an intelligent learning environment (ILE) for a student's understanding of the material being imparted. This model may also be used as a cognitive tool by making it available to categorical learners.

Instructional Model

Instructional models are sets of approaches or recommendations on which the methodologies are operated to teach by instructors. Effective instructional models are based on learning theories primarily. Learning theories describe the ways which theorists believe people learning new ideas and concepts.

Instructional Environment

The instructional setting refers to the instructional, behavioral, and individual features of the classroom experience. An extensive amount of research has linked optimistic academic environments to higher student test scores and qualification rates.

8.7 BENEFITS, LIMITATIONS AND FUTURE PROSPECTS OF ADAPTIVE LEARNING

Adaptive learning improves learner's requirement according to individual learner's need. It provides methods and learning paths that are unique to each learner.

Furthermore, through inherent efficiencies, adaptive learning helps the administrators to meet their goals. Here are six advantages of using adaptive learning in the education system which benefits the learner.

One-to-one Tutoring

Adaptive learning helps in providing focused consideration on an individual. Current e-learning methods organize fall back when it comes to providing personalized feedback. Adaptive learning technology uses algorithms to accustom itself to the learner needs which are to be established on the tasks and responses. This, in turn, emulates one-to-one instruction, which is necessary for today's education system.

Greater Time Efficiency

Adaptive learning supports learners to spend half the amount of time that they take in a standard course if they have a clear understanding of the concepts. A 'personalized approach' is what benefits learners to achieve the same. The important point here is that learner's requirement does not go through the content which they are already aware of. Instead, they focus on the content that helps them become more knowledgeable thereby helping the learners to learn more with less effective time.

Confidence-based Methodology

Adaptive learning improves a confidence-based assessment methodology to test the current understanding of the learners. Learners are questioned to answer on the content they claim to be self-confident about. This methodology is very beneficial in knowing what the learners are aware of consciously or unconsciously and hence it becomes an unintended method of providing personalized feedback.

Generate Personalized Learning Paths

Adaptive learning platforms collect data as the learner's progress through the modules. This data is then used to help personalize goals, learning content and an effective learning path for each learner. The data stored also helps to regulate the training so that they meet the needs of learners. The adaptive learning platform's ability to track the learner's performance makes them ready for a promotion. Thus, adaptive learning increases the efficiency of find a personalized learning path.

Personalized Learning for a Heterogeneous Group

Adaptive learning is best suitable for a group of learners who are dissimilar. Adaptive learning is personalized to suit all types of learners, whether they are novices, intermediate, or forward-thinking in their understanding of the perceptions.

Delivers Focused Remediation

As an alternative to wasting time over learning topics, learners become master or underlearned on the concepts they haven't yet grasped. Adaptive learning helps learners focus on areas of weakness with efficient remediation in the education system.

Adaptive learning systems are computer-based programs that permit computers to 'learn' and adapt to a user's input. But the decisions are made based on previously

compiled user input so that the human interaction becomes lesser. The following problems may occur in that case.
  i. Adaptive learning makes things very easy for individuals which could cut out work for people.
  ii. The decision is taken by the machine based on a database, so will take longer to develop.
  iii. Learning is based on the user here. If the user wishes to alter their choice, it becomes a complicated issue.
  iv. The information is limited to analysis only.
  v. Maintaining database could be problematic to keep up the database used to scan objects due to continuous variations in features.

The best reason for enhancement of adaptive learning is its comprehensiveness. Adaptive learning has made great steps to improve the leading teaching–learning approaches which improve student outcomes. In order to comprehend the everlasting opportunities adaptive learning offers and will offer in the future, the essential part that powers learning systems. Three promising areas of study may be evolved in this course. Natural language processing programs are intended to process and consolidate written content based on the input, listening, and understanding user feedback. Conversational interfaces deliver and empower communication on a more anthropological level while using adaptive learning technologies that are artificial intelligence or virtual reality-powered. This would generate a supplementary meaningful intent from the learner. Machine learning algorithms plans to build personalized pathways, monitor feedbacks and provide dynamic visualizations, which may provide a valuable vision for both teachers and learners.

8.8 ADAPTIVITY AND PERSONALIZATION IN MOBILE LEARNING TOWARDS STUDENT MODELING

Personalization can be realized through two adaptive methods—learner's characteristics (such as learning requirements, styles, performances, status, profiles, and preferences) and context associated with the learners are used to adapt the learning services. Multimedia materials with a visual learning style can be delivered as learning services or step-by-step instructions may be offered to the learners who have trouble in solving problems. Context-awareness abilities are to be developed by learning services. For example, it will be useless to deliver botanical materials inside an art gallery. Two adaptive solution approaches for adopting personalization in mobile learning are presented here. One solution is to use a learner's characteristics such as learning styles and other is to use context-awareness knowledge structure according to the learning objects and domain knowledge surroundings of the learners.

The design approach used in this case is to develop a multi-agent system to integrate and deploy software components, learners, devices, situations, and educational services to form mobile learning communities for collaborative problem-solving. Another approach is to use students modeling agents to capture information on learner's learning styles, location, behaviors, context, performance, and actions. Those modeling agents collect all required data from the relevant services and making the information reachable for all services which are responsible for offering an adaptive mobile learning environment. Location awareness services are used to form face-to-face learning groups and social networking services are also integrated into the infrastructure. Included adaptive mechanisms provide learning materials that fit the personalized learning styles. Available multimedia components often reach the source of interaction in mobile learning. Context-awareness service recognizes the personalized context-aware knowledge structure and directs individual students to learn through automatically generated guidance. Learners are also provided intelligent question–answer knowledge sharing platform and problem-based learning platform in adaptive mobile learning. The learning environment accumulates data on students' usage patterns, interests, progress, knowledge level, problem-solving abilities, location, social closeness, and learning styles for providing adaptivity through these personalized user data supporting learning at any time and any place.

Felder-Silverman learning style model can be used for adaptivity. This learning style distinguishes preferences on four dimensions—active/reflective, sensing/intuitive, visual/verbal, and sequential/global. So, each learner has a preference for each of these four dimensions. The degree of preference can be used to describe a balanced learning style by using dimensions and scales. The students with a high preference for certain behavior can also act sometimes differently according to this style. This model is used and advocated very often for technology enhanced systems.

A student model is the approach to understand students' behaviors, actions, and preferences towards learning and identifying learning styles in an automatic, dynamic, and global way. The students' behavior and actions are used to understand their learning styles and the dynamic part update the model while students are using the system for learning. Thus the model is revised and improved leading to higher accuracy of adaptivity. Mobile learning environment gathers all data on students' behavior and actions through the offered integrated services. Learning style questionnaire may be incorporated for data acquisition on students' behavior and actions towards revision and improvement of the adaptivity and personalization. Calculated information about students' learning styles by the student modeling approaches can be used to offer the best learning experience which incorporates and fits their preferred ways of learning. So learning styles are used as a basis for the design and updating the adaptive mechanisms and activities that fit their personalized learning styles. The question and answer service also incorporates learning styles that fit the personalized way of acquiring information considering the chosen media type.

EXECUTIVE SUMMARY

- The rapid improvement of computer technology and e-learning strengthens the requirement of dynamic adaptation to the requirements of each individual learner.
- Personalized learning supports the diverse variety in educational platforms. Learning objectives, instructional methodologies, and instructions may vary based on learner's requirements. Several student modeling attributes help the learners in adaptation.
- In learner centric approach learning activities are significant and appropriate for the learners, determined by their benefits, and often self-initiated.
- Personalization techniques identify each learner's strengths, requirements, and benefits to customize learning.
- ICT is enhancing learning experiences as well as development of various tools as digital resources, made personalized learning available to wider audiences.

- Learners' profiles, learners' learning paths, competency-based progression, providing flexible learning environments support personalized learning, which improves and enhances 21st century education system in schools.
- Self-regulated personalized learning (SRPL) pedagogical model supports personalized learning in a large extent. Personalization, self-regulation and essential motivation are the main entities of this model. Each of them perform in tandem to achieve the goal.
- SRPL is not a specific learning approach but is flexible. It can be modified according to the prerequisite of the individual learners.
- Adaptive learning is an online educational system supported by different artificial intelligence techniques. Expert, student, instructional models, and instructional environments are the modeling concern of adaptive learning.
- Adaptive learning not only has huge benefits and future prospects but also has some limitations.
- We can build adaptivity and personalization in mobile environments towards student modeling by using appropriate learning styles.

Review Questions

1. Define personalization in the learning environment. Why is personalized learning better than traditional learning?
2. Give example of different technologies that contain ICT towards personalization. Define pedagogical model.
3. Define different entity is used in SRPL. How does SRPL help individual learners in learning?
4. What do you mean by self-regulated learning? State the key components of SRPL pedagogical model.
5. Why is learner profile an important aspect in personalized learning? State the benefits of service-oriented architecture.
6. Why is intrinsic motivation an important aspect in SRPL?
7. What is the difference between teacher-centric and learner-centric approach? Write the benefits of personalized learning.
8. What is adaptive learning? Discuss the different models supporting adaptive learning.
9. Write down the benefits and limitations of adaptive learning. Indicate the future prospects of adaptive learning.
10. How to incorporate adaptivity and personalization in mobile learning towards student modeling?

Chapter 9

Emerging Learning Technologies

Objectives of this chapter
- To explain the importance of emerging technologies in teaching–learning.
- To introduce the different important emerging learning technologies.
- To explain the significance of different important emerging learning technologies in education.
- To mention some examples of applications of the said technologies.
- To explain different entrepreneurial approaches with emerging learning technologies.

Expected outcomes of this chapter

After going through this chapter learners will be able to:
- Understand the definition, elements and working principles of major emerging learning technologies.
- Understand how the emerging technologies are used in teaching–learning process.
- Get themselves aware about the different emerging learning technologies and continue study if they want to proceed further on the selected domain of their interest.
- Identify the opportunities of technological innovations to their respective education system.
- Judge the requirement of technology implementation in their practicing on relevant education system.
- Get motivated towards developing expertise on emerging learning technologies to avail entrepreneurship opportunities attached with this field.

9.1 EMERGING TECHNOLOGIES IN EDUCATION

Because of the availability of more and more technologies inside and outside of our modern classrooms, educators have to be prepared to make the best use of emerging technology-based teaching and learning mechanisms. Students are depending on those technological developments and facilities to build their creative skills, their ability to breed innovative ideas and design solutions for emerging problems. Modern classroom teaching strategies must integrate these technology-enhanced learning paradigms across all content areas of concern. Modern teaching–learning also concentrates beyond the school, college and university walls even outside the day of their degree earning days. Awareness of the latest trends in the teaching–learning will surely advance their learning process.

It has been proved that technology has the potential to improve the teaching and learning process. Technology is rapidly changing the dynamics of education. With the use of computer and internet, the teaching–learning process has changed. Teachers are using modern technology to replace old models of rote learning and creating more personalized, self-directed experiences for their students. There are plenty of mobile applications that instigate learners with special needs into the learning environment by enabling and facilitating them with digital education. Through the use of LMS, students can access online resources to get assistance on-demand beyond the physical reach of their teachers. Fast advancements of computing techniques and ICT are contributing massively towards the design and development of new learning technologies.

9.2 INTELLIGENT TUTORING SYSTEM (ITS)

An intelligent tutoring system (ITS) is a software application that provides individualized tutoring or instruction that gives support to automated learning activities. The concept of intelligent machines for teaching purposes can be traced back to 1926 when Sidney L. Pressey built a machine with multiple choice questions and answers. The machine-guided tutoring is generally implemented through e-learning software like CBT and WBT packages. Each ITS must have three components, namely knowledge of the domain, knowledge of the learner, and knowledge of teaching strategies. The domain refers to the topic or curriculum being taught. The learner refers to the student or the user of the ITS. The teaching strategies refer to the methods of instruction and how the material shall be presented. Although there are many types of ITSs around, each one must behave intelligently, if not actually be intelligent. They must be able to accurately diagnose student's knowledge structures, skills and styles; diagnose using principles rather than preprogrammed responses; decide what to do next; adapt instruction accordingly; provide feedback.

LMS may have some intelligent tasks to perform by incorporating the features of ITS. These ITSs give support to the learning activity through the deliberations of knowledge over the internet. They present new ways of education, which can change the role of human tutor towards offering more facilities. A learner learns from an ITS often by solving problems (kinesthetic learning). The system selects a problem and compares its solution with that of the learner and then performs a diagnosis based on the differences. After getting feedback, the system reassesses and updates the learner's skills and the entire cycle is repeated. As the system is assessing what the student knows, it is also considering what the student needs to know, which part of the content is to be taught next, and how to present the material. It then selects the problem accordingly. The recent trends of ITS application have been observed towards developing sector-specific applications. All ITS must use a paradigm of computational intelligence other than heuristic approaches. This application can be used in a virtual classroom, in distant learning courses through web-based LMS or in the form of CD-ROM format.

ITS Architecture

The following figure 9.1 presents the architecture of an ITS for intelligent learning.

The functions of the six modules are as follows. Learner module is a part of the ITS where the variables retain user information from the interaction with the tutor. Learner's performance module is the module that gives feedback to the adaptation module based on the learner's performance judged through test scores at each stage of the learning. The content materials to be taught are kept in the knowledge module structured as a

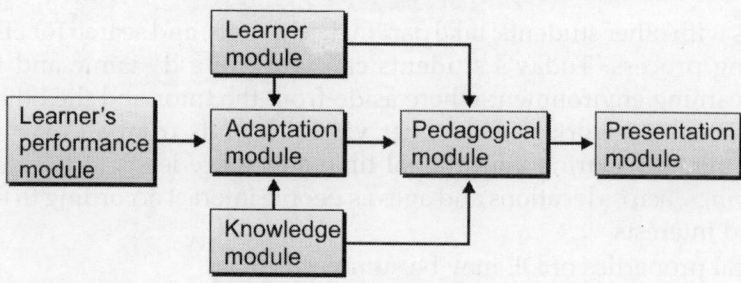

Fig. 9.1: ITS architecture

knowledge map and a set of topics and subtopics. Learner assessment is performed by the adaptation module which combines information from the knowledge module with learner data (from the learner module) for, inferring the learner's state of knowledge using Bayesian network, or neural network or any other soft computing methods. Major emphasize is to be centered on the implementation part of this particular module. The pedagogical module creates a set of suggestions about the student's subsequent activity. These suggestions are based on some pedagogical rules. Pedagogical rules are formed on the basis of the data generated by the last three modules. This module creates a support point for intelligent computing methods. The pedagogical module gives feedback to the adaptation module and adaptation rules are changed in accordance with the intelligent methods. The presentation module works as a visual representation or interface of the other three modules to the users or learners. It is the collection and composition of the topics, subtopics, respective questions, pedagogical suggestions (for example the most likely step) and an indication of knowledge level at each step.

9.3 ICT-BASED DISTANCE EDUCATION (DE)

The phenomenon of distance education is strongly related to the rapid development of ICT. Presently, a huge number of students and teachers have access to advanced ICT leading to a dramatic change in the ways they communicate as well as use and create information. Educational organizations are no longer the sole and most attractive source of information and knowledge. Quick access to unlimited sources of information is obtained due to modern technologies. The ability of the students to read, write and communicate digitally has resulted in a shift in the concept of literacy to multimedia literacy (or digital literacy) where text, graphics, still and moving images, animation and sounds are incorporated along with the traditional means of education.

Distance education can be defined as all forms of education with a focus on the fact that most of the transactions between instructors and learners take place through information and communication technologies in a different space put side-by-side to the traditional learning. Technologies have made remarkable progress since the early days of ICT in education. Digitization of resources has shifted the impact of ICT-based DE mostly to online electronic libraries and rich multimedia resources rather than hardcopy materials. Students can do self-study through aesthetically systemized and interactive multimedia learning materials. They can construct their knowledge, study individually according to their needs, learning styles, skills, interests, and cognitive characteristics, and learn how to learn. Students can control their learning process, work in teams with other students, take part in discussions, and search for effectiveness in the learning process. Today's students can work in a dynamic and interactive multimedia learning environment where aside from the tutor and the other students can communicate and work with his/her virtual friends from all over the world. Learners can think of sharing educational time and space leads to the formation of flexible groupings, across locations and ages as people interact according to their needs, curiosities and interests.

Some typical properties of DE may be summarized as:
- Development effort depends upon the scope and the content of the learning material.
- Self-paced study is possible.
- A high level of motivation is required.
- Minimum technological requirement.
- Minimum requirements for the instructors.
- Less feedback provision.
- Ease of revision and use.
- Versatility in teaching–learning approaches.

9.4 VIRTUAL LEARNING ENVIRONMENTS (VLES) AND AUGMENTED REALITY

Virtual reality (VR) offers a synthesized experience through computer simulation of real world situations. Computer software and some other special hardware are required to get in touch with or experience VR. A learning environment needs to be created for teaching–learning to take place. The learning environment in ICT-based DE often does not have a physical space but is a virtual environment (or VLE) designed and developed to facilitate teaching and learning when teachers and students are separate in time and place. ICT-based DE intends to be focused on design and utilizing VLEs. A very important role in effective use of VLEs is played by the instructional designers who should apply an appropriate learning theory in the design of the VLE. One could use different mental images (metaphors) of teaching and learning while designing a VLE. An extension and a substitute of a physical environment are provided by internet and web in the form of cyber metaphor.

Pedagogical Approaches for VLEs

Behaviorism, cognitivism and constructivism are the three most trending learning theories often referred by instructors while designing VLEs. Nowadays many researchers and professionals refer to constructivism as the most popular theory in the area of ICT-based DE. The theory states that by reflecting on our experiences and participating in social activities (ICT-based web society here) we construct our knowledge about the world around. In a constructivist classroom, the teacher tries to understand the student's prior understanding of the concept, and then structures opportunities for students to refine or revise these understandings. The refinement and revision take place by posing contradictions, presenting novel information, asking queries, encouraging research, and/or engaging students in investigation intended to confront existing concepts.

Types of Media Used

The selection of media options is very important because it is a fact that in distance mode the teachers often do not come in contact with the students. Hence, the choice (careful) of media should be such that it can create the same atmosphere of learning as in the case of a teacher conducted classroom education. Virtual reality headset combined with student's friendly interfaces, gesture control, embedded educational resources and teacher's control facilitates was not cost effective 10 years back. These augmented reality technologies made education more interactive and enjoyable for learners in recent years.

9.5 WEARABLE TECHNOLOGY (WT)

Wearable technology is a smart electronic device that can be attached to our clothing or worn on the body as accessories. Wearable technologies can increase learner's ability and be innovative by interacting naturally with the environment. Information is easily accessible to students without obstructions. A few possible uses of wearable technology in education are given below.

- WT can be used for job training, for special equipment or procedures.
- WT can be used by athletes to supplement workout footage that might be taken by a coach, in order for the athlete to learn to improve.
- WT can be used by coaches to demonstrate a technique from their own perspective.
- WT can be used to augment cooking videos with footage from the perspective of the chef, including voiceover.
- WT language learning tool may be combined with Google Translator.
- WT may be used in distance learning via Glass, instead of on a computer or laptop.

The following are the wearable technologies for classroom use.

- *Autographer*: It allows students to capture direct notes to ensure complete note taking.
- *Keyglove*: These wireless gloves are useful in gaming, design, art, music, data entry, device control, and 3D objects.
- *Muse*: It tracks students' brain activity onto a smartphone or tablet so that it can detect what activities they might need to keep them focused on studying.
- *Virtual reality*: It gives students hands-on experience that allows students to interact with the object in that particular environment.
- *iPod*: It is an effective learning tool that empowered students to creatively think about the subject as well as to allow greater collaboration.
- *GoPro*: It is a camera that can capture a student or teacher's point of view of events, such as a lesson or student behavior.
- *Google glass*: It enables students and teachers to search, take a picture, record video, and answer and translate questions in a foreign language.
- *Smart watch*: It is a wearable electronic device in the form of a wristwatch.

9.6. GAMIFICATION

Games have many ingredients that make them a powerful instrument for human learning. These are normally built for players to solve a problem and develop essential skills needed for the future. It often promotes communication, cooperation, and even competition amongst players. Games can spawn creativity and imagination in its players besides teaching and testing them. So games can act as an incredible package of teaching, learning, and assessment. Gamification (or gameful design) adds game elements such as storytelling, problem solving, aesthetics, rules, collaboration, competition, reward systems, feedback, and learning through trial and error into non-game situations. It has already experienced extensive implementation in the fields such as marketing, training, and consumerism with rampant success. Classcraft, Class Dojo, and Rezzly are few of the good examples of widespread gamification applications. The following are the elements generally found in the gamification application.

- *Mystery*: It requires the learners to fill the gap of known with unknown. For example, finding a hidden key to a closed door is mystery to resolve.
- *Action*: Almost all games instantly begin with an action which forces the learner to make a move. Finding a map, collecting pieces, searching a shelter, etc. are examples of actions. The action is used to engage learners directly.
- *Challenge*: Everybody likes the pleasure in overcoming challenges. Game developers leverage this inherent desire by challenging players at each step.
- *Risk*: A game with no risk of life or chance of winning coins is a piece of boredom. It appears more appealing if it comes with the risk of losing a life (virtual) or to lose all the collected items just because of a wrong move and need to start over again. Thus, the games improve the learner's ability to focus and make a strategic move.
- *Uncertainty*: Learners often hold no idea about what may happen next in their way. Solving puzzle and to move next level is an example of uncertainty.
- *Progress visibility*: Games clearly display where the players are, what must be done, where to start and how long it must go on. These improve their performance and chances of success.
- *Emotional content*: Games bring up the most valuable human emotion of anger, sadness, frustration, enthusiastic, happiness or unlike learning modules. These game elements assist in encouraging and accepting different human emotions.

9.7 MOBILE LEARNING

One of the recent technologies in e-learning paradigm is mobile learning which allows users to use learning resources through mobile phones. Mobiles being very handy nowadays and smart phones being present with almost all the senior students, they can have uninterrupted access to the learning resources through mobile browsers and applications (apps). The main concept of learning at the convenience of the user is characterized through usage of M-learning. M-learning can be achieved through smart phones, mini laptops, tablets and other handheld devices. At the basic levels, most schools are adapting M-learning and are using tablets and laptops as an integral part of education. While laptops and tablets lure the children, for the bigger students, educational apps are becoming more and more popular.

Mobile learning provides flexibility in teaching–learning and can be effective in contemporary pedagogy (digital) design. Mobile learning is gaining popularity and is steadily growing into a long-term as well as more persistent means of education, but provided the constraints of budgetary and human resources, institutional practices, procedures and priorities should be met beforehand.

Some of the emerging categories of mobile learning are:
- Technology-driven mobile learning, where technological innovation is installed within academics to demonstrate technical feasibility and pedagogic possibility.
- Miniature but portable e-learning where mobile, wireless and handheld technologies are used to recreate approaches and solutions already used in 'conventional' e-learning.

- Connected classroom learning in which the same technologies are used in classroom settings to support collaborative learning, perhaps installation of interactive whiteboards in classrooms.
- Informal, personalized, situated mobile learning in which the same technologies are enhanced with additional functionality, for example location-awareness or video-capture, and deployed to deliver educational experiences that would otherwise be difficult or impossible.

Advantage of mobile learning: This learning allows the learner to learn whenever and wherever suitable. It helps in motivating students when they get to know that learning can be enjoyed through their mobiles and that too can be accomplished 'on the move', as learning materials will be always available in the mobiles. Different file formats of the learning resources help in transforming the plain texts into livelier and interesting ones. One of the major benefits of mobile learning is that long distance is not a problem, irrespective of the dispersed geographical location. Students from any place can view the same content and take the same tests at the same time.

Disadvantage of mobile learning: Keeping control of the exposure to mobiles for both children and adults should be a matter of concern. Pupils are easily distracted by longer usage of other irrelevant apps in the name of studying. Focus towards the goal should be clear for the student to fulfill their objectives. It has to be ensured that there is proper internet connectivity to introduce M-learning in classes and in other places.

It has been studied that there are some particular tasks that are suited for mobile learning strategies. Activities that require gathering of information, conducting online tests and quizzes during the class hours, consolidation of learning, personal reflection and skills acquisition are mostly achievable through M-learning. To enhance the mobile learning methodologies further, personal motivational content can be scheduled along with the learning content so that students get self-motivated before starting to learn and further mobiles can also be transformed into devices that helps on-the-move participation in online activities that might be continued or completed at a desktop PC or laptops. Availability of open access mobile apps are increasing by leaps and bounds every day. There are a huge deployment of educational blogs and YouTube videos in the web space which are accessible through mobiles and other handheld devices for learning purposes. Proper choice of such apps, blogs and videos has the huge potential for enrichment of learners' knowledge and skills in varied domains.

9.8 CLOUD COMPUTING

Cloud computing consists of the techniques through which multiple facilities like software, servers and storage are provided over the internet, referred to as 'the cloud'. Users basically pay for the service that they require helping in leveraging the cost yet resourcefully running the organizations and their personal needs. Generally, there are three types of clouds. In public cloud, all the services to be provided along with their infrastructure are possessed and controlled by external cloud service providers like Microsoft, Azure. The second type is the private cloud whose services are exclusively used by a single organization. Hybrid cloud, being the third type, is the mixture of the above two types of clouds. Clouds provide infrastructure (IaaS or infrastructure as a service), platform (PaaS or platform as a service), and software (SaaS or software as a service) as services for users.

The goal of modern e-learning programmes is to achieve 4A, namely anyone, any-time, any-place and anything. The benefits of e-learning include taking an online course, taking examinations, sending feedbacks, projects and homeworks. Cloud computing enhances web-learning platform offering active and flexible learning, a learning-friendly environment and improved learning results. Traditional e-learning networks are usually built, developed and maintained by the user institution, and often found costly. Transferring the creation, maintenance, development and management to vendors, opening it up to numerous subscribers via the internet and allowing them use-on-demand and paying according to the total used servers would help to cut costs for the institutions. The cloud services are particularly useful for supporting lab activities in the teaching–learning process. In classroom, students able to do some activity based on the teachers instructions and hence improve their skills and knowledge using the cloud-based software and services. To implement the cloud on the education, firstly one has to create a cloud system and then upload the required documents, files, images, videos on the cloud. Then one can access it from anywhere. In schools and colleges, teachers, students can prepare their documents and share it with others through the cloud-based storage services. Also by creating dynamic changes in the documents or in the presentations, one can show animations or perform experiments on the documents. The figure 9.2 indicates the education system in a cloud environment.

The key features of cloud computing which are effective in education are as:

- *Portability*: No more carrying around devices, such as thumb drives or CDs. It does not need to worry about losing the device, breaking the CD, or not having your information load properly.
- *Easy access*: Lesson plans, labs, grades, notes, PowerPoint slides—just about anything digital that one can use in teaching is easily uploaded and accessed anytime.
- *Stability*: Cloud computing is now to-the-point of being a very stable technology that one can rely on. Educational resources are stored and may leave it for future use.

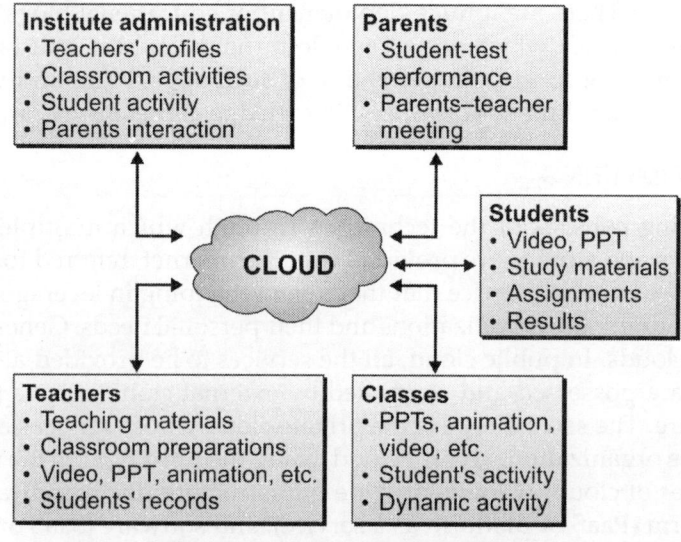

Fig. 9.2: Education system in cloud

- *Security*: The data, content, information, images—anything can be stored in the cloud usually requires authentication (ID and password, for example), so it is not easily accessible by anyone. In addition, if something happens to the technology at the institution, the content will still be available to all if it is stored elsewhere in a cloud.
- *Shareability*: All the files that are stored in the cloud can be shared easily with others. There is no more requirement of an extra thumb drive or burning another CD or DVD, only need to send a link to the file(s) to the intended receiver.
- *Trackability*: There will be no problem if instructor make changes to a lesson and want to change it back. Cloud system will save multiple revisions and versions of a document so that the evolution of an item can be traced back chronologically.

Modernizing learning processes using the latest technologies in classrooms encourage students to develop skills and knowledge necessary for achieving their academic and professional goals. From this perspective, the cloud is a valuable resource for the education sector. Together with other forms of technology implementation, the cloud can substantially increase learning opportunities for learners all over the world.

9.9 INTERNET-OF-THINGS (IOT)

Internet-of-things or IoT, literally means all things available to be connected to the internet. It is an empowering technology for researchers to develop smaller and more affordable wireless systems that consume less power and can be integrated into almost any type of device. There are three IoT components that enable seamless connections. The first one is hardware made-up of sensors, actuators and embedded communication hardware. The second one is middleware on demand storage and computing tools for data analytics. The third one is presentation made of novel, easy to understand, visualization and interpretation tools that can be widely accessed on different platforms and that can be designed for different applications. IoT includes accumulating and transmitting data through the use of sensors from the real world physical objects to the internet.

The unique growth of developing IoT technologies is helpful not only in improving the core values of teaching and quality of research but also developing an IoT society and encouraging a new digital culture. With increasing online degree opportunities and seamless access to instructional content in both structured and unstructured formats, the IoT leads digital momentum into higher education institutions. IoT is a dramatic shift in the traditional instructional paradigm while integrating broader disciplines, including social science to enrich the value of big data available from social media.

Presently at digital age, all the paper documents are moving toward smart phones, tablets and laptops that offer the necessary information at their fingertips, and also the possibility to learn at their own pace. This trend provides convenience also for teachers because teaching activities become more efficient and student-centered. Mobile devices' and tablets–educational apps changed the methods of teaching–learning and can be considered as powerful tools to create 3D graphics presentations and textbooks featuring videos. Also, students are using mobile devices as an educational tool which is allowed the access to eBooks, quizzes, projects and to watch the labs and courses in video format. These are very attractive learning methods for students and new teaching opportunities for teachers.

In recent years, several companies, such as SMART (https://education.smarttech.com/products/smart-learning-suite) and IBM (https://developer.ibm.com/academic/), have demonstrated their interest in introducing IoT into academia, developing 'Smart University' projects. Google launched several applications that could be considered 'things' supporting instructional objectives. Tools such as Google apps allow the students and teachers to share the documents online and make changes in real time on a screen.

With the advancement in IoT-based technology, universities can resolve many challenges such as keeping track of essential resources, develop access to information, build smarter plans, and design safer campuses. IoT systems have tremendous potential to bring significant values to higher education by engaging and motivating the students and staff, and to increase speed of learning. IoT has much other potential across all educational level to address the surveillance, risk and reliability issues of educational distributions administration and management in a cost effective and purposeful manner.

9.10 EDUCATIONAL DATA MINING (EDM) AND LEARNING ANALYTICS (LA)

Educational data mining concerns with developing methods for exploring the increasingly large-scale data that come from educational settings and using those methods to better understand students, and the learning processes. Issues of time, sequence, and context also play important roles in the study of educational data using EDM. Learning medium and environment have evolved from chalk and talk-based face-to-face methods to online open courses in smart learning paradigm with the advancements of ICT and other learning technologies. A smart learning paradigm is defined as the paradigm that is reasonably improved using technology to enhance learning. Traditional assessments of learning process seem to be inadequate with the use of these new smart environments and mediums. Assessing learners in traditional classrooms is not easy and it becomes more difficult in online and open-learning environments. Institutions are being challenged to increase their understanding of learners' needs by regulators with those advancements. LA have been emerged as a very promising field with techniques to effectively use the data generated by learners while learning to assess the learners as well as learning process for corrective actions. It offers institutions to track student's progression, detect students with learning gaps and provide a personalized learning experience. Data collection from various educational resources is a serious concern and it is associated with LA applications.

LA is rooted in data mining, data science, artificial intelligence, practices of recommender systems and business intelligence. The objective of LA is to use of intelligent data, learner-produced data, and analyse models to discover information in a process to produce information for prediction and recommend learning activities. It focuses on the measurement, collection, analysis, and reporting of data about learners and their contexts for understanding and optimizing learning and the environments in which it occurs. LA approaches usually depend on data obtained from learners' interactions with ICT, such as LMS and social media. From an institutional perspective, LA can improve decision making and resource allocation, highlight an institution's

successes and increase organizational productivity. Five latent purposes of LA are (concisely):
- Provide learners' feedback about their learning progress compared to their colleagues.
- Identify at risk students.
- Help instructors to plan interventions when needed.
- Enhance the designed courses.
- Support decision making when it comes to administrative tasks.

The five phase of LA are as follows:
1. Learning phase is where learners can acquire new knowledge, information or skills within the learning environment.
2. Data selection phase is where the learner or the instructor selects the data to be analyzed. Generally, this data is the learner's learning behaviors sketches during the learning process.
3. Data collection phase is where the selected data is collected from the learning environments.
4. Analysis phase is where the collected data is analyzed using different techniques.
5. Intervention phase is where decisions are made based on the analysis results. These decisions can be the personalization of the learning content as well as recommendations for learners or instructors.

A wider selection of methods to extract meaning has emerged with the development of these increasingly large data sets. These are known as educational data mining. The educational data mining and learning analytics experts address many of such research questions, using similar techniques. With the emergence of big data, new extensive educational media, combined with advances in computational methods holds promise for enriching learning processes in formal education, and beyond as well. Very large data sets are increasingly available from students' interactions with educational software and online learning with support for acquisitions, warehousing and mining. Computer scientists, learning scientists, psychometricians, and other researchers are contributing largely towards the development of this field. Technical, pedagogical, and social domains must be brought into the surface to promote such research efforts. Though the ultimate outcomes of LA and EDM are not much distinguishable, but there are some different technological, ideological and methodological orientations for each of them.

9.11 MACHINE LEARNING (ML) AND STUDENT MODELING

ML is based on the concept that a computer program can learn and adapt to new data without human interference. It involves an inbuilt source code or an algorithm that would create a model data generated by it. ML is the induction or compilation of knowledge, normally leading to improvements in the ability of an agent to classify objects or solve problems in its domain.

Student modeling involves the construction of a qualitative representation and adaptation process by learners to the intelligent learning environment (ILE or in a ITS) in terms of relevant learners' attributes such as learning behavior, skill and domain knowledge. These attributes of student behavior are qualifying in terms of existing background knowledge about a domain and about students learning the domain. Such system needs huge amount of student analysis-based tedious manual works having huge time consumption and high error probability. Data mining and machine learning techniques can be adopted for providing the automation in student modeling in e-learning for ILE and reducing the manual work up to a certain level.

A student model is a representation of a student's understanding of material being taught. Application of machine learning and data mining techniques in automatic student model development are the recent burning areas of research. Many important issues of student models are yet to be evolved with machine learning teaching to provide higher degree of automation. Application of data mining techniques for student performance analysis and automated content recommendation are expected to contributing to the modern education system. The machine learning applications may be summarized as follows.

- *Increasing efficiency*: ML has the potential to make educators more efficient by completing tasks like classroom management, scheduling, etc. Educators are liberated to focus on tasks that cannot be achieved by AI, and that require a human touch.
- *Learning analytics*: ML in the form of learning analytics can help teachers gain insight into data that cannot be processed by using the human brain. Computers can perform deep dives into data, sifting through large pieces of content, and making associations and conclusions that positively influence the teaching and learning process.
- *Predicative analytics*: ML in the form of predictive analytics can conclude about things that may occur in the future. It can predict which students are more likely to dropout because of academic failure or even their predicated score on a standardized examination.
- *Adaptive learning*: ML in the form of adaptive learning can be used to remediate struggling students or challenge gifted ones.
- *Personalized learning*: ML in the form of personalized learning could be used to offer each student individualized learning experience.
- *Assessment*: ML in the form of artificial intelligence can be used to grade (with higher validity and reliability) student assignments and examinations more accurately than a human can.

ML has the potential to revolutionize the field of education, whether we want it to or not. A lot more educational applications are evolving with the study of these fields towards students' modeling.

9.12 SENTIMENT ANALYSIS AND DEEP LEARNING

Sentiment analysis or opinion mining is the process in which the perspective of a text is understood automatically by machines. Emotions of texts cannot be understood normally, and hence it is important that they should be mined for a variety of purposes. The recent surge of allowing comments in each and every event on social media has necessitated the need for extracting emotions of users. It becomes easy for organizations to assume the trend on how users portray against a particular occurrence. Based on the data collected from comments, organizations apply methods to improve their brand, product or service. The accumulated comments are often found unstructured in nature.

They need to be processed before mining for the original sentiments. Deep learning is a subpart of machine learning which handles huge amount of data and learns features automatically to yields excellent results in case of supervised learning. Deep learning helps analyze sentiments more accurately and hence it is used extensively to predict emotions of the masses.

The entire education scenario is facing a vast shift to cope up with the aggressive standards of today's fast paced society. The advent of ICT-based education techniques has helped sentiment analysis to be easily used to infer the emotions of learners. As most of the conversations occur through texts, it becomes very easy to supervise the sentiments occurring in the online discussion forums provided in the online courses. Though face-to-face interactions are not possible in these types of courses, there can be a provision of messaging the instructors when there arises a change in the sentiment of the learners. In a way, student retention can be increased by tracking the changes in sentiments in these courses. Sentiment analysis can also be used as a tool to classify the nature of learning graph of the students, categorize the needs of the students and predict their performance. Effective alterations should be made in the instruction approach accordingly. The analyzed results can also be used for other purposes by the institution like planning remedial measures for negative sentiments and giving awards to teachers who receives the most positive emotions of the students. Overall, sentiment analysis in education can help enhancing teaching–learning by easily accumulating student feedback regarding teaching techniques and course contentment.

Teacher performance and course satisfaction (or dissatisfaction) can be analyzed through a sentiment and emotion analysis of a students' feedback system. The system may categorize emotion into eight classes, namely anger, anticipation, disgust, fear, joy, sadness, surprise, and trust and sentiments into two classes, namely positive and negative. From these emotion and sentiment analysis parameters, the system will computes satisfaction and dissatisfaction using a five phase process consists of data collection, data preprocessing, sentiment and emotion identification, satisfaction and dissatisfaction computation, and data visualization. Student feedbacks are collected from both formal sources such as course surveys and informal sources such as blogs and forums in the data collection phase. Data processing phase consists of six sub-processes, namely tokenization, lowercasing, normalization, stemming, removal of irrelevant content and transliteration. Sentiment and emotion identification phase uses natural language processing to classify sentiments and emotions through two sub-process, namely token matching and vector creation. Satisfaction and dissatisfaction are computed from these vectors. Data visualization phase present the analysis results (like satisfaction, dissatisfaction, emotions and sentiments) through graphical (bat line, etc.) aids.

9.13 CYBERNETICS

The potential of cybernetics has not exhausted even after nearly 70 years of its existence for diversified applications. Cybernetics started its journey from electrical and mechanical system automation and control, later it has spread to the social, biological, and learning systems. Cybernetics means governing the system towards its desired goal. The classroom teaching–learning process may be considered as a system where the ultimate goal is the success of learners and learning processes. Classroom cybernetics is comprised of constructivism, conversation theory and a feedback system.

The first one resulted in 5Es, namely engage, explore, explain, elaborate and evaluate. Learner constructs meanings (or knowledge) based on his/her own experience rather than as perceived by others. That is why s/he produces unique sense to a concept in the learning domain. The second one requires interaction between teacher and learner which passes through three levels of language, namely natural language, subject language and meta language. According to these, learning takes place through a conversation about a subject matter of concern between two parties which serve to bring knowledge in the public domain and make it acceptable. The last one is a mechanism for controlling the system to keep up equilibrium, move forward or even reverse it. As per cybernetics, there are three feedback states, namely steady state (equilibrium maintenance), growth state (forward or next level), and change state (backward or reversal). In a steady state when a deviation in the outcomes occurs, the system acknowledges a problem, and returns to normalcy to restore the original situation. To uphold all these three cybernetics components, ICT, and emerging learning technologies can help a lot towards the achievements of their desired goals. An ideal mixture of digital pedagogy and emerging learning technologies have the great potential to achieve these goals of learning cybernetics if instructors and learners both are capable of adopting these technologies.

9.14 CYBER SECURITY

Across all education sectors, educational data collection and analytics are increasing day-by-day. Student retention and performance, intellectual property rights are few of the major areas of data insecurity and field of attacks by hackers. Lack of knowledge and attention among the educational electronic data users is also a serious concern with respect to cyber security to educational activities. Education institutions started to implement security plans with respect to the following.

- *Application security*: Schools are relying on online applications for testing, data collection and analytics. Hackers will take advantage of application vulnerabilities, which means schools, colleges, and universities need to be aware and build their application securities. Incorporating vulnerability scans or penetration tests is the way to root out potential security flaws through firewalls and other security software.
- *Endpoint security*: The number of personal devices is increasing as a number of students and instructors are increasing. These expansion is increasing the number of vulnerable endpoints. Cyber security education is crucial to ensure users take appropriate initiative for security through software and hardware applications.
- *Patching modulation*: Updating security software is essential. Initial patching and continuous regular patching by security software helps educational users keep themselves safe from malicious attacks.

Over the next few years, most if not all information will be stored online in electronic databases. Cyber security has not kept up with the shift of electronic storage in the education system. Hackers are scarily good at stealing school and student data and they are going to get better and more efficient and sneakier. Local institutions will have to safely share sensitive information with state and federal level stakeholders. There needs to be a faith and assurance that this information is safe and is stored in a tightly secure database. There has been a tightening up of security in the education sector. There must have proof such as how they are applying new security rules and how it will be monitored in the lead up to a more secure education system. Using white-hackers is a smart idea as they know all the techniques that the hackers will use to creep their way into this sensitive information. Security is always changing and the education sector has to go a long way with securing their sensitive information with advanced use of new technological innovations.

9.15 BIG DATA

Big data includes a large variety of information that arrives in increasing volumes and velocity. It incorporates both processed and raw data and is more voluminous than traditional data. Generally, this data is too huge and too multifaceted to be processed by conventional software. This huge collection of data brings many opportunities for analysis from many different perspectives or concept. Five attributes of the big data explain its characteristics given below.

- *Volume*: Big data is accumulated from thousands of diverse resources. So, they usually are of low density and unstructured. The volume (amount) of big data may be in the figure of terabytes (240 bytes) to petabytes (250 bytes).
- *Velocity*: This attribute describes the pace of data coming in and getting exchanged or shared. The speed of big data is generally calculated in real time.
- *Variety*: Big data may have types like raw, unstructured, structured, and verified data. Some of these require further evaluation and analysis while others are ready to use.
- *Veracity*: It identifies the credibility of the incoming data. It means concentrating on eliminating bias, flaws, inconsistencies, and duplication that convey no value (originality is a primary requirement in education).
- *Variability*: This aspect describes the variety and consistency of ways through which big data is received. Data comes in periodic peaks. It may be seasonal and triggered by a specific phenomenon online.

Big data has brought noteworthy changes to many characteristics of education. The most important is the ability to monitor educational systems. The feature of automation, brought by these big-data-based systems, has itself resulted in many other benefits, like, credible grading, more dynamic grading programs, improved student performance, and better learning experience. The massive volumes of data bring much value for both educators and students. Here are some examples of how it works:

- Students data come from heterogeneous sources like social networks, studying students' blogs, to understand how much they are interested in a specific course, how is their progress, how instructors are performing at teaching courses. The attributes of these data match with big data characteristics.
- Students' activity (click) and performance tracking data are also huge and have enough variety, etc. that may reveal their mistakes if analysed with appropriate tools.
- LMS allows the instructors to create assignments and tests using the information that is uploaded online using automation, these are distributed to varied students. These multimedia and interactivity actions data are of big-data nature.
- Big-data technology is supporting the emergence of new educational models with provisions of customising curriculum. Educators use big-data technology to collect information about students and develop customized learning plans to generate enhanced learning outcomes.

- Educators use big data technology to discover students' problem areas, rather than relying on standardized tests to reveal issues nowadays. By using adaptive learning technology based on those big-data analytics, students can practice through challenging subject matter, while continuing to keep pace with the rest of the class. Big-data systems help educators to assess students accurately, while continuously monitoring their progress and likelihood of advancements.
- Using big-data systems, educators can measure student performance continuously and advance students accordingly. Big-data systems can assist students to learn on a higher level in improved educational models.

The analysis of big data relies on many factors, like transparency, value to the learner and the educator, expense, and openness. Big-data technology in education allows us to get benefited from this data to the maximum extent considering these features into consideration.

9.16 ENTREPRENEURSHIP USING EMERGING LEARNING TECHNOLOGIES

Entrepreneurship came from the business or commercial discipline where technological innovations are used for generating revenue from the market by their commercial use. Technology entrepreneurs use their specific knowledge and expertise to conduct technology focused entrepreneurial activities efficiently and effectively. Technology entrepreneurship is becoming a lucrative field with the globalization and liberalization of economy activities along with the spread of ICT. The level of acceptance and distinction of ICT not only deviates the nature of knowledge but also reforms higher education system, research activities and learning approaches. Variations and expansions in various technology sections such as personal computers, integrated circuits, digital subordinates, several storage mediums and devices, internet and web, broadcastings (emails, telecommunication), the software applications, fashioned thrilling potentials for creation of new businesses and also for the extension of existing industries. Colleges and universities are investing seriously in the development of their student's entrepreneurial skills and have a tremendous effect on innovation and entrepreneurial development. The evolution of ICT and other learning technologies opened a new dimension to those entrepreneurial activities. Following entrepreneurial activities may be planned with knowledge and skill of digital pedagogies (teaching–learning) and critical understanding of ICT (emerging learning technologies):

1. *Online school*: Online schools are very popular nowadays since students acquire knowledge on a topic online. This is both time and cost effective. So, we can offer online educational platforms to serve course materials and video lectures directly to learners.
2. *Tech video channel*: If someone loves to talk in front of cameras and edit video, video channel about technology will be a good idea for him/her. We can earn revenue and get endorsed by others online. The video content may be on any technical subjects, like computer training.
3. *Live streaming influencer*: Live streaming services are available on the social media channel including YouTube. We can take advantage of these services to serve as an influencer, motivator or knowledge provider. Students learning activities may be accelerated through these services and service providers can earn revenue.

4. *Online research service/internet research*: It is about using our expertise to perform research or generating new knowledge and inferences. We can use different research tools for specific businesses. The research will discover multiple specific insights to help businesses and generate revenue.
5. *Online podcasting platform*: People may like to learn via audio services. We can help them with a service platform where we will upload and share podcasting content to the potential learners to learn.
6. *Online coach/online tutoring*: If someone is passionate about something (niche) and possess an excellent knowledge on that thing, s/he can start a career as an online coach. This is a very lucrative way of earning revenue through blog, YouTube channel, learning portal or services via LMS, etc.
7. *Online teaching assistant*: Here an expert offers virtual assistance to the learner by assisting in their learning may be by solving their exercises and assignments. The expert helps the students remotely and charge for their services.
8. *Online english and other language teaching*: If someone is native speaker of language or bilingual, s/he can go for teaching the languages online to other people and make good revenue.
9. *Online translator*: Similar kind of services may be offered by a bilingual language expert for translation from one language to other online.
10. *Online vocational consultant*: Someone may have the potential to offer consultation to several people who want to learn how to ace a promotion interview or ask for a raise, or simply land a high paying job. S/he may go for a startup in the web platform. The experiences, tricks and useful tips will be shared to the intended recipient and earn good revenue.
11. *Online courses*: If someone is good at anything, chances are that there are people who would like to know how to do exactly that, no matter which field it is. People are willing to pay money to learn things online without having to get them from traditional educational institutes such as schools and colleges since they can learn at their own pace.
12. *YouTube channel*: YouTube is currently the 2nd largest search engine and the largest video site in existence. 300 hours of videos are uploaded to YouTube and 3.25 billion of video content are consumed each month. Someone with good knowledge of any niche may prepare video content on learning or entertainment and earn excellent revenue through this digital marketing platform.
13. *Online music teacher*: If someone is a musician and loves teaching music, s/he could be a music teacher online and earn money. The coaching may be offered through YouTube channel, Skype or any other video calling/conferencing services.
14. *Online fitness coach*: Like online music teacher, online coaching may be offered through similar services on health and fitness issues and earns revenue.
15. *Online Yoga and meditation instructor*: Similar to fitness, yoga and meditation instructors are required by people and such services (classes) may be offered by an expert through similar online services.
16. *Online freelance proofreading and editing*: Proofreading and copy editing are services prone to education. These services may be offered through online service channels to earn good revenue.

17. *Virtual and augmented reality*: Online platforms may be used for offering virtual and augmented reality-based training on high cost and risky experiments using multimedia applications and people are ready to pay for such experience through web-based VLE.

EXECUTIVE SUMMARY

- Emerging technologies in education helps us to complete our learning tasks more effectively and efficiently through the technically improved applications.
- Intelligent Tutoring System is a software application that provides individualized tutoring or instruction that supports the automated learning activities using artificial intelligence, soft computing and machine learning techniques.
- Distance education is all forms of education where the transactions between instructors and learners take place through information and communication technologies in a different space put in tandem with the traditional learning. It brings all learners in touch with the instruction system often unreachable due to their different geographical locations.
- ICT offers a variety of simulate real world's situations, known as virtual reality, to provide virtual learning environments. Costly and risky experiments may be simulated to provide students an experience of those essential learning facilities using these augmented realities.
- Wearable technologies are smart electronic devices that increase learner's ability and to be innovative by interacting naturally with environment.
- Gamification adds game elements such as storytelling, problem solving, aesthetics, rules, collaboration, competition, reward systems, feedback, and learning through trial and error into non-game situations and improves learner's knowledge, skill and abilities.
- Mobile learning allows education to be imparted through handheld devices so that learner can access all educational requirements through those devices.
- Cloud computing consists of the techniques through which multiple facilities like software, servers, storage are provided over the internet, referred to as 'the cloud'.
- Internet-of-things literally means all things available be connected to the internet. It is empowering technology researchers to develop smaller and more affordable wireless systems that consume less power and can be integrated into almost any type of device.
- Educational data mining concerns with developing methods for exploring the increasingly large-scale data that come from educational setting and using those methods to better understand students. Learning analytics use of intelligent data, learner-produced data, and analysis models to discover information, process that information for prediction and recommend on learning activities.
- ML is based on the concept that a computer program can learn and adapt to new data without human interference. A student model is a representation of a student's understanding of material being taught and such modeling is done using machine learning techniques nowadays inside ITS.
- Sentiment analysis is the process in which the perspective of a text is understood automatically by machines based on the data collected from comments, organizations, interactions, etc. It helps enhancing teaching–learning by easily accumulating

student's feedback regarding teaching techniques and course contentment and analyzing thereof often using deep learning techniques.
- Ideal mixture of digital pedagogy and emerging learning technologies has the great potential to achieve the goals of learning cybernetics if instructors and learners both are capable of adopting these technologies.
- Educational institutions started to implement security plans with respect to application security, endpoint security and virtual patching with advanced use of new technological innovations.
- Big data includes a large variety of information that arrives in increasing volumes and velocity. Using big data systems, educators can measure student performance continuously and advance students accordingly.
- There are many entrepreneurship activities that are evolving using emerging learning technologies.

Review Questions

1. Write the name of different emerging technologies in education.
2. Compare the advantages and disadvantages of mobile learning.
3. What is ITS? Briefly describe the system architecture of ITS.
4. What is a VLE in ICT-based distance education? How is VR different from augmented reality?
5. What do you understand by wearable technology? Give few possible uses of wearable technology in education.
6. What is gamification? What are the different elements normally found in an educational gamification application?
7. Describe the advantages and disadvantages of mobile learning.
8. What is cloud computing? Discuss how an education system can be modeled using cloud services.
9. What is educational data mining? Write down the purposes of learning analytics. Give the five phases of learning analytics.
10. What is student modeling? How does machine learning help in student modeling?
11. Write the characteristics of big data. How do big-data technologies assist education industry?
12. What is sentiment analysis? How does it help education? Write how does a typical sentiment analysis system work using student feedback.
13. Write the definition, components and importance of the following with respect to their function as emerging learning technologies (or write short notes on):

    (a) Learning technologies, (b) ITS, (c) ICT in distance education, (d) VLE and augmented reality, (e) wearable technology, (f) gamification, (g) mobile learning, (h) cloud computing, (i) IoT, (j) educational data mining, (k) learning analytics, (l) machine learning and student modeling, (m) sentiment analysis, (n) cybernetics, (o) cyber security, (p) big-data technology.
14. Write down the different entrepreneurship opportunities using emerging learning technologies.

Chapter 10

Courseware Engineering

Objectives of this chapter

- To introduce the concepts of courseware engineering (CE).
- To discuss the problem with traditional approaches to courseware development.
- To present the practical goals and development dimensions of CE.
- To present the pedagogical model of CE.
- To explain the content structure, layout, steps necessary to create tools used to design, factor for real use and standards of courseware.
- To present courseware development process.
- To discuss the evaluation techniques of courseware as well as courseware engineering methods.
- To present the courseware development life cycle model and different aspects therein.
- To introduce the concept of courseware quality assurance.

Expected outcomes of this chapter

After going through this chapter learners will be able to:
- Understand the problem of traditional approaches to courseware development and use appropriate knowledge of CE for courseware development.
- Describe practical goals, development dimensions and pedagogical model of CE.
- Explain content structure, layout, steps necessary to create tools used to design, factor for real use and standards of courseware.
- Identify appropriate software tools for courseware development, both for media editing and integration or authoring.
- Follow the systematic courseware development process and apply ADDIE model courseware development for their development works.
- Evaluate the developed courseware and the methods for courseware development.
- Understand the concept of quality assurance of courseware product.

10.1 INTRODUCTION TO COURSEWARE ENGINEERING

Courseware means any instructional system delivering content or activities via computers in order to support learners as well as teachers in their educational efforts, in all technical and instructional ways. It is also software blended instructional material intended as kits for teachers or as tutorials for students, usually packaged for use with a computer. Basic needs of educational courseware are to create valuable, compelling, empowering information and experiences to organize and present information to develop knowledge and understanding through interactions, presentations and experiences using engineering principles towards ICT-based learning.

It is important that pedagogy is one of the major concerns of courseware construction. To produce quality courseware, course creators aim to apply specific pedagogical principles to courseware. Courseware validation allows the course creator to specify the pedagogical rules and principles that courseware must conform to. ICT has influenced every aspects of human livelihood and it has brought a lot of innovation in the field of education. A fast growing aspect of lifelong learning process is e-learning which offers new form of teaching–learning that force educators to rethink when designing a courseware for that. Digital pedagogies should be taken into consideration while designing an e-learning courseware.

Courseware engineering can be considered as an emerging discipline with a set of practices, methods, tools and procedures whose primary goal is to improve the efficiency and effectiveness of courseware production. Courseware engineering provides a coherent framework for the variety of tools and production methodologies.

10.2 PROBLEM WITH TRADITIONAL APPROACHES TO COURSEWARE DEVELOPMENT

Courseware engineering method (CEM) differs from traditional courseware methodologies in many ways. There are some demerits associated with traditional approach to courseware development given below.

- Deficiency of prototyping facilities to allow early evaluation of the study.
- Deficiency of separation of the various components of the development process.
- Support for reuse is missing.
- Deficiency of a method for interfacing and hypermedia modeling.

An engineering approach to courseware development is desirable to overcome these drawbacks.

10.3 PRACTICAL GOALS AND DEVELOPMENT DIMENSIONS

With the advancement of internet and web technology along with the use of computer, the technology-enabled learning is getting more importance especially in continuing education of the workforce. One of the main drawbacks of a broader use of the new learning opportunities is the non-availability of high-quality courseware. The major goals for courseware engineering should be focused on improvement of the quality of courseware and of the efficiency of courseware development. Another scope of improvement in courseware engineering is the integration of courseware into the curriculum. It will not solve in itself the problem of the integration of technology into the curriculum.

Basically, there are four different dimensions of a courseware in the courseware development process—its content, its content presentation style, its instructional strategy, and its functionality. The development of 'electronic learning environment (ELE)' is the objective of study for courseware engineering (CE). ELE is composed of tasks, agents, courseware products, tools and contexts. It aimed at supporting learning processes in which learning processes take place mostly through interaction between learners, courseware products, and tools. The instructional system is the object of study of instructional development. This system consists of instructional tools, instructional materials, learners, product developers and an instructional environment aimed at supporting learning and development processes.

Increasing the effectiveness and efficiency are the two main foci of CE research and development activities. We can set the following practical goals for CE as a discipline.

- To promote the effective organization of courseware.
- To promote the ability to develop courseware products that has specific product characteristics.
- To promote the efficiency of the processes of development and use.
- To assure the educational quality (i.e. performance) of courseware products.

10.4 PEDAGOGICAL MODEL

The objective of the design process of courseware engineering is to produce a pedagogical model. This incorporates objective definition, assessment definition, and instructional strategies definition. The objective definition depicts the learning outcomes of the intended courseware. Once the objectives have been fixed, the best possible sequence of the instruction is reached. After defining the learning objectives, the next task is to identify how learners' attainment of the objectives will be tested. Maturity of assessment follows the objectives' identification. Evaluation of learning is a critical part of an instruction process. There is a requirement to evaluate student performance to judge whether the newly designed courseware has met its design objectives. There are various types of strategies available in CEM to evaluate students' performance. The judgment on what type of testing to use is identified by the students' needs, the purpose of the course, and the skills required. Guidelines are required to be provided in CEM for designers to choose the most appropriate assessment strategies for their learning objectives. The drafting of instructional strategies follows the assessment criteria identification. Instructional strategies to be used are identified by the type of learning required. Once the instructional strategies are fixed, the development of instructional messages can commence. This completes the design process. The output is the pedagogical model (a blueprint of the courseware) to be developed. The pedagogical model produced so far is self-determining of any medium of instruction. It may be utilized to deliver on any selected medium.

10.5 CONTENT STRUCTURE AND LAYOUT OF COURSEWARE ENGINEERING

The structuring of the total content is much more important in this context as the learning process immensely depends upon the way of delivering the information. Total content should be organized so that it can be easily gone through and assimilated. Following aspects are to be considered during arrangement of the total information.

- How do the learners interact with the material?
- What is the sequence of major concepts?
- What is the course timeline as well as how long should the modules take to complete?
- Are modules linked to other modules? How?

Functional Steps Needed to Prepare a Courseware

The courseware development process in large projects has been forced to mature from the previous ad hoc production of 'small scale lessonware' to the progressively more organized development of large-scale courseware. The main steps in this process are:

- Firstly, it is necessary to define the content as a 'rule set'. Detailed analysis of the content and target group (i.e. the background of the learners) is required.
- Detailed description of procedures and concepts are to be specified next. It will help the developer to give the learner a vivid outline of the subject.
- Then the learning steps are to be decided. It will help developer to prepare a blueprint of the total organization of the courseware according to the learning strategy.
- Then the sequence/branching of screens, perhaps with flowcharts, are to be decided.
- Next, the screens should be designed as storyboards.
- Finally, implementation code to be produced using a programming language or authoring language (production).

Tools Used for Designing Courseware

Following are the widely used tools for making courseware more effective.

Concept Maps

The first and foremost task to design courseware is to decide the subject matter. The topic should be chosen in such a way that it can be described adequately using various other media apart from text. After deciding upon the topic, its scope needs to be fixed. For doing that, the target audience needs to be specified. Side-by-side, the objectives of the content presentation need to be decided. This implies specifying how much the target audience is expected to get out of the content.

Semantic Maps

Semantics refers to the concepts or ideas conveyed by words. Semantic mapping is the process of structuring information in graphic form. It is known as concept webbing, concept networking, and plot maps. Semantic mapping is a tool by which students can represent the relationships among words and concepts, and in doing so they are able to reinforce the associations and categories that structure meaning.

Flowcharts

A flowchart depicts the flow of interactivity within a presentation. It shows at a glance how different modules and pages of the presentation are lined to each other and how user can navigate to different parts of the presentation starting from a particular point within it.

Schematic Diagram

A schematic diagram is a representation of the elements of a system using abstract, graphic symbols rather than realistic pictures drawing that shows all of the significant components of a course, flow process or device. It uses a standard set of symbols. A schematic diagram usually omits all details that are not relevant to the key information. It is also intended to convey, and may include over simplified elements in order to make the essential meaning easier to grasp.

Graphical Presentation

It is a method to analyze and represent numerical data with pictorial representation. It displays the relation between data, ideas, information and concepts in a diagram. It always depends on the type of information in a particular domain. It is the visual display of data through charts and graphs. There are different types of graphical representation, like line graphs, bar graphs, histograms, line plot, frequency table, circular graph, etc.

Story Boards

The story board depicts the layout of each and every screen or frame of the presentation to be decided upon. This includes issues like where the text and images should be placed, what should be their dimensions and appearances such as font, color and style, what should be the background music or voice over, etc. It is usually presented in graphically form with each screen presented by a rectangular outline containing the distribution of the media elements like text, image, video, etc. Each screen should be labeled sequentially and the elements within it should be represented as icons with appropriate labels.

Diagram

A diagram is a simple drawing consists mainly of lines which act as a symbolic representation of information using visualization techniques. Sometimes, the technique uses a three-dimensional visualization which is then projected onto a two-dimensional surface. The word graph is used occasionally as a synonym for diagram.

Venn Diagram

A diagram that demonstrates all possible logical relations between finite collections of different sets is called Venn diagram. These diagrams represent elements as points in the plane, and sets as regions inside closed curves. This diagram has a multiple overlapping closed curves, usually circles, each representing a set.

Important Factors for Real World Use of Courseware

The web is a fluid medium which may be strong or weak. The considerations of web materials are critical. Updating the content regularly to reflect recent changes helps to retain and increase readers' credibility. Strategies like portability and scalability should be kept in mind in order to move the course material to another system or platform and to change its content.

Standards

The term interoperability refers to content from multiple sources being able to work inside different LMS. Reusability refers to content developed in one context being transferable to another context. A significant issue in relation to online content development is the ability to develop content in a cost effective manner. As much online courseware is delivered via LMS, most systems are using a standards-based approach to allow for interoperability and reusability of the content. Another, major initiative which may revolutionize how content may be developed in the future is learning objects. Using this approach, content is broken down into small, independent, self-contained and reusable chunks (known as learning object) with each chunk confined to a specific task or role. There are specific guidelines and standards as to what defines a learning object, the main objective being that learning objects can both work within any LMS and be reused again and again.

10.6 COURSEWARE DEVELOPMENT PROCESS

Improvement of the quality of courseware and of the efficiency of courseware development should be major goals for courseware engineering. The efficiency of the courseware development process can be increased by following an industrial approach, in contrast to an individual or team approach. This approach indicates that mass production techniques, incorporating project management and quality assurance approaches, should become the major characteristics for the development process. The two phases, one design and another technical implementation, are seen as separate activities. For executing those phases different hardware systems and development tools are to be considered. In this concept, the use of hardware in the design phase should be much more powerful than the hardware necessary to run the final product. As a result, powerful design tools could be used to support the design phase, the development of a prototype and the iterative work to optimize the prototype.

A methodology based upon courseware engineering, a combination of instructional systems' development and software engineering, has emerged over the last 10–15 years. This methodology is used to improve the quality of courseware products and the efficiency of the courseware development process. Presently, software engineering approaches have gained extra dimension. The continuing developments in hardware and software are opening new perceptions for courseware engineering and related research.

A selected state-of-the-art technique, including object orientation and use cases from software engineering is incorporated to CEM. This method provides guidelines and methods for hypermedia and interface development. The various techniques are integrated from various disciplines within a framework of interrelated models. The modular approach facilitates designers to focus on particular aspects of the development process one at a time.

There are many specific advances within the methodology that include the development of courseware learning objectives, the use of conceptualization for needs analysis, separation of domain from instructional strategies, the modeling of hypermedia courseware applications, support of reuse through design patterns and interface modeling. The development of courseware engineering modules is generally a non-linear process, as shown in Fig. 10.1.

There are multiple multimedia software available based on simulation, sculpting, representation and authoring functions that they perform. The entire methodology initiates with the identification of the engineering matter for execution, followed by replication of the problem or circumstance that demonstrates the topic. The result is then transformed from the replication to the corresponding precise diagrammatic format. An animation is also described to explain the system which is made incorporating text and audio elements. In the end, the navigation format is described and the entire thing is incorporated with the help of an authoring package. Processes necessitated for every module depends entirely on the nature of the topic. Software packages like Working Model or Strata Studio Pro has the potential to execute multiple tasks concurrently.

In the modern day practices, the evaluation concept is directed from the process of making judgment and coining to decisions as regards to value of experiences. Evaluation is not a collection of techniques but a continuous process that is to be supplemented by feedback programmes. If a good result is expected, evaluation is to be made as an integral part of the total instructional objectives. Evaluation is the last step in the construction phase of CEM. Lessons are evaluated for their overall quality, their applicability to a curriculum, performance, and usability. Another purpose of evaluation is to assist in lesson development and maintenance. On the contrary, evaluation is part of an iterative cycle of designing, evaluating, and revising. It is carried out in all of the processes involved.

The students' performance and lesson effectiveness are the two types of evaluation measures in CEM. CEM provides a very detailed and comprehensive plan for formative evaluation of the courseware produced. The three steps involved are quality review, pilot testing, and field testing. During quality review, the materials developed are reviewed to assess the content, appearance and attention to good instructional practice.

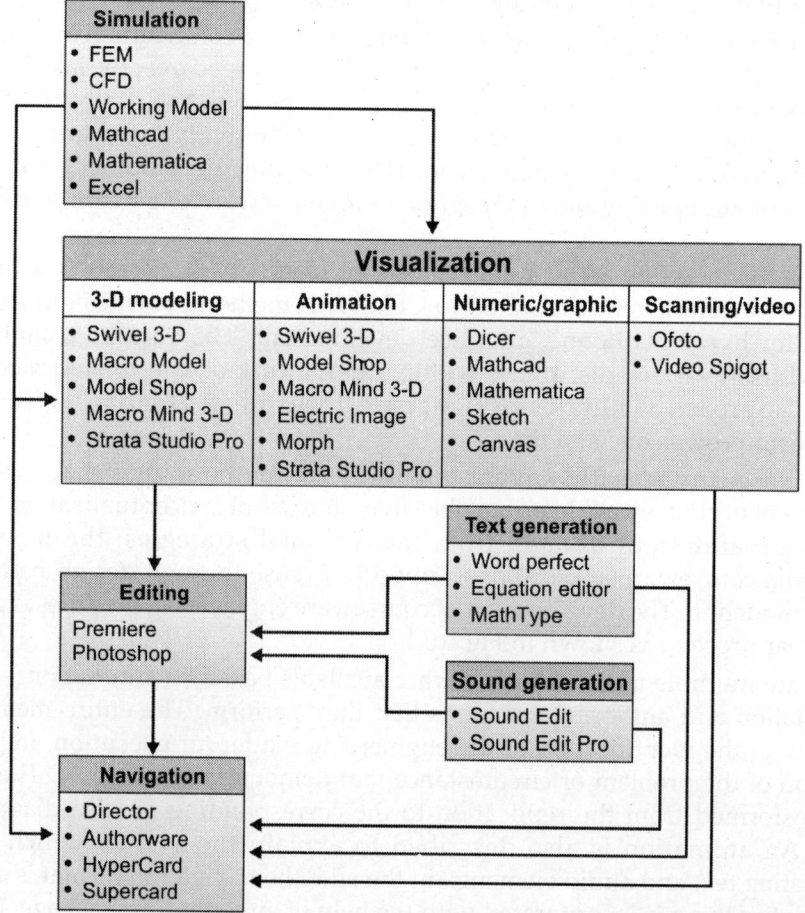

Fig. 10.1: Flowchart of courseware engineering development processes (with software examples)

The analysis of effectiveness of the learning process involved with students and use of the courseware product is the main objective of pilot testing.

The checking procedure of lesson works in the real instructional setting is validated by field testing. It is conducted only after full and thorough evaluation that the courseware can be released for deployment. The main aspects of courseware to valuate are:
- Whether the content achieves learning objectives or not?
- Whether the structure and navigational facilities are good or not?
- Whether the appearance of presentation design is attractive or not?
- Does it give good return for money or is it cost effective or not?

Evaluation of Courseware

The evaluation of courseware consists of the systematic description, analysis and decision of the effects of courseware. It includes procedures for gathering information to assess the worth of an event or process. It is a measure of effectiveness of different methods for different purposes. It verifies whether the production involves planning and also scope of applying judgment.

Courseware products should be evaluated at least for four different aspects. The first aspect is usability which measures the effectiveness at the interface and its functions. The second aspect is learnability which measures the case with which the product functions are learned and remembered. The third aspect is educateability which measures the product's educational effectiveness. The fourth aspect is utility which measures the usefulness of the product in terms of productivity gains.

Formative evaluation takes place at each stage of analysis, design and prototyping using different methods. Earlier stages test the courseware design in isolation whereas later stages of evaluation involve the systematic description, analysis and discussion of the impact of courseware. Revision done after each evaluation or wait for several results. Summative evaluation does final overall assessment for selection justification or accountability. It also monitors and judges the learning outcomes with respect to its use and ultimate testing objectives.

CEM Evaluation

The CEM evaluation methods are categorized into three groups, namely testing, inquiry, and inspection. The usability issues are tested for efficiency, satisfaction and effectiveness of the application. The testing approach usually involves the evaluation of prototype or the system through the observation of users working on general task. The inquiry involves communication between the participants in the test and the experimenters. The experimenters question the users about their thoughts on the interface or prototype. The participants may suggest ways to improve the application or discuss the effectiveness of the application. Inspection is the analysis of the application's user interface by usability specialists, software engineers and users. Some of the important methods of courseware evaluation are given below.

Expert and Peer Review

Content, pedagogy and interface, all three, are reviewed by an expert. Inconsistencies, if any, are identified and removed during educational review of the whole course.

It provides simple methods for busy experts giving background, analysis and a check list and leaves them to do it. It also includes cooperative evaluation by peer members.

Quality Review

It is a systematic exercise on a complete draft before pilot use, using checklist. It also helps us to select readymade packages. There exist readymade checklists for performing this task. The checklist should be modified to create an appropriate evaluation tool. The quality review process awards score to the courseware packages.

Quality Check Lists

To assess content and usability we need an evaluation instrument such as a check list. For example, MEDA evaluating training software check list are used to verify main features, usage, effects and purpose.

10.7 COURSEWARE DEVELOPMENT LIFE CYCLE

Course development comprises a set of steps. The steps incorporate methods, tools and procedures. These steps are referred to as life cycle model. The life cycle analysis also calls for defining the methods and procedures to be applied and the sequence in which such method would be enforced.

Courseware Development Life Cycle Model

The figure 10.2 shown below is a courseware development life cycle model used to develop the multimedia courseware. This model is a combination of the waterfall and prototype software development life cycle model. The Table 10.1 shows the methods used to implement each steps of life cycle.

ADDIE Model

In 1996, Ritchie and Hoffman introduced a popular life cycle model for course development called ADDIE. It is an instructional systems design (ISD) framework

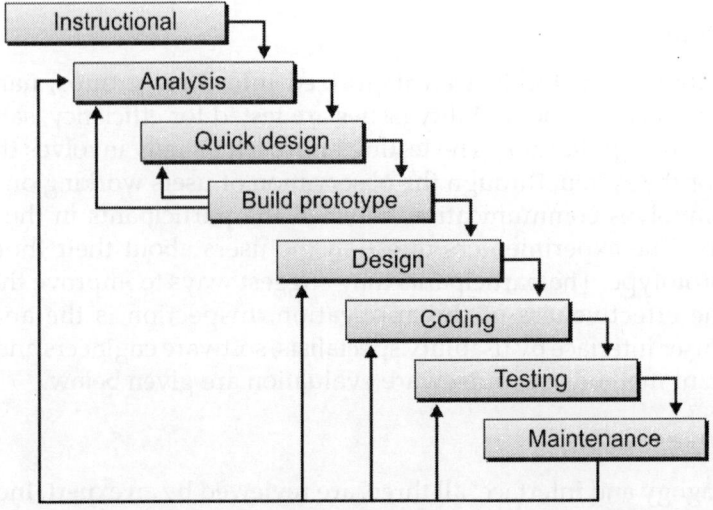

Fig. 10.2: Courseware development life cycle model

Table 10.1: Courseware development life cycle and methods

S. No.	Steps	Title with description	Method
1.	Instructional design	The process by which learning products like online courses, instructional manuals, video tutorials, learning simulations are designed, developed, and delivered.	Story board
2.	Analysis	This is required to understand the correct requirements for the product development. Two distinct activities here are requirements gathering and analysis, and requirements specification. The first one is to collect all relevant information regarding the product to be developed. The identified product requirements are then organized into requirement specifications (SRS).	Object-oriented authoring
3.	Quick design	A quick design is carried out to build a prototype. The prototype is submitted to the user for feedback. Based on the feedback, the requirements are refined and the prototype is modified accordingly.	Object-oriented authoring
4.	Build prototype	The prototyping model requires that before carrying out the development of the actual product, a working prototype (a miniature of the system) of the product should be built. It is usually built using several short cuts like using inefficient, inaccurate, or dummy functions. It is a very crude version of the actual system, possibly exhibiting limited functional capabilities, low reliability, and inefficient performance as compared to the actual product.	Object-oriented authoring
5.	Design	The goal of the design phase is to transfer the SRS documents into a structure form. This is appropriate for implementing in some programming language. Two approaches like traditional design approach and object-oriented design approach (OOD) are used. Most popular traditional design approach is based on the data flow-oriented design approach. OOD is the other new technique where various objects that occur in the problem domain and the solution domain are first identified and the different relationships that exist among these objects are established.	Object-oriented authoring
6.	Coding	The coding phase is nothing but an implementation phase since the design is implemented into a workable solution. The purpose of the coding phase is to translate the software design into source code.	Authoring environment
7.	Testing	The developed system and the codes are to be gone through unit testing which involves testing each module in isolation from other modules, then debugging, and documenting it. Unit testing involves a precise definition of the test cases, testing criteria, and management of test cases. The main objective here is to check the individual modules in an accurate working condition.	Debugging
8.	Maintenance	The product maintenance requires more effort than the effort necessary to develop the product itself. There are three types of activities involved in maintenance. These are corrective maintenance, perfective maintenance and adaptive maintenance. Corrective maintenance involves correcting errors that were not discovered during the product development phase. Perfective maintenance involves improving the implementation of the system. Adaptive maintenance enhances the functionalities of the system after feedback analysis.	Steps 1–7

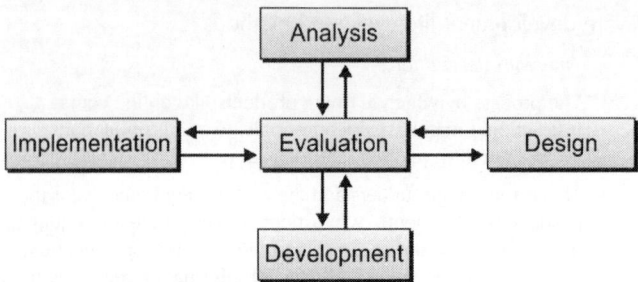

Fig. 10.3: ADDIE Model

that many instructional designers and training developers use to develop courses. Here 'A' stands for analysis, 'D' stands for design, the next 'D' stands for development, 'I' stands for implementation and 'E' for evaluation.

Purpose of the ADDIE model is to provide a systematic approach, identifying the actual problem and its content before moving into a solution and implementing it, identifying the purpose of the project, providing a method to look at the whole rather than part and avoiding wasted time and resources.

Analysis Phase

In analysis phase, three kinds of initial situations may arise. Those are a performance problem, new technology and an administrative mandate. What are the needs for the development of courseware are assessed in the need assessment subphase of analysis phase. Knowledge level and requirement of target audience are analyzed properly in audience analysis subphase of analysis phase. The content of the subject matter is analyzed and also instructional goal and resources are analyzed in the subject matter analysis subphase of the analysis phase. Analysis tool includes interviews, observation, surveys, and focus groups. Sources of data for analysis phase are learner audience, faculty/content experts, administrators and library.

Design Phase

After the analysis phase, we consider the design phase. The designers draft objective, draft test item to measure performance, specify instructional strategies and select media in this phase. Content, subject matter analysis and lesson planning are conducted here. Design phase consists of verification at all possible stages. The design phase should be specific and systematic. This phase may also include writing design document through proposal, concept and structure note to assist final development.

Development Phase

The development phase is used to develop the product by content experts and technologists by assembling content assets. The steps used for development, are writing down the story, creating script, drawing flow line and writing story board. Testing, reviewing and revising the project are carried out here according to feedbacks.

Script, flowchart and story board are used as tool in the development phase. Scripts are paper-based documents that provide a detailed description of the courseware content and how this is to be implemented within the final product. Script is also used to understand the flow of the application. Flowchart is used to see the virtual blue print and story board is an expression of everything that will contain in the program. Scripts and story boards are usually prepared by the courseware designers.

Implementation Phase

During the implementation phase, the developed material such as books, hands-on equipments, digital camera, image scanner, microphone, speaker, video capture card, CD/DVR storage and software are ensured by project manager and learning application or website become functional. There are two kinds of software usually used—editing tools and authoring tools. Editing tools include Adobe Photoshop, Corel Draw (image editing), Sound Forge (audio editing), Adobe Premere, After Effect, Cooledit (video editing) and Flash, Animator Studio, 3D Studio Max (animation). On the other hand, authoring tools are following different authoring metaphor or paradigm such as MS PowerPoint (Slideshow metaphor), Textbook (Book metaphor), MS Visual Basic (Window metaphor), Director (Timeline metaphor), Media Script (Network metaphor), Dreamweaver, Frontpage (Web metaphor), Authorware (Icon metaphor).

Evaluation Phase

An evaluation has two perspectives. One is that the courseware products should have at least the quality to achieve their goal. The other is that they should look and feel good, work efficiently and reliably and lastly be fit for the purpose for which they were designed. In evaluation phase, the product should be evaluated in terms of usability, learnability, educability and utility.

10.8 COURSEWARE QUALITY ASSURANCE

Quality of a courseware depends on multifaceted perceptions. The quality of a product can either be derived directly from the results emerged from it or its performance can be measured through the feedback provided by the person using it. Factors like knowledge outcomes, inspiration, bugs, exhaustion, etc. are some of the criteria anticipated to form the quality assurance vector as perceived by its users. Ideally, courseware products shall comply with the quality characteristics predefined by its designers, but the product performance in its entirety should be simplified before critically considering value assurance.

Quality of course product is concerned with four dimensions, namely the content of learning material, the presentation of the material, the way in which they are taught (pedagogic content), and the overall functionality of a courseware. The courseware engineering life cycle model in some methodology is accompanied by four engineering methods that assure the quality of the output artifacts of each perspective-based inspections, prototyping, tests along with formative and summative evaluations. Thus, the whole life cycle is encompassed by verification tasks and validation tasks.

EXECUTIVE SUMMARY

- The term courseware is the blending of 'course' and 'software', which means that it contains contents to assist teachers and students to teach a course through the use of computer software. Courseware engineering refers to the techniques of designing effective courses of varied disciplines.

- Courseware engineering aims to help beginners guide the way an ideal course be prepared through proper software development principles and processes.
- Courseware engineering method has many advantages over traditional approaches to courseware development.
- Courseware products should be evaluated based on its usefulness, educational efficiency, learning capability and production gains. It has a pedagogical model for development.
- Courseware development life cycle model helps in designing an efficient courseware. ADDIE is model for courseware development where 'A' stands for Analysis, 'D' stands for design, the next 'D' stands for development, 'I' stands for implementation and 'E' for evaluation.
- Evaluation of a courseware depends on various parameters set by the user or predefined by the designer. Thus, quality of a courseware depends on multifaceted factors like knowledge outcomes, inspiration, bugs, exhaustion, etc. Four engineering methods that assure the quality of the courseware product are artifacts of each perspective based inspections, prototyping, tests along with formative and summative evaluations.

Review Questions

1. What is courseware engineering?
2. What does the effect courseware have on pedagogy?
3. What were the problems associated with the traditional approach of developing a courseware?
4. Write down the practical goals and development dimensions of courseware engineering.
5. Discuss the pedagogical model of courseware engineering study.
6. What are the function steps to be followed while preparing a courseware?
7. Describe courseware engineering development processes with a flowchart. Also give examples of software used.
8. Name and explain some of the tools required for designing a courseware.
9. Write the important factors of real world use of courseware.
10. Briefly describe the courseware development life cycle process.
11. Explain some of the courseware evaluation metrics.
12. Describe the ADDIE Model used to develop courses.
13. How to ensure quality of a courseware product?

Chapter 11

Outcome-based Education and Regulatory Practices

Objectives of this chapter

- To introduce the concept of outcome-based education and its requirements.
- To introduce the concept of accreditation and usefulness to measure the quality of teaching–learning process in present education system.
- To explain the parameters of OBE and its attainments.
- To illustrate the concept of continuous improvements in teaching–learning process.
- To explain the concept of bridging curriculum gaps in OBE.
- To discuss the processes of teaching–learning quality improvements.
- To explain the role of FDP in OBE.
- To explain the role of ICT in OBE.

Expected outcomes of this chapter

After going through this chapter learners will be able to:
- Understand the parameters and processes of OBE.
- Practice OBE system for quality improvements and accreditation.
- Understand the requirements of accreditation and its national and international trends.
- Design the OBE-focused curriculum of the course of their teaching expertise.
- Move towards continuous improvements of teaching–learning.
- Analyze the curricular gap and take appropriate remedial measures.
- Follow different processes to improve the quality of the teaching–learning.
- Understand the importance of FDP with respect to their career progress and institutional demands.
- Analyze the importance of ICT usage towards OBE implementation.

11.1 OUTCOME-BASED EDUCATION AND ITS REQUIREMENTS

Output is the direct, short-term results associated with an activity whereas an outcome is the result of those outputs in the long term. Outcomes are not seen immediately after the end of the activity, but there are measures to evaluate outcomes. The effectiveness or impact of the activities is indicated by the outcomes, not by outputs. Outcomes also reflect the level of achievements or performances. Outcome-based education (OBE) is a learner-centric approach that focuses on student performances, known as outcomes. Traditional education primarily focuses on the resources that are available to the learner which is called inputs while OBE often introduces a host of many progressive pedagogical models and ideas, like project-based learning, cooperative learning, etc. It does not specify or require any particular learning style. Instead, OBE requires learners to do something with the acquired skills and knowledge. OBE is a system that leads towards outcome-based curriculum (OBC), outcome-based learning (OBL) and outcome-based assessment and evaluation (OBAE). It is a closed-loop cycle that enables continuous improvement towards excellence. The key components of OBE are vision, mission, program educational objectives (PEOs), program outcomes (POs), and course outcomes (COs). OBE is also called performance-based education that is achievable and measurable. The emphasis is given on measuring 'outcomes' which can be set as per individual institutional requirements. In brief, OBE is a learner-centric approach by which learners are able to do something successfully at the end of their learning experiences. Following figure 11.1 demonstrates some perspectives of OBE.

The figure 11.2 presents the present structure of OBE.

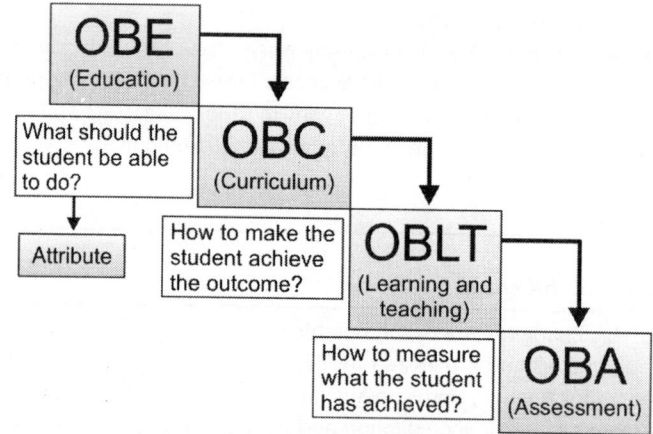

Fig. 11.1: Outcome-based systems

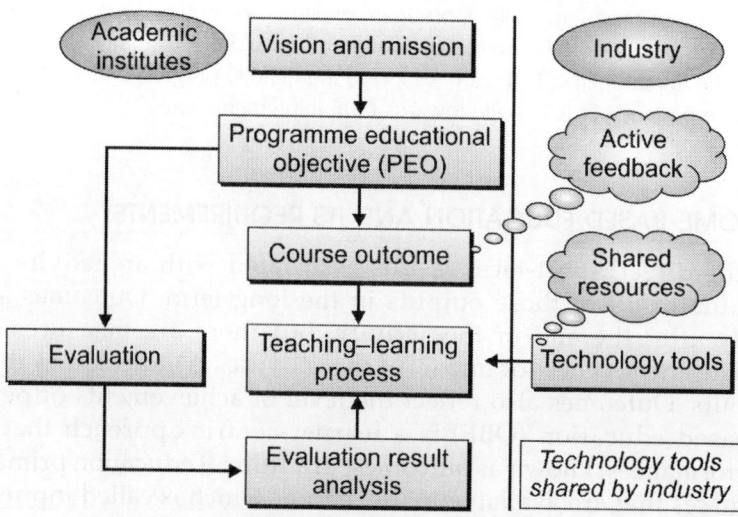

Fig. 11.2: Present structure of OBE

Traditional Input–output-based Education *vs* Outcome-based Education

Input–output-based education is the traditional education system. It is an open-loop teacher-centric approach focusing on inputs and outputs. It requires a close relationship with the core curriculum. The output measures only the knowledge of the learner. The figure 11.3 demonstrates the attributes of the traditional input–output-based education system.

Advantages and Disadvantages of Input–output-based Education

Input–output-based system is relatively easy to maintain and it makes accreditation process uniform and potentially fair. Its criteria are unambiguous and often numeric and hence success lies in adherence to those clear unambiguous criteria or rules.

On the other hand, it is difficult to establish as well as update and it does not encourage continuous improvement in curriculum. It lacks innovation and creativity in the curriculum whereas it assesses and evaluates knowledge only.

Outcome-based Education

It is a learner-centric closed loop process that focuses on outcomes achieved by learners which can be measurable and achievable. It concentrates on developing four parameters, like knowledge, skill, attitude, and abilities. The most detailed articulation of the theory underpinning OBE is given in Spady (1994, 1998). In Spady's words, "OBE means clearly focusing and organizing everything in an educational system around what is essential for all students to be able to do successfully at the end of their learning experiences. This means starting with a clear picture of what is important for students to be able to do, then organizing the curriculum, instruction, and assessment to make sure this learning ultimately happens."

Important Features of OBE

OBE offers a highly configurable learning path for students to provide learning outcomes with multilevel, multidimensional capabilities. Learner's knowledge, skills, competencies, attitude, and values are mapped to the student's learning outcomes. It

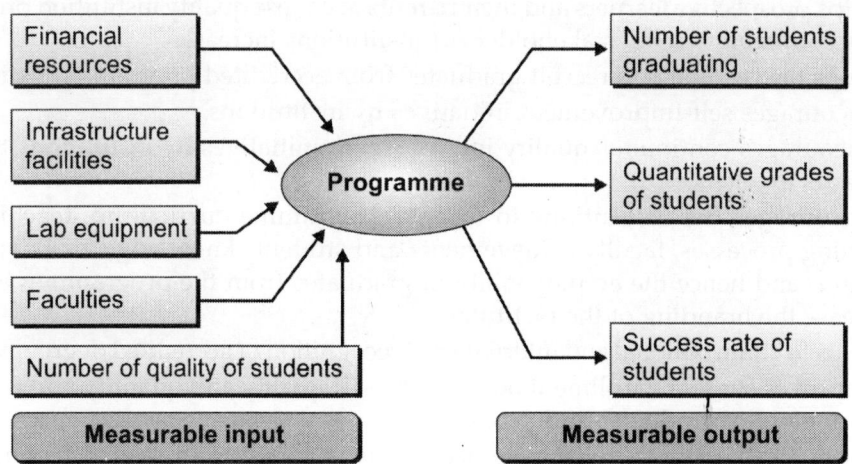

Fig. 11.3: Attributes of traditional input–output-based education system

allows continuous improvement in curricula and incorporation of better educational resources (maybe open) to ensure effective teaching for producing industry-ready professionals as the outcome. It promotes ICT-based pedagogy for improved collaboration and interactions between students, faculty, and peers through the discussion forum, quizzes and surveys. The main focus here is to strive for continuous quality improvement through different pedagogic tools and customizable rubrics for student's evaluation and implementation of corrective measures. The continuous student's progress tracking through data visualizations using powerful reporting tools are compulsory in OBE. It also advocates formative and summative student's evaluation system through examination to reinforce teaching–learning process. It also incorporates attributes for ensuring the lifelong learning of a student undergoing through these ideal OBE.

How is OBE Different from Other Learning Models?

OBE is student-focused educational system with clearly defined criteria for measurements and achievements of student's competencies and system improvements. Learner's support is provided at every stage through the adoption of different mechanisms for personalization and adaptive learning. Learners are provided adequate time to achieve mastery of some skills in this system. The use of disruptive technologies may lead to malfunctioning of OBE, otherwise, it has the potential to revolutionize the education system with appropriate use of ICT and other learning technologies.

11.2 ACCREDITATION AND ITS USEFULNESS

Accreditation is an assessment process of the performance of the programme/institution that assures programme/institution meets established quality standards. Accreditation of educational institutions/programmes is a global practice and its need has been felt by various developing and developed countries for one or more of the following purposes.

- Accreditation gives the institution a structured mechanism to assess, evaluate and improve the quality of their program, i.e. quality assurance of educational programmes.
- It helps prospective learners and their parents to choose quality institution programs, i.e. accountability to all stakeholders of institutions increases.
- It helps the recruiters to recruit graduates from accredited program or institutions.
- It encourages self-improvement initiatives by institutions.
- It encourages continuous quality improvement initiatives by institutions to move towards excellence.
- It encourages the institutions to update programme curriculum, teaching and learning processes, faculty achievements and students knowledge/skill/attitude/abilities and hence the employability of graduates from the programmes and will increase the branding of the institutes.
- It helps to attain national and international recognition of accredited degree awarded.
- It improves student enrollment both in terms of quality and quantity and facilitates the mobility of graduates and professionals.
- It motivates faculty to participate actively in academic and related institutional/departmental activities.

- It facilitates capturing grants from government and non-government regulatory bodies or agencies.
- It helps to create sound and challenging academic environment in the institution and contributes to the social and economic development of the country by producing high-quality technical manpower.

Various Accreditation Bodies in India

Accreditation of programs/institutions is basically done by the following organizations/bodies in India.
- Accreditation Board for Engineering and Technology (ABET)
- National Board of Accreditation (NBA funded by AICTE)
- National Assessment and Accreditation Council (NAAC funded by UGC)

Accreditation Board for Engineering and Technology (ABET)

ABET accreditation is a form of quality assurance, not a ranking system, declaring to the relevant professional community and to the world at large that a program meets the quality standards set by the technical profession. It is applied to programs only, not degrees, colleges, institutions or individuals.

ABET was found in 1932 as the Engineers' Council for Professional Development (ECPD) dedicated to the education, accreditation, regulation and professional development of the engineering professionals and students in the united states. The headquarter was at Engineering Society Building in New York City and it was reallocated to Baltimore in 1996. The organization was founded by seven engineering societies. The first degree program was evaluated by ECPD in 1936 and ten years later by 1947, 580 undergraduate programs at 133 institutions were accredited by ECPD. In 1980, ECPD has renamed the Accreditation Board for Engineering and Technology (ABET). In 1989, ABET has established international accreditation boards and became a founding member of the multinational Washington Accord. Since 1997, ABET has been recognized by the Council for Higher Education Accreditation (CHEA) in the USA. In 1997, ABET adopted Engineering Criteria 2000 (EC2000), considered at the time of a revolutionary approach to accreditation criteria. EC2000 focused on learner-centric approach. Different international accords for educational standardization and quality improvements are given below.

- The **Washington Accord** was first signed in 1989. It recognizes substantial equivalence in the accreditation of qualifications in professional engineering, normally for 4 years of duration.
- The **Sydney Accord** signed in 2001 and recognizes substantial equivalence in the accreditation of qualifications in engineering technology normally of 3 years of duration.
- The **Dublin Accord** is an agreement for substantial equivalence in the accreditation of tertiary qualifications in technician engineering, normally of 2 years duration and it commenced in 2002.

National Board of Accreditation (NBA Funded by AICTE)

NBA is an autonomous body with effect from January 2010. The NBA became a provisional member of the Washington Accord (WA) in 2007. NBA established by the

Ministry of Human Resource and Development (MHRD) under the aegis of All India Council of Technical Education (AICTE). The objective of the NBA is for external review of the overall quality of academic programmes and institutions.

NBA covers the following courses in the area of engineering, technology, management, architecture, pharmacy, hotel management and catering technology, applied arts and crafts. Courses under accreditation by NBA were PG courses, UG courses, and diploma courses primarily. It is a program-based accreditation. Presently, the revised accreditation programs are:
- Diploma engineering programs
- UG engineering programs
- PG engineering programs
- MCA programs
- UG pharmacy programs
- Management/MBA programs

NBA accreditation is valid for 3 years or 6 years for a programme. The norms and regulations for the accreditation changes from time to time and updated in their website.

National Assessment and Accreditation Council (NAAC Funded by UGC)

NAAC was set-up in 1994 with the recommendation of National Policy of Education (1986) as an autonomous organization funded by the University Grants Commission (UGC) with its Headquarter in Bengaluru. The purpose of the NAAC is for external review of the overall quality of academic programmes offered by higher education institutions (HEIs). NAAC is an institutional accreditation to assess overall institutional quality. NAAC grades institutes in a four-point scale on an eight-grade ladder (Table 11.1).

Table 11.1: NAAC eight grade letters

Range of institutional CGPA	Letter grade	Performance descriptor
3.51–4.00	A++	Accredited
3.26–3.50	A+	Accredited
3.01–3.25	A	Accredited
2.76–3.00	B++	Accredited
2.51–2.75	B+	Accredited
2.01–2.50	B	Accredited
1.51–2.00	C	Accredited
≤1.50	D	Not accredited

The accreditation for an institution is valid for 5 years during which a compliance report has to be sent to NAAC each year.

11.3 PARAMETERS OF OBE AND ATTAINMENTS

OBE starts with a clear statement on what knowledge, skills and attitudes, and abilities the learner will be able to demonstrate as having acquired on successful completion of a program of study. These should be clearly measurable. These are stated as program outcomes (POs) and course outcomes (COs) and are related to the vision, mission and programme educational objectives (PEOs) statements. The next step of OBE is designing an appropriate outcome-based curriculum. A carefully planned teaching–learning process has to be put in place next. Suitable assessment methods and tools are to be used at appropriate times involving the concerned stakeholders to monitor and improve teaching–learning on a continuous basis (Figs 11.4 and 11.5).

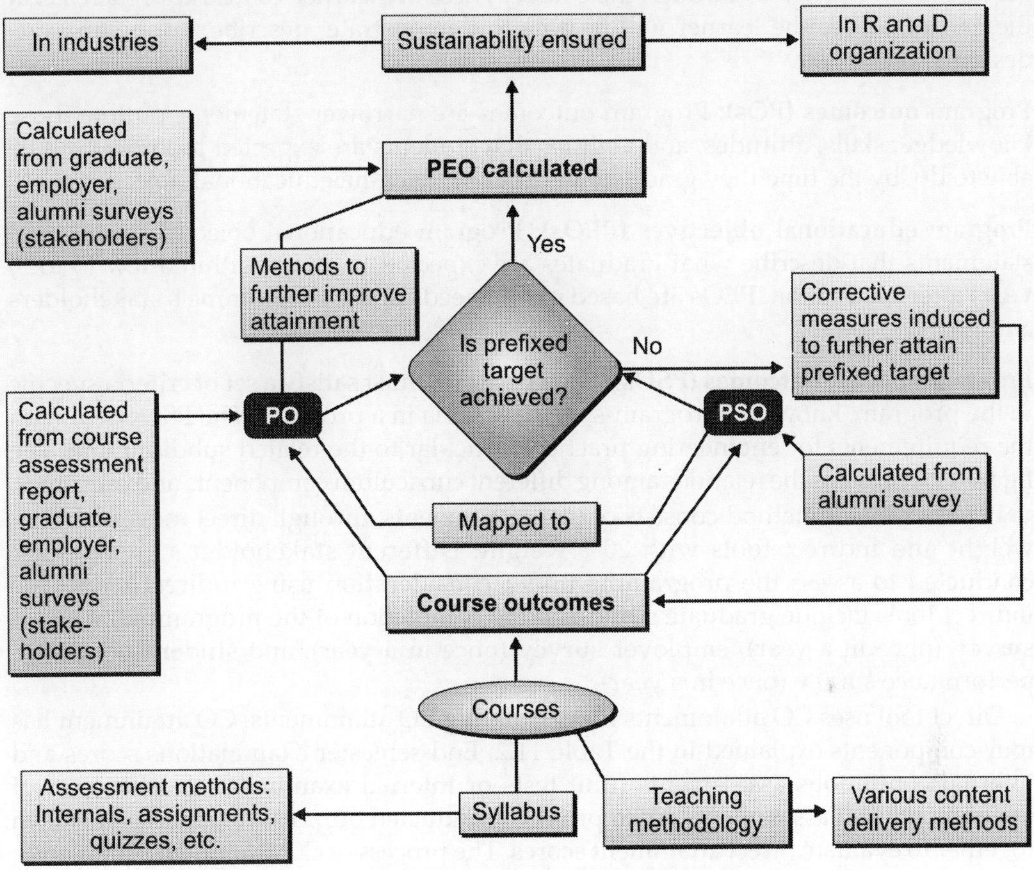

Fig. 11.4: Relations among different curriculum components and outcomes

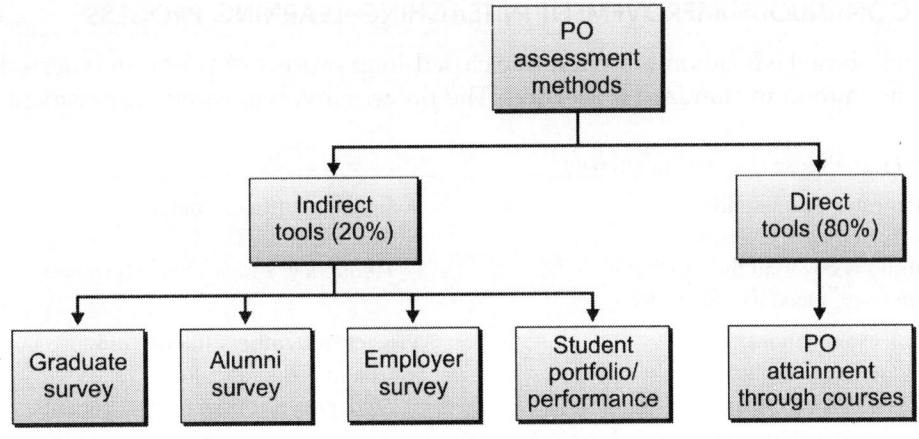

Fig. 11.5: PO assessment tools

COs, POs, PSOs, PEOs and their Correlations

Course outcomes (COs): Course outcomes are narrower statements that describe what students are expected to know and be able to do at the time of completion of the course. These relate to the skills, knowledge, attitude, and abilities that the learners acquire as they progress through the course. These are learner-centric approach, i.e. at the end of course the learner will be able to demonstrate, describe, apply, analyze, design, develop, etc.

Program outcomes (POs): Program outcomes are narrower statements outline those knowledge, skills, attitudes, and abilities that students are expected to know, and be able to do, by the time they graduate in order to meet the educational objectives.

Program educational objectives (PEOs): Program educational objectives are broad statements that describe what graduates are expected to attain within a few (3 to 5) years after graduation. PEOs are based on the needs of the programme's stakeholders and goals.

Program-specific outcomes (PSOs): Each program must satisfy a set of criteria specific to the program, known as program-specific criteria in a program. The PSOs deal with the requirements for engineering practice particular to the related subdiscipline. The figure 11.4 presents the relations among different curriculum components and outcomes.

PO assessment method consists of two components, through direct tools with 80% weight and indirect tools with 20% weight. Different stakeholder's surveys are conducted to assess the programme under consideration using indirect tools. The indirect tools include graduate survey (at the completion of the programme), alumni survey (once in a year), employer survey (once in a year), and student portfolio/performance survey (once in a year).

Direct tool uses CO attainments for calculating PO attainments. CO attainment has four components explained in the Table 11.2. End-semester examinations scores and internal continuous assessments (unit tests or internal examination, assessment of assignments and assessments given projects, conducted quizzes, etc.) marks are taken together to evaluate direct attainment scores. The process of CO attainment calculation is explained in the Fig. 11.6.

11.4 CONTINUOUS IMPROVEMENT IN TEACHING–LEARNING PROCESS

Outcome-based education is an iterative closed-loop process. A program is accredited once the minimum standard is reached. The process involves careful assessment and

Table 11.2: Course outcome attainment

End-semester examination:	Assignments (theory only):
• Conducted by University	• Conducted by faculty
• Questions cover all the COs	*Frequency*: At least twice a semester
Frequency: Once in a Semester	
Internal examinations:	**Project/quiz/others (theory only):**
• Conducted by Institute/Faculty	• Conducted by faculty
• Questions are CO based	*Frequency*: At least twice a semester
Frequency: Twice a semester	

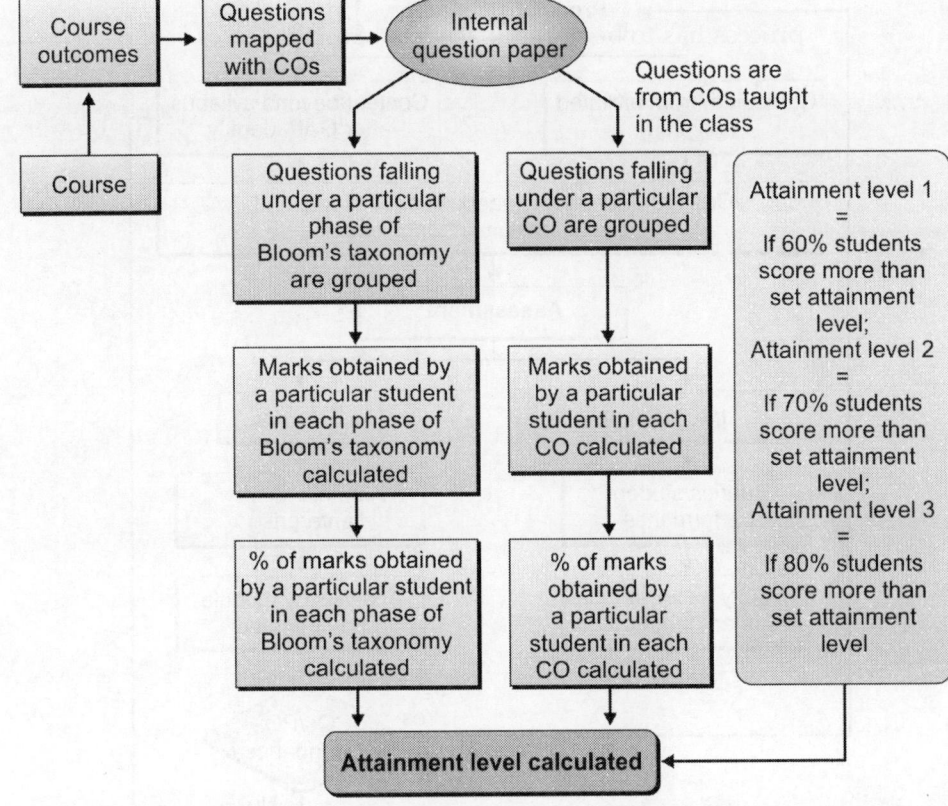

Fig. 11.6: Process of calculating CO attainments

evaluation of all major components and recording the results systematically. Appropriate changes are required to be introduced to improve the system. The changes are needed to be focused on continuous improvement in teaching–learning process. The figure 11.7 presents the iterative closed-loop process of continuous improvements in the teaching–learning processes.

11.5 CURRICULUM AND TEACHING–LEARNING IN OBE

Curriculum design is focused on outcomes in OBE. First course outcomes (COs, normally 4–6 in number) of each course (included in the curriculum) are to be designed keeping in mind the POs and PSOs. Maximum correlations are required to be matched with COs and POs as well as COs and PSOs as best as possible considering the present infrastructure for reaching better attainments from these courses. Based on COs, prerequisites have to be analysed before setting the course objectives. Thus, topics and subtopics are to be decided based COs, prerequisites, course objectives besides taking into consideration authentic assessment methods. Topics or subtopics which cannot be assessed with respect to outcomes should be given less importance in the curriculum. The set topics will be delivered through the different pedagogic components such as lectures, lectures with discussion (flipped class), interactive, presentations, project, handouts, e-resources (OER), group tasks, and tutorials. These components need to be mentioned in the lesson plan.

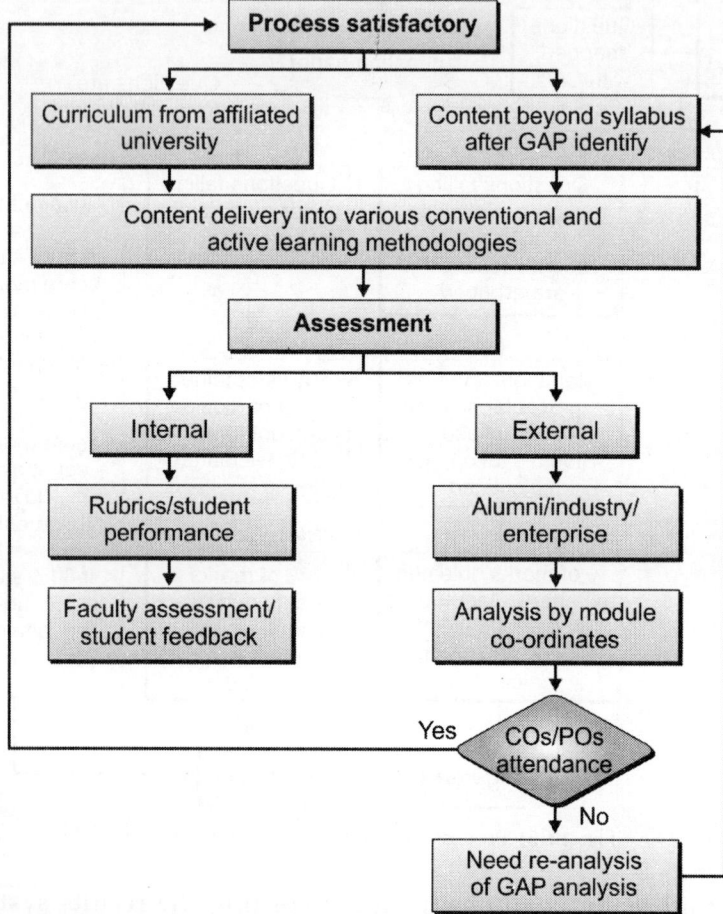

Fig. 11.7: Flow diagram for continuous improvement in teaching–learning

Delivery of Syllabus Contents and Compliance of the Curriculum for the Attainment of POs

Each faculty determines the level of their courses studying the elements of POs. Further, the revised Bloom's taxonomy is a tool that can be adopted to determine the level of expected attainment. According to that taxonomy courses may be divided into three levels.

- The introductory courses are termed as level I covering Bloom's levels 1 and 2, where students are exposed to the topics.
- The competency courses are termed as level II covering Blooms levels 3 and 4, where students gain competency in the topic.
- The expertization courses are termed as level III covering Bloom's levels 5 and 6, where students gained mastery in the topic.

Curriculum Gap Identification Process

Three courses of action are taken to identify curricular gap:
- Through CO/PO attainment

- Through syllabus comparison of reputed academic institutes
- Through Stakeholders' feedback

The COs and POs (CO–PO) mappings are to be designed first. The weak areas are to be pointed out and probable gaps are to be identified. The designed CO–PO mapping table is to be reviewed by the concerned faculty member (or team of faculty members) to determine which components of PO are either not met or met to level I only. If the faculty members feel that the above design is not adequate and institute need to develop more beyond syllabus topics, then additional electives, laboratory experiments, etc. may be introduced to improve the level. Feedbacks from industry, training placement department, alumni, and other stakeholders may be consulted for developing content beyond the syllabus. Other parallel university syllabus may be taken as input in this process. Ultimate all such curriculum-related inputs are to be placed before the academic committee or board of studies and topic/content beyond syllabus are to be determined and finalized to bridge the curriculum gaps. The process is diagrammatically represented below in two figures (Figs 11.8 and 11.9).

Implementation Process and Effectiveness Analysis

Identified contents beyond the syllabus in both theory and practical are to be included in lesson plan and covered in the classroom by the subject teacher. If internal resource person is not available, external expert from academia and industry should be hired to cover those topics. Effectiveness of this process should be analyzed through feedbacks from the students and their performance in examinations, from the alumni, from industries and other stakeholder. It is a continuous improvement process which requires more and more fine tuning through regular feedbacks from students and other stakeholders.

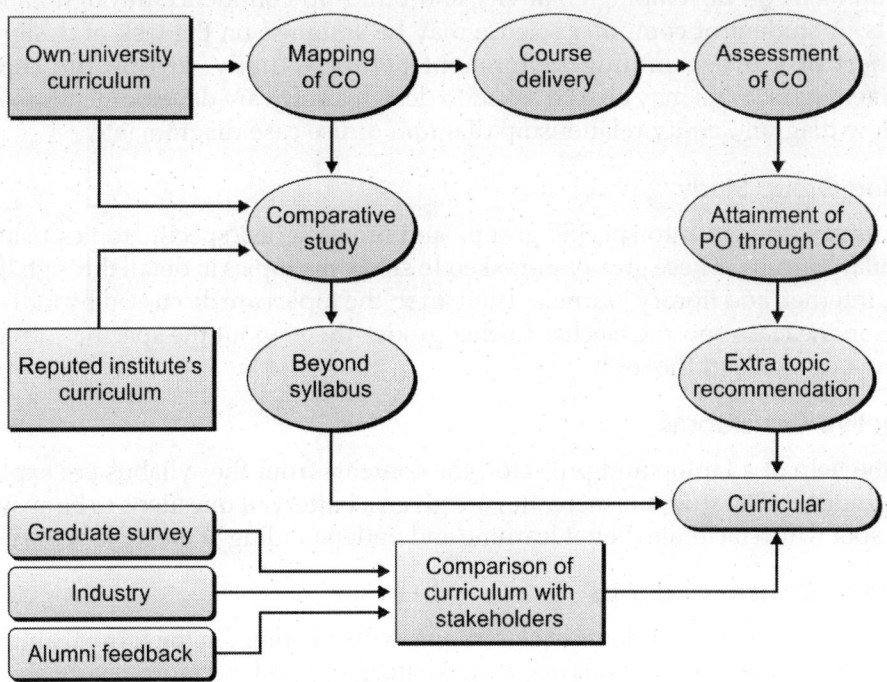

Fig. 11.8: The analysis process of curriculum gap identification

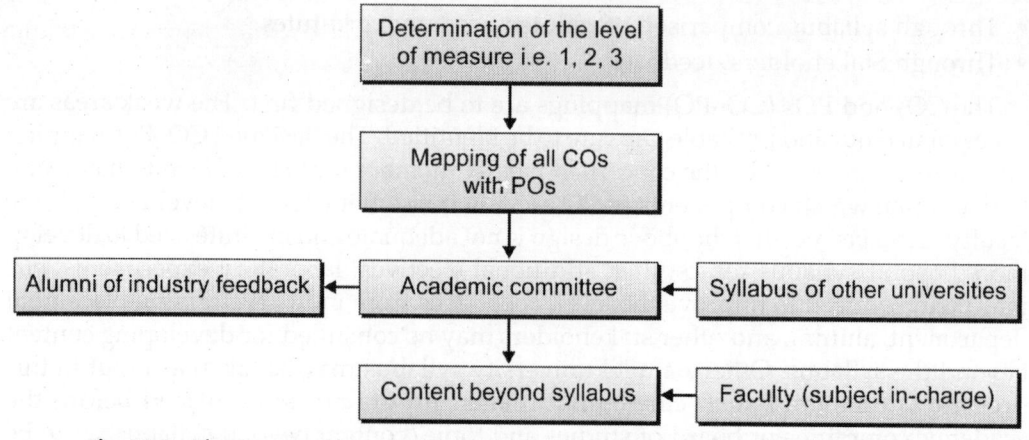

Fig. 11.9: The process of curriculum gap identification through academic committee

11.6 PROCESSES FOLLOWED TO IMPROVE QUALITY OF TEACHING–LEARNING

According to the present scenario of the teaching–learning process, modern techniques have to be adopted in every institution for the upliftment of the students and for the achievement of POs, PSOs, PEOs and ultimately mission and vision as described in a different chapter of this book. Some of the relevant points are given below for a quick review from OBE perspectives.

Design Thinking to Optimize Student Learning

Students are assigned to design a project and asked to make their plan of work so that they can focus on developing creativity and build-up confidence through hands-on projects. A student of computer science may be assigned on the task of designing a flowchart of a programming assignment before actually writing the code for implementation. S/he may also be asked to design a software development project by data flow diagram, entity relationship diagram or use case diagram, etc.

Focused Group Study

Students are divided into specific groups and are assigned specific topics related to curricular learning. These groups are asked to study the topics in detail through library books, internet, and library journals. Thereafter, the topics are discussed by individual groups in the class and the teacher further guides them about the specific corrections and enhancements of the topic.

Interactive Classrooms

With the help of a laptop and projector, the contents from the syllabus are explained to the students. The students thereafter are given a battery of questions to be answered on the spot which facilitates better learning and understanding of the topic being taught.

Simulation Classes and Labs

Topics are explained to students in classrooms with e-content in the form of animation and working pictures from YouTube to make them understand more clearly about the concepts and mechanisms and their application in real life.

ICT Usage

Students are provided with knowledge and proficiency in the usage of a simulation software like MATLAB, SCILAB, SPSS and subject-specific design software like AUTOCAD for civil engineering. This software are available online and students can use it for various analysis purposes. Special training should be provided to the students in the lab on a regular basis.

Problem-based Student-directed Learning

Attempts are made to create excitement in the classroom through posing problems related to the topic and finding solutions thereby presenting and learning the topic, which ensures students do more than listening through the active participation.

Flipped Classroom

The teachers put the material on a specific topic online on WhatsApp study groups for students to go through the material in advance, bring questions and queries about the topic and build additional knowledge on the subject during the class. This provides the opportunity for learning beyond syllabus also.

Away from Rote Learning (Memorization by Repetition)

Emphasis is given on logical learning wherein real life examples related to application, analysis, synthesis and evaluation/creation is given to the students so that their learning is formed permanently instead of mugging up.

Develop Lifelong Learning Attitude

Focus is given on developing abilities/skills which are central to the discipline and help to prepare the student on what is important to the discipline which develops lifelong learning skills. This ability developed by giving specific assignments that help students learn/unlearn/relearn and adapt new technology/knowledge as the field evolves.

Web-based Learning

The internet is an open information system from where the students can obtain various kinds of information, media and materials as texts, images, video sequences that can help them in a diverse way for generating self-learning environments. Due to its interactivity, learners can gather information which is important in learning and helpful in accomplishing their learning objectives. Hence, the potential of the internet self-learning mode is considered to be very high and therefore, the institute has to provide internet facility in both the academic and hostel campuses 24×7 mode. These will allow students to learn and to gather information from a worldwide network without any interruption.

Presentations

Every course allows students to prepare and present any topic from the curriculum and also on any non-technical topics. The teacher will guide during the presentation by suggesting corrections and scope for improvements.

Soft Skill Classes for Personality Development

Understanding the need for one's personality enables an individual to act more genuinely and effectively in a team environment. Students are encouraged to deliver presentations in the class which helps them to develop the ability to gather information, make decisions and interact with others. Soft skills classes empower students with confidence, boldness, expressiveness, etc. Also, the students' personality is developed as a whole.

Pedagogical Initiatives

Following are some pedagogical initiatives taken by the department in addition to chalk and talk lectures, assignments, PowerPoint presentation, and tutorials.
- Seminars/presentations.
- Lab experiments beyond the syllabus
- Group discussions
- Working model/visual charts/videos
- An analogy with live examples from industries and surroundings
- Lecture interspersed with discussions among students
- E-tutorial
- Group assignments and projects with defined individual roles
- Quizzes (conventional/technical)
- Designing and problem solving through simulation.

Apart from the methods listed above, while developing and delivering the course/lecture, the teacher should take into account other pedagogic aspects, especially Bloom's taxonomy for the development of intellectual skills.

Quality of Laboratory Experiments

All laboratories are to be equipped with relevant equipment with standard operating procedures. Students have to conduct experiments in a group of 2–3 candidates. Each student has to prepare a lab record which is assessed by the teacher using the laboratory rubrics immediately after the completion of the experiment or before the commencement of the next practical. The practical record indicates the collection of data and analysis along with the conclusion. The students have to submit the developed product(s) wherever applicable.

Weak and Bright Student Identification

Weak and bright students are to be identified by the teachers through classroom interactions, practical viva, group discussions, assignments, quizzes, sessional exams, etc. Moreover, each faculty (mentor) is assigned the responsibility of 10–15 students for guidance through all academic, career related, extracurricular and cocurricular activities during the full course of study. The mentor identifies the advanced learners and slow learners of his/her group.

The above pedagogic strategies definitely have the potential to enhance the learning outcomes. Since many of them are associated with digital pedagogy and ICT, we advocate the full use of the same for increasing different outcome attainments for the benefit of all stakeholders of education. Modern education systems are moving towards getting the full benefits of OBE and these are rationally possible with a real implementation of digital pedagogy with ICT.

11.7 PEDAGOGY OF FACULTY DEVELOPMENT PROGRAMMES (FDPS)

The proper implementation of OBE is very much dependent on the faculty competencies. The outcomes can be improved if the institution has well trained faculty members. Thus OBE audit system has components incorporating faculty training (commonly known as FDP) initiatives by the institutes. The aim of the FDP is to provide an opportunity to acquire knowledge and other competencies by the faculty members on contemporary developments that are taking place in various areas of their interest and in line with curriculum changes. These programmes normally help participants to upgrade their domain knowledge as well as on the latest pedagogical practices to achieve sustainable growth in their educational environments. Usually, two types of FDP are conducted, orientation courses and refresher courses. Orientation courses are focused on teaching skill development through the latest knowledge and awareness on pedagogical practices. A newly joined faculty should attend at least two orientation courses during first 5 years of their service and later on need basis. On the other hand, refresher courses are conducted to refresh the knowledge and skill on the latest development on their domain of subject teaching. A faculty member should attend the refresher courses normally but at least once in a 3 years duration. A training need analysis task must be conducted by the institution to arrange FDPs required for their faculty members. The need analysis must incorporate feedback analysis reports of different stakeholder's survey. Because faculty teaching development efforts are contextual, there is no best, one-size-fits-all model; all have their advantages and disadvantages. The following are the key issues to be planned beforehand by the resource person of the FDP.

- Syllabus/course design
- Writing objectives
- Constructing assessments
- Rubrics design
- Grading strategies
- Student motivation
- Learning disabilities
- Classroom management
- Active learning
- Presentation and communication skills
- Self reflection
- Searching and evaluating evidence.

The latest practices of digital pedagogy should be adhered to promote teacher's learning more effective. Since faculty members are adults and advanced learner, self-learning and activity-based learning will be enjoyable for them. Which teaching style and learning style will fit into the specific FDP, will depend on the trainer, the trainee and the subject area. It has been observed that the hybrid pedagogical model often is found suitable in these situations.

11.8 ROLE OF ICT ON OBE

If ICT is incorporated for OBE implementation, it will enlighten all the facets of the teaching–learning process. ICT focuses on learner's capability enhancement, as desired in the OBE philosophy, by rejuvenating their thinking power. Effective use of ICT will

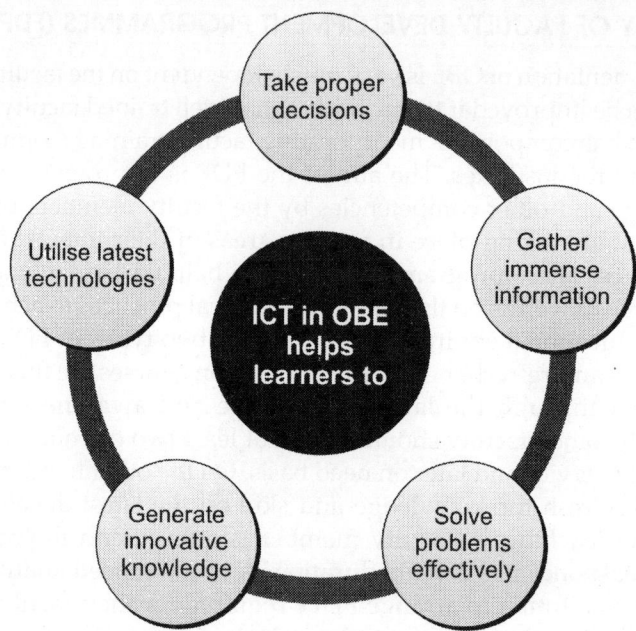

Fig. 11.10: How ICT helps learners in OBE

help students to be self-learner and constructive. It will definitely bridge the communication gaps often occur due to limited resources. The students will have increased access to the latest development in the field and make them productive to real-life activities which are supposed to be the ultimate outcome of their study. Having access to international instructors and world-class materials (knowledge too), they will be in a position to emerge greater outcomes in their future professional life and higher studies. The openness of ICT will teach them better life skills and contribute to society as demanded in OBE. ICT, as a modern tool, will provide learners the experience of conducting experiments and practical works in a simulated environment at less cost and time. Such experience will help them survive in complex real world situations. The knowledge and skill they acquired through ICT usage, will build their career for lifelong sustainability. Managing time and presenting precise queries are two of the characteristics which can be enhanced while associating with the course mentors through this ICT system. When students enroll for courses and learn together in a team, they understand the proper distribution of resources, acknowledge and respect an innovative idea of team members, help them by giving proper advice and collectively solve the issues raised by them. The true spirit of this type of education emphasizes on the performance, acquiring data, managing time, sharing information, deciphering problems efficiently and taking combined decisions yet retaining ethical values. Thus the roles of ICT in OBE are enormous as demonstrated above and maybe justified through programme outcomes definitions. Some of the important roles are demonstrated in the figure 11.10 for remembering.

EXECUTIVE SUMMARY

- OBE is a learner centric approach that focuses on student's long-term performances, known as outcomes. OBE is governed by different outcomes of educational

programmes like POs, PSOs, COs besides PEOs and mission-vision, all of which are measurable through direct and indirect tools.
- OBE provides continuous students tracking and improvements which are the key concepts that have revolutionized the traditional input–output based system.
- Accreditation is a global practice to assess the performance of the educational programme/institute with respect to set quality criteria and standards based on OBE nowadays all over the world.
- National and international accreditation bodies are set-up to fix the quality standard of educational programmes/institutions and institutions should approach towards accreditation for ensuring quality certificates regarding their processes and outcomes.
- Accreditation criteria and OBE both put emphasis on teaching–learning process and its continuous improvements realized through different attainments along with identifying and bridging the curriculum gaps.
- There have been a number of processes to improve quality of teaching–learning process and most of which are based on digital pedagogy and ICT.
- FDP plays very crucial role in OBE implementation and increasing outcomes of the teaching–learning processes. Pedagogic considerations for FDP are heterogeneous and need practicing hybrid pedagogic model depending on the trainer and trainee.
- ICT integration in teaching–learning processes greatly influences learning outcomes. Appropriately designed digital pedagogy using ICT tools and practices definitely increases the effectiveness of OBE.

Review Questions

1. What are the differences between output and outcome? Explain the differences between input–out-based education and outcome-based education. Write down the advantages and disadvantages of input–output-based education system.
2. Define outcome-based education (OBE). Write down the important features of OBE. How OBE is different from other educational models?
3. What is accreditation? Discuss its usefulness with respect to quality improvement. Discuss various accreditation bodies in India.
4. Write down the different parameters of OBE. How are the attainments calculated in OBE system?
5. What are the differences between direct and indirect tools of attainment calculation? Give examples.
6. Write down the process of continuous improvements of teaching–learning in OBE.
7. Briefly describe the process of designing a course curriculum. Why is curriculum a most important component in teaching–learning process?
8. Describe the process of identifying and bridging curricular gaps in OBE.
9. What do you understand by soft skill? Why is it essential for a student undergoing a professional course?
10. Discuss the processes of improving quality of teaching–learning in OBE. How do digital pedagogy and ICT help towards these quality improvements?
11. Discuss the process of identifying weak and brighter students and corresponding actions to be taken.
12. What is the role of FDP in OBE? Write down the different pedagogic practices for FDP.
13. Discuss the role of ICT in OBE.

Chapter

12

Rubrics-based Students' Assessment Planning

Objectives of this chapter

- To introduce the concept, importance and types of students' assessment.
- To discuss the significance of examination systems reforms in higher education with respect to introduction of OBE.
- To explain the concept of rubrics-based students' assessment system.
- To present the indicative rubrics for continuous assessment, assignment works, practical works, seminar presentation, mini project, major project works and viva-voce examinations.
- To explain the use of ICT for students' assessment.

Expected outcomes of this chapter

After going through this chapter learners will be able to:
- Understand the significance of different students' assessment schemes and their validity.
- Aware of examination system reforms in higher education in India with respect to introduction of OBE.
- Understand the importance of performance indicators and performance descriptors of various rubrics for assessment of different pedagogic activities.
- Apply well designed rubrics for students' assessments and performance analysis of various pedagogic activities like continuous assessment, assignment works, practical works, seminar presentation, mini project, major project works and viva-voce examinations.
- Find and use ICT tools for students' assessments and analysis assessment data.

12.1 STUDENTS' ASSESSMENT

Students' assessment or evaluation is one of the most important academic processes to be designed by curriculum planners and must be accomplished during curriculum execution. Assessment can also be on a learning community (class, workshop, or other organized groups of learners), a course, an academic program, the institution, or the educational system as a whole but we will concentrate on learner's assessment in this chapter. It is a systematic process of measuring student's performances on and after various pedagogic activities through different tests and/or examinations. The objectives of various examinations and activities are different and presented here for comprehensive understanding. All the examinations are focused on the assessment of students' works towards achieving learning outcomes of that course of pedagogic activities. Learning outcomes varies with respect to course and programmes and set specifically for evaluation. Two generic methods of defining the said outcomes are based on fulfilling Bloom's (revised) taxonomy of educational objectives and competency development for the benefit of the profession, industry, society and humanity at large. OBE system dictates enforcing outcome focused examination and student evaluation must incorporate transparent and measurable performance indicators inclined to fulfill educational objectives (Bloom's), the achievement of course and programme outcomes, and developing competency factors (knowledge, skill, attitude and ability). This is possible through well designed rubrics of that specific assessment activity. The systematic collection, analysis and interpretation of the students' assessment data will determine how well the students learning matches expected outcomes through attainment calculation as well as these will indicate scope for improvements and corrective actions. Assessment practices also depend on practitioners and their beliefs and assumptions about the nature of the human mind, the origin of knowledge, and the process of learning. The various classes of assessment are discussed below.

Placement, Formative, Summative and Diagnostic Assessments

Assessment is often divided into diverse categories for the purpose of considering different objectives for assessment practices.

Placement Assessment

This is known as preassessment or initial assessment conducted before instruction or intervention for assessing readiness and place students into their initial classes (like average learners, advanced learners, etc.) according to their prior achievements and personal characteristics. The objective is to formulate an appropriate instructional sequence or strategy by the teachers. This establishes a baseline of individual student depending on which the growth can be measured.

Formative Assessment

Formative assessment, also known as 'educative assessment,' generally carried out throughout a course or project to assist learning. This might be conducted by a teacher, by peers, by himself or herself as a feedback (on progress) of his/her learning and usually not much used for grading purpose. It may be in the form of standardized tests, oral questions, quizzes or draft works. The object is to see if the learners understand the instruction before appearing in summative assessments.

Summative Assessment

It is conducted at the end of a course or project typically through assigning grades (e.g. pass/fail, 0–100) to students. This summarizes what the students have learned. It also decides whether the students' have achieved the learning outcomes. Students identify how well they have attained the outcomes too late for it to be of use.

Diagnostic Assessment

It deals with the whole difficulty that occurs during the learning process at the end of the course.

Objective and Subjective Assessments

Assessment can also be classified into objective and subjective evaluation. Objective assessment questions have a single correct answer. These include multiple-choice (MCQ), true/false, multiple-response and matching type questions. This is becoming popular with the expansion of ICT tools because computerized and online tests are under this category. Subjective assessment questions have more than one way of expressing the correct answer. Extended-response type questions and essay type questions are under the category of subjective assessment. It seems subjective assessments have a better scope of testing the achievement of the last four levels of Bloom's taxonomy (revised) than the objective assessment. But practically both have the potential to fulfill the desired achievement tests of all levels of the said taxonomy with proper planning.

Formal and Informal Assessments

The formal assessment generally involves a written document, such as a paper, quiz, or test. A numerical score or grade is awarded on a formal assessment. Informal assessment often conducted in a more casual way and may include observation, checklists, inventories, rubrics, rating scales, participation, performance and portfolio assessments, peer and self-evaluation, and discussion. It does not contribute much to the student's final grade.

Internal and External Assessments

Internal assessment is set and marked by the teacher from the institution itself. Students get scores or grades along with the feedbacks regarding their assessments. External assessment is set by the institutional management and the objective here is to assess students through marks and grades by non-biased personnel. The weightage of external assessment is normally less compared to internal assessment. Students are provided detailed feedbacks regarding their learning achievements and weaknesses so that the students themselves and the teachers' concern can plan for the future.

Validity

The validity of an assessment measures the fulfillment of its intended purposes. It is generally determined through examination of evidence in the following.
- *Content*: It measures the content of the test to fulfill the stated objectives.
- *Criterion*: It correlates scores to outside references like helping next level tasks to perform.
- *Construct*: It checks whether the assessment corresponds to other significant variables like speaking power with writing skills.

12.2 EXAMINATION SYSTEMS REFORMS IN HIGHER EDUCATION

Higher education in India has observed a paradigm shift through the implementation of choice-based credit system (CBCS) system where all summative assessments was required to be conducted semester-wise. Partial implementations of OBE are already in place especially in engineering and professional education. Now, it is on the verge of full implementation of OBE for student's assessment purposes in higher education. Examinations or assessments of students play a very important role in deciding the quality of education. They not only assesses student's achievement (and grades) but also measure whether the desired learning outcomes have been achieved. The achievements of objectives and program outcomes are crucial that need to be verified through accurate and reliable assessment methods. The academic quality of examinations (question papers) in the higher education system has been a matter of concern for a long time. The question papers that require simple memory recall only cannot ensure full proof learning. The examination system needs to be reformed to meet the challenges on an emerging higher education landscape. Several educational experiences and assessment opportunities are identified to overcome the said challenges.

Adaptation of OBE Framework

In OBE framework, the educational outcomes of a program are clearly and unambiguously specified. These determine the curriculum content and its organization, the teaching methods, teaching strategies and the assessment process.

Importance of Higher-order Abilities and Professional Skills

The assessment process must also test higher level skills, viz. ability to apply knowledge, solve complex problems, analyze, synthesize and design. Further, professional skills like the ability to communicate, work in teams, lifelong learning have become important elements for better employability. It is important that the examinations should give appropriate weightage to the assessment of these higher-level skills and professional competencies.

Assessment Strategy for OBE

In outcome-based education, a 'design down' process is employed which moves from POs to COs. Outcomes at each successive level need to be aligned with, and contribute to, the POs. For each PO we have to define competencies (i.e. different abilities implied by the PO statement) that would generally require different assessment measures. We can bring clarity to POs by a two-step process, (1) identify competencies to be attained, and (2) define performance indicators (PIs).

The method is demonstrated with an example of PO qualifying the design and development of solutions linked very much with higher order skills.

PO-X: Design/development of solutions—design solutions for complex engineering problems and design system components or processes that meet the specified needs with appropriate consideration for public health and safety, and cultural, societal, and environmental considerations.

- Competencies (C) of the PO-X are given below.

    C-X.1: Demonstrate an ability to define a complex open-ended problem in engineering terms.

    C-X.2: Demonstrate an ability to generate a diverse set of alternative design solutions.

    C-X.3: Demonstrate an ability to select the optimal design scheme for further development.

    C-X.4: Demonstrate an ability to advance an engineering design to defined end state.

- Performance indicators (PI) for competency C-X.2 of PO-X are given below.

    PI-X.2.1: Apply formal idea generation tools to develop multiple engineering design solutions.

PI-X.2.2: Build models, prototypes, algorithms to develop a diverse set of design solutions.
PI-X.2.3: Identify the functional and non-functional criteria for evaluation of alternative design solutions.

Once the above process is completed for the program, the assessment of COs for all the courses are designed by connecting assessment questions (used in various assessment tools) to the PIs in figure 12.1.

Improving Structure and Quality of Assessment

For improving the structure and quality of assessment, the following points need to be remembered.
- The design of question papers needs to go beyond a simple test of 'memory recall'. It should include the issues of testing higher order abilities and skills.
- A wide range of assessment methods like term papers, complex problem-solving assignments, lab projects, portfolios, etc. need to be employed to ensure assessment methods matching with learning outcomes.
- Assessment method to be adapted considering the alignment of assessment with learning outcome and achievement of Bloom's cognitive levels.

Assessing Higher-order Abilities and Professional Skills

The present education system focuses on teaching knowledge remembering and understanding hence the assessment is limited to those abilities. Participation in a set of classes is not sufficient to achieve professional outcomes. Rather, these outcomes are more often acquired or influenced through sources both in and outside the classrooms. Following are the few educational experiences that are recommended to teach and assess professional outcomes and higher order cognitive abilities.
- Course projects, open-ended experiments in labs, project-based learning modules.
- MOOCs, cocurricular experiences, mini/minor projects, major projects.
- Internship experiences, e-portfolios of student works.

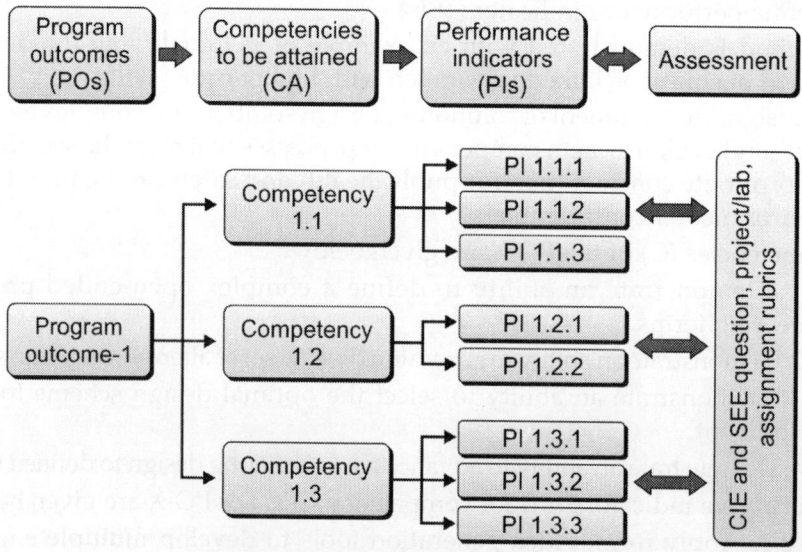

Fig. 12.1: Connecting POs to assessment

Open-book Examinations

The traditional written examination promotes the superficial application of knowledge in spite of encouraging active learning. Open book examination has the potential to uphold active learning. Students are allowed to consult class notes, textbooks, and other approved materials while answering questions. They are particularly useful for the students to self-test their skills in application, analysis and evaluation particularly achieving higher levels of Bloom's taxonomy. Here, there are fewer demands of memory recall and hence less stressful to students. Assessment questions in open book examination reflect real life situations that require comprehension, information retrieval and synthesizing skills of the students to solve problems. However, in a program, the curriculum areas that are best suited to an open book examination are to be carefully chosen. Following are some suggestions for setting open book examination.

- Set questions that require students to do things with the information available to them, rather than simply locating the correct information and then summarize or rewrite it.
- The questions in an open book exam must take advantage of the format, and give more weightage to the application of knowledge, critical thinking and use of resources for solving real complex professional problems.
- As the nature of questions is complex, it is to be ensured that the students get enough time compared to traditional examinations. It is advisable either to set less number of questions that encompass 2 or 3 concepts already taught and allocate longer duration of time for the examinations.

12.3 RUBRICS FOR ASSESSMENT

Bloom's revised taxonomy (of educational objectives) framework is a popular approach to plan and design student's assessment. While using this tool, we should consider the first three levels (remembering, understanding and applying) and to some extent the fourth level (analyzing) for continuous internal evaluation (CIE) and end-semester examinations (ESE). The last three criteria (analysis, evaluation and creation) can be assessed or in a variety of student works like minor/major projects, internship experience, extended course works and final year projects.

The following check list is to be confirmed to ensure OBE's success before moving on to designing evaluation rubrics.
- Alignment of assessment questions (internal and end-semester test papers) with COs.
- The entire COs are to be tested (sometimes some COs are over-emphasized at the expense of others).
- Each of Bloom's levels to be distributed to overall weightage in the assessment as discussed above.
- Assessment methods should adequately review the content and COs fitness.

A well-planned examination paper expected to include various difficulty levels to test the different capabilities of students. Bloom's framework helps the teachers to set test papers well balanced to test the different cognitive skills without an inclination towards a tough or easy paper perception. Cognitive levels in the test papers will vary from course to course as the nature of every course is different and thus the weightage will be different.

OBE always recommends all assessment methods should be measurable and transparent. Thus all students' assessment methods must have some criteria based on which the evaluation will take place. A rubric is a well accepted tool for teachers to set up grading of all students' activities and tasks (assignments, etc.). It defines what is expected from the student to get a particular quality grade on a specific task in a transparent written form. It also provides scoring guidance to evaluate the quality of students' responses fabricated by the said evaluative criteria.

There are three components within rubrics, namely
- Criteria
- Descriptors
- Scale

Scale (or Level of Performance)

It indicates the level of performance of a particular student. It is a rating scale that defines students' level of mastery within each criterion. The following Table 12.1 gives the scale in percentage form.

Descriptors

Descriptors are some characteristics associated with each dimension or performance indicators. We considered two classes of descriptors, one to qualify educational objectives defined by revised Bloom's taxonomy and the other is to qualify outcome proficiencies developments defined through competency parameters. According to revised Bloom's taxonomy, the levels in the cognitive domain are used as descriptors given in the following Table 12.2 and Table 12.3 provides the competency descriptors.

Table 12.1: Rubrics scale in percentage form

Quality scales	Performance levels				
	Very poor	Poor	Average	Good	Very good
Distribution of score in %	Up to 20%	Up to 40%	Up to 60%	Up to 80%	Up to 100%
Example: PI-Articulate Problem Statement and Identify Objectives	Problem statement and objectives are not identified	Problem statement and objectives are not clear	Problem statement is clear and objectives are not in line with problem statement	Problem statement is clear and objectives are not completely defined	Problem statement is clear and objectives are completely defined

Table 12.2: Bloom's descriptors with level of attainments

Level ID	Descriptors	Descriptions
B1	Remembering	Recalling from memory of previously learned material.
B2	Understanding	Explaining ideas or concepts.
B3	Applying	Using information in another familiar situation.
B4	Analyzing	Breaking information into part to explore understandings and relationships.
B5	Evaluating	Justifying a decision or course of action.
B6	Creating	Generating new ideas, products or new ways of viewing things.

Table 12.3: Competency descriptors with level of attainments

Level ID	Descriptors	Descriptions
C1	Knowledge	It is the theoretical or practical understanding of a subject.
C2	Skill	It is the ability to carry out a task with determined results within a given amount of time and energy.
C3	Attitude	It specifies what we actually tend to do.
C4	Ability	It is the inborn physical or mental power to do or accomplish something.

Criteria (or Performance Indicator)

Criteria are the performance indicator (PI) based on which the rubrics work. These are the characteristics of performance that will be assessed actually. The following section presents the performance indicators for the evaluation of different pedagogic activities of students, namely continuous comprehensive evaluation (CCE), assignments, laboratory works, seminar/presentation, mini project (project phase-I), major project (project phase-II) and viva-voce/interview. While evaluating the performance indicators of a specific activity, allocated full marks to be distributed among the performance indicators of that specific activity. The performance indicators required to be mapped to the said two descriptors (Bloom's descriptors and competency descriptors) to justify and rationality, usefulness and importance of the descriptors with respect to descriptors in the rubrics. Descriptor mapping and weightage distribution (in % form) are given below based on the literature review of present regulatory practices and authors' academic experiences. This may vary depending on the course, teaching environment, infrastructure and other pedagogic issues.

12.4 CONTINUOUS COMPREHENSIVE EVALUATION (PEACOCK CCE MODEL) RUBRICS

Right of Children to Free and Compulsory Education Act (2009) mandates the Indian States and Union Territories to implement Peacock CCE. It foresees all-round development of the student by allowing them to learn and progress in fear and anxiety free environment. Therefore, while excluding any external examination till elementary stage (Class I–VIII), it mandates using CCE as a school-based activity to ensure the right of each child to full time elementary education of satisfactory and reasonable quality. CCE enables students to perform according to the performance indicators given in Table 12.4 and teachers have to award score/marks according to the weights distributions (rubrics) given therein on individual daily class/activity basis.

Table 12.4: Peacock CCE model descriptors mapping and weightage distribution of PIs

PI ID	Performance indicators	Descriptors mapping		Weightage (%)
		Bloom	Competency	
PICCE-1	Participation	—	C3, C4	30
PICCE-1	Inquisitiveness	B1, B2	C3	30
PICCE-1	Analytical and application ability	B3, B4	C2, C4	20
PICCE-1	Teamwork	—	C3, C4	10
PICCE-1	Creativity	B6	C3, C4	10

12.5 ASSIGNMENTS RUBRICS

Spoon feeding practically ruins the learning capabilities of students and makes the education useless. Hence it is not recommended for a healthy education system. Educational institutes offer learning environments along with the teachers who clear the concepts and advice the students to learn on their own may be at home. These tasks to perform by the students themselves are called assignments. These often become displeasure for the learners who think studying in the classroom time is enough for them. The prime objective is to enhance the learning abilities of the learners. It is a proven fact that the more we use our brains, the more they develop. This is the theory behind giving extremely creative and involving assignments to the learners. Learners learn a lot more when they read and practice (both) something by themselves successively in an open book system. The practice also makes students ready for exams and similar unseen situations or problems. It also helps students to manage time and schedule by prioritizing the tasks at hand like a professional. Table 12.5 presents the PIs of the rubrics of submitted assignments for assessment by the evaluator or teacher along with its mapping with descriptors and weightage distribution.

Table 12.5: Assignments rubrics

PI ID	Performance indicators	Descriptors mapping		Weightage (%)
		Bloom	Competency	
PIA-1	Approach	B3	C2, C3	15
PIA-2	Explanation	B2	C1, C3	25
PIA-3	Completeness	B4, B5	C1, C4	25
PIA-4	Quality	B5, B6	C4	10
PIA-5	Organization and style	B3, B6	C2	10
PIA-6	Evidence	B5	C2	10
PIA-7	Timely submission	B5	C3, C4	5

12.6 LABORATORY/PRACTICAL WORKS RUBRICS

Experience of conducting hands-on laboratory experiments is highly essential for all programmes almost particularly for the courses prone to science and engineering disciplines. Beginning from kindergarten to research programmes all encompasses courses in the curriculum with hands-on experiments. These courses are considered under laboratory or practical works. These may be conducted under the roof in closed environments or in an open field environment. Students who engage in well-designed laboratory works develop critical-thinking skills and problem-solving abilities, as well as gain exposure to materials, reactions, and equipment in a laboratory setting. These skills development help students to find real life exposure essential for employment. The real laboratory works must be guided by educators adhere to safety and security principles. Web-based or computer-simulated activities may help students to enjoy the laboratory experiences with reduced costs, and eliminated hazardous waste and safety concerns. However, these tools cannot be considered as equivalent replacements for hands-on laboratory experiences. The society expects sustained investments to provide the facilities, curricula, equipment, and professional development needed for effective hands-on laboratory or practical works. Following Table 12.6 presents the

PIs of the rubrics of laboratory/practical works for assessment by the evaluator or teacher along with its mapping with descriptors and weightage distribution.

Table 12.6: Laboratory/practical works rubrics

PI ID	Performance indicators	Descriptors mapping		Weightage (%)
		Bloom	Competency	
PIL-1	**Continuous assessments**	—	—	40
PIL-1.1	Attendance (continuous)	—	C3, C4	5
PIL-1.2	Experimentation (continuous)	B3, B4	C2, C4	15
PIL-1.3	Documentation of lab works in lab copy (continuous)	B4, B5	C1, C2	15
PIL-1.4	Accuracy of the results (continuous)	B4, B5	C2, C4	5
PIL-2	**End-semester examination**	—	—	60
PIL-2.1	Experiment performance (examination)	B3, B4	C2, C4	20
PIL-2.2	Data tabulation in answer script (examination)	B4, B5	C1, C2	10
PIL-2.3	Accuracy, conclusion and interpretations (examination)	B4, B5	C1, C4	10
PIL-2.4	Experiment and course-related viva-voce (examination)	B1, B2	C3	20

12.7 SEMINAR/PRESENTATION RUBRICS

Every day starts with something new and everything is getting advanced in the field. Plenty of research and studies are conducted around the whole world on various subjects. These modernizations or modifications in different fields cannot be incorporated in the student curriculum every time. But the students have to always keep their minds on what new things are arriving day-by-day. Seminars are of great significance in those situations. By participating and presenting in seminars students will be keeping themselves updated with the research and development in their field of study. Seminars provide the latest information about the happenings in the fields along with the latest trends. So students must take part and prepare for the presentation of recently emerging topics in the field. Seminars also assist them to present their innovative ideas to their friends and teachers. They will initiate thinking about new things which they believe could be implemented practically. The teachers have the responsibility of making the students aware of the latest topics and remain present on the seminars not only to assess the students' performances but also rectify their mistakes before, during and after the presentation. The topic to be decided by the students after consultations with their mentors based on their strengths and weaknesses on subjective knowledge. This way, the interpretivism principle of pedagogy will come into practice. The student will also learn and practice how to be narrative, communicative, interactive, productive, adaptive and integrative useful in their later life. It will also encourage new principles of digital pedagogy (consumption to creation, correct to correcting and content to the conversation) through the appropriate use of ICT tools and resources. Table 12.7 presents the PIs of the rubrics of the seminar presentation for assessment by the evaluator or teacher along with its mapping with descriptors and weightage distribution. It is to be noted that the teachers can always present something as seminars to their students. Inviting eminent speakers and professionals who have achieved some feat in the field to take some seminars for the students greatly helps them interact with present and ongoing advancements in the fields. The educational institutions should take initiatives towards these practices. So the seminars have a very important role to play in the curriculum.

Table 12.7: Seminar/presentation rubrics

PI ID	Performance indicators	Descriptors mapping Bloom	Descriptors mapping Competency	Weightage (%)
PIS-1	**Content and document evaluation**	—	—	40
PIS-1.1	Introduction and objective	B1, B2	C1	7
PIS-1.2	Literature review	B1, B2, B4	C1, C4	8
PIS-1.3	Methodology/approach/technique	B3	C2	20
PIS-1.4	Conclusion	B4	C2, C4	3
PIS-1.5	References	B1	C1	2
PIS-2	**Presentation evaluation**	—	—	60
PIS-2.1	Time management	B4, B5	C2, C4	5
PIS-2.2	Presentation skill including multimedia and PowerPoint use	B3, B6	C2, C3	10
PIS-2.3	Adequacy in delivery	B1, B2	C1, C4	20
PIS-2.4	Understanding and explanation of the subject matter	B1, B2	C1, C4	20
PIS-2.5	Question and answering	B1, B5	C1, C3	10

Rubrics may also include the life skills like narrative, communicative, interactive, productive, adaptive, integrative, and ICT usage as PIs if the concern program of study deserve so as feel by the curriculum planners.

12.8 MINI PROJECT/PROJECT PHASE-I RUBRICS

A project is an activity to meet the creation of a unique product or service. Mini projects give students an edge over the race of recruitment to ensure a good career. Besides employments, students are progressively taking up mini projects to pad up their skill-set. They can showcase these mini projects during internship and placements opportunities appearing before final year major projects. Students acquire hands-on practical knowledge and skills through such projects. It can also be considered as a subsidiary of practical assignments to a course of study. Bloom's last four levels of cognitive abilities (applying, analyzing, evaluating and creating) can be developed through mini projects. It will enlighten the students about professional practices at micro level. Special emphasis is given to mini projects during internship works and value added domain knowledge training due to time constraints. It has been observed that mini projects increase productivity among students in many ways. It will also boost the major project at the final year by the gained experiences of identifying their problem area through literature reviews, articulation of their creative ideas through synopsis planning, defining their scope of the project, team building, identifying the solution domains and tools related to the problem areas, unique design approaches and convincing the board of examiners on the appropriateness of their objectives, approaches, etc. Mini projects will also build students profiles for higher educationals applications and writing a statement of purpose as well as justifying their attitude and potential for the higher study. Rubrics for mini project are given on Table 12.8.

Table 12.8: Mini project rubrics

PI ID	Performance indicators	Descriptors mapping		Weightage (%)
		Bloom	Competency	
PPI-A	**Internal assessment segmentation**	—	—	
PPI-A1	Project progress evaluation criteria	—	—	30
PPI-A1.1	Planning suited with the allocated time	B6	C2	6
PPI-A1.2	Faculty interaction	B2	C3	6
PPI-A1.3	Teamwork	—	C3, C4	6
PPI-A1.4	Technical approach	B3, B4, B5	C2, C4	6
PPI-A1.5	Achievement of objective	B5	C4	6
PPI-A2	Synopsis content evaluation criteria	—	—	30
PPI-A2.1	Abstract	B1, B2	C1	3
PPI-A2.2	Objective, scope, and problem statement	B1, B2, B5	C1	6
PPI-A2.3	Literature review	B1, B2, B4	C1, C4	6
PPI-A2.4	Methodology, approach, technique, software and hardware requirement, problem identification	B3, B4	C2, C4	10
PPI-A2.5	Conclusion	B4	C2, C4	3
PPI-A2.6	Reference	B1	C1	2
PPI-B	**External assessment segmentation**	—	—	40
PPI-B1	Synopsis demonstration evaluation criteria	—	—	20
PPI-B1.1	Synopsis planning	B6	C2	5
PPI-B1.2	Design and methodology	B3, B4	C2, C4	7
PPI-B1.3	Acceptability of the proposal	B5, B6	C1, C2	5
PPI-B1.4	Creativity and uniqueness	B6	C4	3
PPI-B2	Presentation evaluation criteria	—	—	20
PPI-B2.1	Time management and presentation skill	B3, B4	C2, C4	5
PPI-B2.2	Accuracy in delivered presentation	B4, B5	C2	5
PPI-B2.3	Understanding of subject matter	B2	C1	5
PPI-B2.4	Question and answering	B1, B5	C1, C3	5

12.9 MAJOR PROJECT/PROJECT PHASE-II RUBRICS

Quantity and quality of works to be performed in a major project are much higher than that of a mini project. The objective and importance of major projects remain in line with mini projects but with longer duration, enhanced creativity and contribution to the developments. The skills and abilities developed through the major projects are mapped to the solution building of real world problems under the field of study. These skills and abilities will help them to be productive during employments and serving the industry, society and nation. This is the place where students will apply the knowledge and understanding acquired during the whole period of study through different courses. The student will design, implement, evaluate their designs along with implementations and enhance their designs and implementations of the solution to the problem identified in the project phase I or mini project towards striving for more creativity. It is the part of the full programme that prospective employers will most likely ask at an interview as the student is supposed to developed skill and hand-on experience of work as a specialist in this domain. Hence, it will increase the productivity and employability of the students. The students will learn here how to work in a team in a productive way so that all of them together can contribute reasonably to the success of the project. Rubrics for major project are given in Table 12.9.

Table 12.9: Major project rubrics

PI ID	Performance indicators	Descriptors mapping		Weightage (%)
		Bloom	Competency	
PPII-A	**Internal assessment segmentation**	—	—	60
PPII-A1	**Project progress evaluation criteria**	—	—	30
PPII-A1.1	Project suited with course expectation	B4, B5	C4	4
PPII-A1.2	Project scope suited with problem statement	B2, B5	C1	5
PPII-A1.3	Objective of project scope suited with problem statement	B1, B2, B5	C1	5
PPII-A1.4	Faculty interaction and regularity	B2	C3	4
PPII-A1.5	Teamwork competency	—	C3, C4	4
PPII-A1.6	Suitable application of methodology, approach and technique	B3, B4	C2, C4	4
PPII-A1.7	Achievement of objective	B5	C4	4
PPII-A2	**Project content evaluation criteria**	—	—	30
PPII-A2.1	Abstract	B1, B2	C1	3
PPII-A2.2	Objective, scope, and problem statement	B1, B2, B5	C1	7
PPII-A2.3	Literature review	B1, B2, B4	C1, C4	5
PPII-A2.4	Methodology, approach, technique, software and hardware requirement, problem solution	B3, B4	C2, C4	10
PPII-A2.5	Conclusion	B4	C2, C4	3
PPII-A2.6	Reference	B1	C1	2
PPII-B	**External assessment segmentation**	—	—	40
PPII-B1	**Project demonstration evaluation criteria**	—	—	20
PPII-B1.1	Project planning suited with the allocated time	B6	C2	2
PPII-B1.2	Suitable design for methodology, formula and approach	B3, B4	C2, C4	5
PPII-B1.3	Acceptability of the system to address problem statement and project objective	B5, B6	C1, C2	5
PPII-B1.4	Error in system, approach or configuration	B4	C2, C4	4
PPII-B1.5	Creativity and uniqueness of project	B6	C4	4
PPII-B2	**Presentation evaluation criteria (20)**	—	—	
PPII-B2.1	Time management and presentation skill	B3, B4	C2, C4	5
PPII-B2.2	Accuracy in delivered presentation	B4, B5	C2	5
PPII-B2.3	Understanding of subject matter	B2	C1	5
PPII-B2.4	Question and answering	B1, B5	C1, C3	5

12.10 VIVA-VOCE/INTERVIEW RUBRICS

Viva-voce or interview is an oral test where the examiner asks questions to the student in spoken form. The student has to answer mostly in spoken form to demonstrate sufficient knowledge and understanding of the subject within a stipulated time. Though the knowledge and understanding are tested through written examination, still such type of questions are asked in the viva-voce examination. But the primary focus here is to test the attitude of the candidate for a particular purpose. There are two situations where viva-voce type tests are conducted. One is at the end of a course or programme and another is during the recruitment process for a job. The perspectives for these two situations are different but they are under a single thread. The course or programme-end-viva-voce test primarily focuses on the development of core competencies whereas recruitment interviews assess both core competencies and professionalism for the particular job. The Table 12.10 includes both the PIs for the viva-voce assessment rubrics given below.

Table 12.10: Viva-voce/interview descriptors mapping and weightage distribution of PI

PI ID	Performance indicators	Descriptors mapping		Weightage (%)
		Bloom	Competency	
PIVV-1	**Core competencies**			60
PIVV-1.1	Knowledge	B1	C1	15
PIVV-1.2	Technical skill (trade) and experience	B3, B4, B5	C2	10
PIVV-1.3	Attitude/positivity/motivation	—	C3	25
PIVV-1.4	Ability	—	C4	10
PIVV-2	**Professionalism/soft skills**			40
PIVV-2.1	Communication skill	B3, B4	C2	3
PIVV-2.2	Body language	—	C3	2
PIVV-2.3	Cooperation/teamwork	—	C3, C4	2
PIVV-2.4	Goal-oriented/ambition	—	C3, C4	2
PIVV-2.5	Flexibility/adaptability	—	C3	3
PIVV-2.6	Dependability	—	C3, C4	2
PIVV-2.7	Integrity/honesty/ethics	—	C3	2
PIVV-2.8	Creativity	B6	C4	2
PIVV-2.9	Organization and time-management	B3, B4	C2, C4	2
PIVV-2.10	Intelligence/critical thinking/problem solving	B4, B5, B6	C2, C4	2
PIVV-2.11	Confidence	—	C3	2
PIVV-2.12	Enthusiasm and passion	—	C3	2
PIVV-2.13	Responsiveness	B4	C3	3
PIVV-2.14	Personality	B4	C3	3
PIVV-2.15	Responsibility	—	C3	2
PIVV-2.16	Leadership	—	C3, C4	2
PIVV-2.17	Decisiveness	B5	C3	2
PIVV-2.18	Negotiation/conflict resolution	—	C3, C4	2

The above rubrics are based on the authors' experiences on OBE implementation and following regulatory guidelines. These are developed after brainstorming by the authors and with their colleagues following the said guidelines. The presented rubrics are indicative and may vary with respect to regulatory changes, institutional academic infrastructures, students' quality, stakeholder's demands and faculty interests. Concern board of studies (BOS) or academic council or any other body like IQAC (depending on the institutional management policy) will finalize and approve the rubrics after detailed skillful brainstorming among faculty members and experts.

12.11 USE OF ICT FOR STUDENTS' ASSESSMENTS

Pedagogy integrated with technology enhances the higher-order thinking skills of students such as analyzing, synthesizing, drawing inferences, predicting, comparing, evaluating, etc. The use of multiple teaching strategies demands multiple forms of assessment. In the present activity-based learning, ICT is used in the classroom not only for learning experiences but also for carrying out student assessment. ICT can be used also as an assessment tool for evaluating the achievements of learners and finding out their grades. There are various types of ICT-based assessment tools. They are classified as:

- Computer-assisted assessment or computer-aided assessment (CAA) and
- Computer-based assessment (CBA).

CAA refers to the use of computers to manage or support the assessment process and evaluate assignments. CAA is mostly used for scoring multiple-choice questions and questions with short-answer responses using optical mark reader (OMR). On the other hand, CBA means the use of digital tools for conducting the assessment-related activity. CBA can be implemented using laptops, tablets, and even smart phones. The most common ways of CBA are the following.

- *Assessment embedded within e-learning modules*: This type of online assessment is conducted through e-learning modules so that students' learning activities could be assessed on the module itself. A student will complete a full e-learning module with a final test at the end.
- *Standalone online assessments*: In this, an instructor uses an online assessment dashboard to develop quizzes and tests, which students take using as an online platform. Online or web-based assessments can also be used to engage students in the teaching-learning process and measure their continuous progress. For example, a teacher after completion of his/her teaching may conduct a short quiz that students take on their laptops, tablets, and even on smart phones.

Tools for Assessing Objective Items

Technology driven learning environment provokes educators to apply a computer in students' assessment. CBA may be treated here as the use of digital technology to collect, process, and report the results of the assessment. The four components of CBA may be categorized as (1) assessment generation, (2) assessment delivery, (3) assessment scoring and interpretation, and (4) storage, retrieval and transmission. E-assessment uses computer and information technology to make the assessment process more efficient automatically. Objective questions like multiple choice, fill in the blanks, multiple responses, text box and matrix can be developed online. The format of each objective type question is framed as follows:

- *Objective type questions*: There are various types of objective type questions such as multiple choice, fill in the blank, multiple responses and text box.

- *Text box*: Here, the text box with the answers is marked manually by the evaluator. Student responses are presented anonymously to the evaluator and there is an option for these responses to be marked second time by the evaluator. The system automatically highlights the discrepancies between the first and second marking. The final mark is then selected manually. This system has a similarity with reviewing in MS Word.
- *Quizzes*: There are various software that can be used to assess objective test items in the form of quizzes. Quizzes that are conducted at the end of the module (i.e. 'summative') are referred to as e-examinations and these are designed to help students check their understanding and identify areas to focus on (referred to as 'formative').

Online/Web-based Assessment in Subjective Tests

Technology has made it possible to conduct subjective tests online. The essay writings are generally evaluated through a subjective test. For assessing student answers through subjective tests, there are various online assessment tools such as question mark perception, e-rater, calibrand marker and intelligence essay assessor.

Other Assessment Supports

Apart from objective and subjective tests, user might be thinking about other uses of computer for assessment purposes. In addition to using electronic packages to create unique tests, it is possible to use the computer applications to generate different tests automatically. A question database (bank) may be created with questions taking from several institutional expert teachers in collaboration. Electronic selection of questions from the bank is one possibility for the electronic generation of tests and thus a huge number of different tests can be generated.

Technology also offers tools for assessment-related activities like recording, analysis, general storage and management of results. There are some software packages like spreadsheets (Excel, Lotus 1-2-3), statistical packages (SPSS, Minitab) and database packages (Access, Oracle, MySQL) where inclusion, maintenance and interpretation of students' assessment data can be conducted without much difficulty. There are varieties of diagnostic tools like DIAGNOSYS, THESYS which are used by teachers for student assessment and diagnosis (DIAGNOSYS is a knowledge-based package to investigate mathematics skills on entry to university and the diagnostic report can be made available for either the student or the teacher; THESYS is another diagnostic tool used as formative self-assessment tool for students preparing a project report). Video conferencing and email systems help students to reach their teachers and external evaluators through multimedia communication. The peer group formative evaluation is also conducted through the same channels.

A blog (website with reflective entries) allows individual students to keep a record of their learning progress. A teacher can follow each student's blog, adding supportive comments as appropriate. This can, of course, be done at any time, and at any place where there is access to the internet. A blog also offers interaction with reflective comments and interlinks-related ideas. Other members of the community can also comment on a blog entry to suggest additional considerations and explorations of the idea presented. Thus, it promotes further reflections and thoughts regarding a stated viewpoint. All these comments, reviews, responses, suggestions, reflections, reactions, thoughts, ideas, encouragements and viewpoints are pedagogically very sound and develop a student's portfolio for assessment by expert teachers.

EXECUTIVE SUMMARY

- Student's assessment is a systematic process of measuring student's performances on and after various pedagogic activities through different tests and/or examinations.
- There are various types of assessments such as placement, formative, summative and diagnostic; formal and informal; internal and external, but their validity depends on content, criterion and construct.
- Recent regulators of Indian higher education introduced examination system reforms towards proper implementation of OBE for educational quality improvements. Along with the traditional methods, such reforms initiated advocating for the use of digital online, self-learning, and open-book examination systems for developing higher order cognitive abilities of the students.
- OBE and examination system reforms both are enforcing the rubrics-based student's assessments to inculcate quality and transparency in the evaluation system.
- An assessment rubrics have three components, criteria (or performance indicators), descriptors usually taken from Bloom's cognitive levels and competency factors, and scale (or level of performance) usually classified into five classes namely very good (>80%), good (>60%), average (>40%), poor (>20%) and very poor (<20%).
- While planning the rubrics, the curriculum designers must distribute the total marks allocated for a specific activity into various appropriate PIs. This appropriateness will be reflected by its mapping with the performance descriptors.
- The assessment rubrics must be finalized and approved by appropriate body of the institutes before execution. The rubrics may vary with respect to regulatory requirements, institutional academic infrastructures, students' quality, stakeholder's demands and faculty interests.
- ICT-based tools have great potential to implement quality student-assessment strategies. Present-age students also feel comfortable in appearing tests through these tools. Automatic self evaluation using intelligently designed tools assists students to identify their learning gaps and tune their learning activities and thus ICT tools will definitely promote digital pedagogies.

Review Questions

1. Why students' assessment is an important academic activity? Write down the different traditional methods of students assessments.
2. Differentiate these: (a) Placement, formative, summative and diagnostic assessments; (b) objective and subjective assessments; (c) formal and informal assessments; (d) internal and external assessments.
3. What do you understand by the validity of a student assessment method?
4. Briefly illustrate the recent examination system reforms in Indian higher education. How could higher-order cognitive abilities be inculcated through such reforms?
5. What is relation between OBE and rubrics-based assessment system?
6. Discuss the necessity and importance of open-book students' assessments.

7. What do you understand by rubrics-based student evaluation? What are the different criteria that must be ensured before proceed to the designing assessment rubrics?
8. What are the different components of an assessment rubric? Discuss these components briefly with examples.
9. What are the differences between performance indicators and performance descriptors? Give examples.
10. Distinguish between scale of the rubrics and PI-weightage distribution. What is their relation?
11. Discuss briefly the assessment rubrics for (a) continuous comprehensive evaluation, (b) assignments, (c) practical works, (d) seminar presentation, (e) mini project work, (f) major project work, and (g) viva-voce or interview examination.
12. How to use ICT for students' assessments? How are web blogs used for students' assessments?

Bibliography

1. Abascal J, Civit A, and Nicolle C (2013). Universal accessibility and the digital divide. In the Proceedings of the 14th IFIP TC13 Conference on Human-Computer Interaction, INTERACT 2013 Workshop on Rethinking Universal Accessibility: A broader approach considering the digital gap.
2. Abbhilash M (2019). 4 things you need to know about Outcome-Based Education in India. https://www.myklassroom.com/blog/4-things-to-know-about-outcome-based-education/, 1st July.
3. Ackermann E (2001). Piaget's constructivism, Papert's constructionism: What's the difference. Future of Learning Group Publication, 5(3), 438.
4. Anderson L W and Krathwohl D R (2001). A Taxonomy for Learning, Teaching, and Assessing. Abridged Edition.
5. Anderson R E and Plomp T (2002). Proposal for IEA SITES module 3. Amsterdam: IEA.
6. Anonymous (2019). About SWAYAM, https://swayam.gov.in/about, SWAYAM.
7. Anonymous (2019). Digital Pedagogy, https://en.wikipedia.org/wiki/ Digital_pedagogy, Wikipedia, 24 May.
8. Anonymous (2019). Faculty Development Programme on Pedagogy, http://mtu.ac.in/faculty-development-programme-on-pedagogy/, 1st July.
9. Anonymous (2019). Faculty Development Programme on Pedagogy, http://stanley.edu.in/faculty-development-program/, 1st July.
10. Anonymous (2019). Flipped Classroom, https://facultyinnovate.utexas.edu/ flipped-classroom, The University of Texas at Austin.
11. Anonymous (2019). https://docs.moodle.org/37/en/About_Moodle, 15th July.
12. Anonymous (2019). https://www.instructure.com/canvas/?newhome = canvas, 16th July.
13. Anonymous (2019). Internet Access and Education: Key considerations for policy makers, https://www.internetsociety.org/resources/doc/2017/ internet-access-and-education/, 18th May.
14. Anonymous (2019). Internet of Things (IOT), https://internetofthingsagenda.techtarget.com/definition/Internet-of-Things-IoT, 17th May.
15. Anonymous (2019). Massive Open Online Courses, http://mooc.org/, edX.
16. Anonymous (2019). Massive Open Online Courses, https://en.wikipedia.org/ wiki/Massive_open_online_course, Wikipedia, 22 May.
17. Anonymous (2019). National Mission On Education Through Information And Communication Technology (ICT), https://www.aicte-india.org/ downloads/National%20Mission%20on%20education.pdf, 17th May.
18. Anonymous (2019). National Policy on Information and Communication Technology (ICT) In School Education, https://mhrd.gov.in/sites /upload_files/mhrd/files/upload_document/revised_policy%20document%20ofICT.pdf, 17th May.
19. Anonymous (2019). Open Educational Resources, https://en.unesco.org/themes/building-knowledge-societies/oer, @UNESCO 2019, 17 May.

20. Anonymous (2019). Open Educational Resources, https://en.wikipedia.org/ wiki/ Open_educational_resources, Wikipedia, 15 May, 2019.
21. Anonymous (2019). Open Educational Resources, https://hewlett.org/ strategy/open-educational-resources/.2019 William and Flora Hewlett Foundation, 17 May.
22. Anonymous (2019). Open Learning, https://en.wikipedia.org/wiki/ Open_learning, Wikipedia, 20 May.
23. Anonymous (2019). Techopedia, Information and Communications Technology, https://www.techopedia.com/definition/24152/information-and-communications-technology-ict, 17th May.
24. Anonymous (2019). What is cloud computing?, https://azure.microsoft.com/ en-in/overview/what-is-cloud-computing/, 18th May.
25. Anonymous (2019). Wikipedia, https://en.wikipedia.org/wiki/ Google_ Classroom, 15th July, 2019.
26. Anonymous (2019). Wikipedia, https://en.wikipedia.org/wiki/Moodle, 15th July.
27. Anonymous (2019). Wikipedia, M-learning, https://en.wikipedia.org/ wiki/M-learning, 17th May.
28. Atkin J M, Black P, and Coffey J (2001). Classroom assessment and the national science education standards. Washington, DC: National Academy.
29. Aviram A, Ronen, Y, Somekh S, Winer A, and Sarid A (2008). Self-Regulated Personalized Learning (SRPL): Developing iClass's pedagogical model. eLearning Papers, 9(9), 1–17.
30. Aviram R, Ronen Y, Somekh S, Schellas Y, Dotan I, and Winer A (2007). iClass Pedagogical Model and Guidelines, report published by Information Systems Technologies under contract to the iClass Consortium.
31. Bikfalvi A, Pages J L, Kantola J, Marques Gou P, and Fernandez N M (2007). Complementing education with competence development: an ICT-based application. International Journal of Management in Education, 1(3), 231–250.
32. Blewett C (2016). From Traditional Pedagogy to Digital Pedagogy: Paradoxes, Affordances, and Approaches. In Disrupting Higher Education Curriculum (pp. 265–287). Brill Sense.
33. Bloom B, Englehart M D, Furst E J, Hill W H, and Krathwohl D R (1956). Cognitive domain. Engineering Education, 67, 68.
34. Brooks J G and Brooks M G (1999). In search of understanding: The case for constructivist classrooms. ASCD.
35. Capterra (2019). Content Management Software (CMS), https://www.capterra.com/ content-management-software/, 18th July.
36. Carver C A, Howard R A, and Lane W D (1999). Enhancing student learning through hypermedia courseware and incorporation of student learning styles. IEEE transactions on Education, 42(1), 33–38.
37. Clark R E (1994). Media will never influence learning. Educational Technology Research and Development, 42(2), 21–29.
38. Coffield F, Moseley D, Hall E, and Ecclestone K (2004). Learning styles and pedagogy in post-16 learning: A systematic and critical review.
39. Conole G, Beetham H, and Sharpe R (2007). Rethinking Pedagogy for a Digital Age: Designing and Delivering E-Learning. London: RoutledgeFalmer.
40. Daniel Nations (2019). What Is Facebook?, https://www.lifewire.com/what-is-facebook-3486391, 20th July, 2019.
41. Diana I D and Schaik P V (1993). Courseware engineering outlined: An overview of some research issues. Educational and Training Technology International, 30(3), 191–211.
42. Douglas N and Arnold A B (2017). "Computer Aided Instruction", Microsoft online Encyclopedia, 2007.
43. Duffy T M and Cunningham D J (1996). 7. Constructivism: Implications for the design and delivery of instruction.

44. El Saadawi G M, Azevedo R, Castine M, Payne V, Medvedeva O, Tseytlin E, and Crowley R S (2010). Factors affecting feeling-of-knowing in a medical intelligent tutoring system: the role of immediate feedback as a metacognitive scaffold. Advances in Health Sciences Education, 15(1), 9–30.
45. Favre L (2009). Kinesthetic instructional strategies: Moving at-risk learners to higher levels. Insights on learning disabilities, 6(1), 29–35.
46. Gafoor K A and Abidha K (2015). Development of Academic Goal Orientation Inventory for Senior Secondary School Students of Kerala. Online Submission, 3(1), 352–360.
47. Gamboa H and Fred A (2002). Designing intelligent tutoring systems: a bayesian approach. Enterprise Information Systems III. Edited by J. Filipe, B. Sharp, and P. Miranda. Springer Verlag: New York, 146–152.
48. Grasha A F (1996). Teaching with Style: Pittsburgh, PA: Alliance Publishers.
49. Grasha A F (2002). Teaching with Style: Pittsburgh, PA: Alliance Publishers.
50. Gubbi J, Buyya R, Marusic S, and Palaniswami M (2013). Internet of Things (IoT): A vision, architectural elements, and future directions. Future generation computer systems, 29(7), 1645–1660.
51. Gubbi J, Buyya R, Marusic S, and Palaniswami M (2013). Internet of Things (IoT): A vision, architectural elements, and future directions. Future generation computer systems, 29(7), 1645–1660.
52. Guraya S Y and Chen S (2017). The impact and effectiveness of faculty development program in fostering the faculty's knowledge, skills, and professional competence: a systematic review and meta-analysis. Saudi journal of biological sciences.
53. Hodgson V (1989). Open learning and technology based learning materials. Distance Education, 10(1), 119-126.doi:10.1080/0158791890100109
54. Jin D (2012). Application of Internet of Things in Electronic Commerce. International Journal of Digital Content Technology and its Applic, 6, 222–225.
55. Kele A, Ocak R, Kele A, and Gülcü A (2009). ZOSMAT: Web-based intelligent tutoring system for teaching-learning process.Expert Systems with Applications, 36(2), 1229–1239.
56. Lancaster J W, Stein S M, MacLean L G, Van Amburgh J, and Persky A M (2014). Faculty development program models to advance teaching and learning within health science programs. American journal of pharmaceutical education, 78(5), 99.
57. Landry Lauren (2018). Open Learning: What it is and how you can benefit. https://www.northeastern.edu/graduate/blog/what-is-open-learning/2019 Northeastern University.
58. Lee Watanabe-Crockett (2019). 10 Of The Most Useful Digital Age Skills Every Learner Need, https://www.wabisabilearning.com/blog/10-useful-digital-age-skills, 18th May.
59. Linways Team, ICT enabled education, https://stories.linways.in/ict-enabled-education-d190bcc91bf0, 1st July, 2019.
60. Margaret Rouse (2019). Content Management System (CMS), https://www.wpbeginner.com/glossary/content-management-system-cms/, 17th May.
61. Matt Powell (2019). What is Learning Management System (LMS)? https://www.docebo.com/blog/what-is-learning-management-system/, 17th July.
62. McClintock R (1992). The educators manifesto: Renewing the progressive bond with posterity through the social construction of digital learning communities. New York: Institute of Learning Technologies.
63. Meishar-Tal H, Kurtz G, and Pieterse E (2012). Facebook groups as LMS: A case study. The International Review of Research in Open and Distance Learning, 13(4), 33–48.
64. Moonen J and Schoenmaker J (1992). Evolution of courseware development methodology: Recent issues. International Journal of Educational Research, 17(1), 109–121.
65. Moore M G (2003). Preface. In M G Moore and W Anderson (Eds.), Handbook of distance education. Hillsdale, NJ: Lawrence Erlbaum Associates, Inc.

66. Murray T (1999). Authoring intelligent tutoring systems: An analysis of the state of the art.
67. National Mission in Education through ICT. https://mhrd.gov.in/technology-enabled-learning-0
68. New National Policy on education coming (2011, August). The Hindu. India: The Hindu. http://www.ncert.nic.in/oth_anoun/npe86.pdf
69. Nikolov R (1997). Distance Education via Internet-Education without Borders, invited paper. In Proceedings of the Twenty Sixth Spring Conference of Bulgarian Mathematicians, Plovdiv (pp. 22–25).
70. Pahl C (2003). Managing evolution and change in web-based teaching and learning environments. Computers and Education, 40(2), 99–114.
71. Papert S (1980). Mindstorms: Children, computers, and powerful ideas. Basic Books, Inc.
72. Parthasarathy Bhattacharya (2019). The Digital Divide, http://lisp1.epgpbooks.inflibnet.ac.in/chapter/the-digital-divide/,17th May.
73. Rao V V (2015). Outcome Based Education and Accreditation, VRV Consultants.
74. Reigeluth C M (2013). Instructional-design theories and models: A new paradigm of instructional theory, Volume II. Routledge.
75. Robert Kilner (2019). Principles of Multimedia and Contiguity, https://www.slideshare.net/bobkilner/principles-of-multimedia-and-contiguity, 18th May.
76. Singer E R (1996). Espoused teaching paradigms of college faculty. Research in Higher Education, 37(6), 659–679.
77. Spady W G (1994). Outcome-based Education: Critical Issues and Answers. American Association of School Administrators, 1801 North Moore Street, Arlington, VA 22209 (Stock No. 21-00488; $18.95 plus postage).
78. Spady W G (1998). Paradigm Lost: Reclaiming America's Educational Future. AASA Distribution Center, 1801 N. Moore St, Arlington, VA 22209 (Item No. 236–001; $24.95, non-member; $19.95, member; $4.50 postage and handling; quantity discounts).
79. Thowfeek M H and Jaafar A (2011). Pedagogical approach to design an e-learning courseware. In 2011 International Conference on Pattern Analysis and Intelligence Robotics (Vol. 2, pp. 207–210). IEEE.
80. Uden L (2002). Courseware engineering methodology. Journal of Computing in Higher Education, 14(1), 50–66.
81. van der Akker J, Keursten P, and Plomp T (1992). The integration of computer use in education. International Journal of Educational Research, 17(1), 65–76.
82. Vangie Beal (2019). Google Classroom, https://www.webopedia.com /TERM/G/ google-classroom.html, 15th July.
83. Voogt J, Knezek G, Christensen R, and Lai K W (Eds.) (2018). Second handbook of information technology in primary and secondary education. Springer.
84. Will Kenton (2019). Social Networking, https://www.investopedia.com/ terms/s/ social-networking.asp,18th May.
85. Xu D, Huang W W, Wang H, and Heales J (2014). Enhancing e-learning effectiveness using an intelligent agent-supported personalized virtual learning environment: An empirical investigation. Information and Management, 51(4), 430–440.
86. Zealand H N (2003). Recipe for an intelligent learning management system (ilms). In Workshop Scientific Committee.

Index

A

ADDIE Model 164
Allinson and Hayes' cognitive style index 33
Accreditation 9, 169, 171–174
Activist 32
Adaptive learning 126, 132, 136, 148, 152, 172
Adaptivity 54, 134, 135
Andragogy 2
Artificial intelligence 132, 134, 136, 146, 148
Auditory learning 22, 27, 29, 31, 45
Augmented reality 140, 141, 154
Authoring language 159
Autocracy 52

B

Berlo's model 82
Bloom's taxonomy 17, 20, 24, 178, 182, 188, 191, 192
Behavioral attitudes 38
Behaviorism 24
Big data 147, 151
Blended instruction 156
Blended learning 7, 59, 60, 100
Blogs 84, 102, 109, 110, 143, 149, 151, 153, 201

C

CC-BY-SA 80, 101
Camcorder 83
Canvas 104, 111, 118, 121
Cloud 117, 127, 143, 144, 145
Cognitive domain 17, 50, 192
Cognitive style index (CSI) 33
Cognitive theory 14
Competencies 36, 69, 81, 99, 129, 171, 172, 183, 189, 199
Computer age 47
Computer-assisted instruction (CAI) 35, 56, 61, 106, 124
Concept maps 159
Consortium 122–124
Constructivism 15, 24, 57, 85, 140, 149
Continuous comprehensive evaluation 193
Course file 38, 39
Course outcome 40, 170, 174, 176, 177
Course specifications 39
Courseware 156–158
Curriculum 177–181, 183, 186, 189, 191, 194
Cyber security 150
Cybernetics 149
Continuous improvement 112, 172, 176–179

D

Dunn and Dunn model 31
Deep learning 148
Descriptor mapping 193
Digital age 35, 47, 48, 63, 77, 78, 92, 145
Digital camera 83
Digital contents 2
Digital pedagogy 6, 48, 51, 54, 55, 57, 60, 62, 90, 103
Distance learning 79

E

edX 6, 80, 97, 99, 111
Educational data mining 146
Educational psychology 14, 24, 55
E-learning 70, 79, 107, 108, 110, 111, 128, 133, 142, 144, 157, 200
Emotional content 142
Entrepreneurship 9, 152, 155
Expert model 132

F

Felder-Silverman 34
Faculty development program (FDP) 98, 183, 185
Feedback system 124, 149
Flexibly stable 31
Flipped classroom 100, 128, 181

G

Gagne's Approach 20
GitHub 6, 99, 104
Google classroom 111, 117, 118
Google docs 85
Google groups 85
Gregoric's Mind Styles 30
Gamification 4, 141–142

H

Honey and Mumford model 32
Homeocracy 52
Hybrid pedagogy 59, 60

I

ICT 65, 67
IoT 145
Information age 47
Information society 2
Instructional environment 132, 158
Instructional model 26, 132
Instructional scaffolding 15

Intelligent tutoring system (ITS) 24, 132, 138
Interactive whiteboard 84
Internship 22, 23, 190–191, 196

K

Kolb's model 31
Kinesthetic learning 22, 27, 31, 138

L

Learning analytics 147, 148
Learning designs 88
Learning guidance 20
Learning management system (LMS) 62, 89, 90, 104, 105, 107, 108, 110, 111

M

MOOC 6, 80, 90, 93, 94, 97, 99, 190
Moodle 105, 112
Microsoft Access 74
Microsoft Excel 74
Microsoft Office 71
Microsoft PowerPoint 71, 73
Microsoft Publisher 75
Microsoft Windows 70
Microsoft Word 71, 84,
Machine learning 134, 147–149
Media age 47
Media fidelity 82
Message Currency 82
Mobile-learning 79

N

NAAC 174
NBA 173
NMEICT 10, 68, 69
NPTEL 10, 80, 98, 101
National mission on education 10, 68, 101
National policy on education (NPE) 8
Non-verbal communication 21

O

Office 70
Open educational resources (OERs) 6, 95, 96, 102, 103
Operating systems 65, 70, 78
Outcome-based education 3, 169, 171, 176, 189

P

PEACOCK CCE model 193
Pedagogical model 26, 123, 129, 130
Pedagogy 1
Peer review 163
Perceptual preference 30
Performance indicator 193
Personalized instruction 35
Personalized learning 133, 135, 146, 148
Platonic epistemology 13
Power principles 52
Pragmatist 32
Professionalism attitudes 38

Programme educational objective (PEO) 40, 176, 178, 180, 185
Programme outcome (po) 184, 187
Programme specific outcome (pso) 40, 176, 178, 160, 185

Q

Quality assurance 10, 40, 161, 167, 172–173
Quality review 164
Questionnaire 32, 96, 135
Quizzes 38, 58, 79, 97, 97, 101, 115, 143, 172, 176, 182, 187, 200, 201

R

Rubrics 186, 188, 191

S

SRPL 130–132
SWAYAM 101
Schematic diagram 159
Self-regulated learning 130
Semantic maps 159
Sentiment analysis 148
Sequential learner 35, 135, 160
Social constructivism 15
Socratic method 2
Spoken tutorial 69, 101
Spreadsheets 59, 73, 74, 85, 201
Stakeholders 6, 150, 172, 175, 176, 179
Story boards 160
Student modeling 134, 135, 147–149
Student-centered approach 42

T

Tacit knowledge 2
Teacher's responsibility 36, 37
Teaching styles 31, 41, 44
Technology push 2
Technopedagogic skills 81
Theorist 13, 22, 32, 132
Theory of recollection 13
Transformative theory 16, 27

V

Virtual learning environments (VLE) 4, 140
Visual learning 22
Vulnerability principles 52
Validation principles 52
Virtual university 80, 93
Virtual reality 140
Venn diagram 160

W

Wikipedia 80, 93, 111
Wearable technology 141
Web-based assessment 201
Web-browser 85, 110

Y

YouTube channels 94, 102, 104